Students Learn Carpentry, Jaroslaw, Poland, 1922. Courtesy of the Library of Congress.
One of many vocational training programs set up in response to economic hardship after the First World War. Classes were run by the Organization for Rehabilitation through Training (ORT) and sponsored by the American Jewish Joint Distribution Committee (JDC). Photographed by Emil Tenzer.

Jaroslaw Book: a Memorial to Our Town (Jarosław, Poland)

Translation of
Sefer Yaroslav: gal-'ed le-zekher 'irenu

Original Book Edited by:
Yitzhak Alperowitz
Originally published in Tel Aviv 1978

JewishGen
מרכז עולמי לגנאלוגיה יהודית
The Global Home for Jewish Genealogy

A Publication of JewishGen, INC
Edmond J. Safra Plaza, 36 Battery Place, New York, NY 10280
646.494.5972 | info@JewishGen.org | www.jewishgen.org

MUSEUM OF
JEWISH HERITAGE
A LIVING MEMORIAL
TO THE HOLOCAUST

Jaroslaw Book: a Memorial to Our Town (Jarosław, Poland)
Translation of *Sefer Yaroslav: gal-'ed le-zekher 'irenu*

Copyright © 2021 by JewishGen, INC All rights reserved.
First Printing: November 2021, Kislev 5782

Editor of Original Yizkor Book: Yitzhak Alperowitz
Project Coordinator: Susan Rosin
Layout and Name Indexing: Jonathan Wind and Rachel Kolokoff Hopper
Reproduction of Photographs: Sondra Ettlinger
Cover Design: Nina Schwartz, Impulse Graphics

Printed in the United States of America by Lightning Source, Inc.

Library of Congress Control Number (LCCN): 2021949048

ISBN: 978-1-954176-22-5 (hard cover: 268 pages, alk. paper)

About JewishGen.org

JewishGen, an affiliate of the Museum of Jewish Heritage - A Living Memorial to the Holocaust, serves as the global home for Jewish genealogy.

Featuring unparalleled access to 30+ million records, it offers unique search tools, along with opportunities for researchers to connect with others who share similar interests. Award winning resources such as the Family Finder, Discussion Groups, and ViewMate, are relied upon by thousands each day.

In addition, JewishGen's extensive informational, educational and historical offerings, such as the Jewish Communities Database, Yizkor Book translations, InfoFiles, Family Tree of the Jewish People, and KehilaLinks, provide critical insights, first-hand accounts, and context about Jewish communal and familial life throughout the world.

Offered as a free resource, JewishGen.org has facilitated thousands of family connections and success stories, and is currently engaged in an intensive expansion effort that will bring many more records, tools, and resources to its collections.

Please visit https://www.jewishgen.org/ to learn more.

Executive Director: Avraham Groll

About the JewishGen Yizkor Book Project

Yizkor Books (Memorial Books) were traditionally written to memorialize the names of departed family and martyrs during holiday services in the synagogue (a practice that still exists in many synagogues today).

Over the centuries, as a result of countless persecutions and horrific atrocities committed against the Jews, Yizkor Books (Sefer Zikaron in Hebrew) were expanded to include more historical information, such as biographical sketches of famous personalities and descriptions of daily town life.

Following the Holocaust, the idea of remembrance and learning took on an urgent and crucial importance. Survivors of the Holocaust sought out other surviving residents of their former towns to memorialize and document the names and way of life of those who were ruthlessly murdered by the Nazis. These remembrances were documented in Yizkor Books, hundreds of which were published in the first decades after the Holocaust.

Most of these books were published privately, or through landsmanshaftn (social organizations comprised of members originating from the same European town or region) that still existed, and were often distributed free of charge. Sadly, the languages used to document these crucial histories and links to our past, Yiddish and Hebrew, are no longer commonly understood by a significant percentage of Jews today. As a result, JewishGen has undertaken the sacred responsibility of translating these books into English so that the culture and way of life of these communities will be preserved and transmitted to future generations.

In 1986, a group of farsighted JewishGenners started a project to pool their efforts together in groups based upon their ancestors from each town and donate money to get the Yizkor books of their ancestral towns translated into English. As the translated material became available, it was made accessible for free at www.JewishGen.org/Yizkor. Hardcover copies can be purchased by visiting www.JewishGen.org/Press (see below).

It is our hope that the translation of these books into English (and other languages) will assist the countless Jewish family researchers who are so desperately seeking to forge a connection with their heritage.

Director of JewishGen Yizkor Book Project: Lance Ackerfeld
Director of JewishGen Press: Joel Alpert

About the JewishGen Press

JewishGen Press (formerly the Yizkor Books-in-Print Project) is the publishing division of JewishGen.org, and provides a venue for the publication of non-fiction books pertaining to Jewish genealogy, history, culture, and heritage.

In addition to the Yizkor Book category, publications in the Other Non-Fiction category include Shoah memoirs and research, genealogical research, collections of genealogical and historical materials, biographies, diaries and letters, studies of Jewish experience and cultural life in the past, academic theses, and other books of interest to the Jewish community.

Please visit https://www.jewishgen.org/press/ to learn more.

Director of JewishGen Press: Joel Alpert
Managing Editor: Jessica Feinstein
Publications Manager: Susan Rosin

Notes to the Reader

The images in the original book were reproduced from photographs from the time of the first edition. These reproductions were already of poor quality, being pre-war and at least 30 or more years old. As a result the images in the book are not very good and the best achievable.

A reader can view the original scans of the book on the websites listed below.

The original book can be seen online at the New York Public Library site:

https://digitalcollections.nypl.org/items/aa74e940-79b1-0133-6e8a-00505686d14e

or

at the Yiddish Book Center web site: https://tinyurl.com/42ew6wy4

To obtain a list of all Shoah victims from Jaroslaw (Jarosław), the reader should access the Yad Vashem web site listed below; one can also search for specific family names using family name option. These lists are continually updated by Yad Vashem, so it is worthwhile to periodically search these lists.

There is more valuable information (including the Pages of Testimony, etc.) available on this website: http://yvng.yadvashem.org

A list of all books available from JewishGen Press along with prices is available at: https://www.jewishgen.org/press/

Acknowledgements

Big great thank you goes to Mr. Dan Rottenberg whose financial support made this project possible.

I would like to thank Lance Ackerfeld, JG Special Projects Director who guided me every step of the way to bring this project to a successful completion.

Last but not least special thanks go to Sara Mages who volunteered her excellent translations talents to get us over the finish line.

Susan Rosin
November 2021
Brea, CA

Credits for Book Cover

Front Cover:

Orsetti Tenement, c.1905. Public domain. Source: Polish National Archives. Built in the late 16th century; rebuilt as a burgher's tenement in 1633 by Krakow merchant Wilhelm Orsetti. Since 1945, home of the Museum in Jaroslaw. The photographer romanticized this photo (accepted practice at the time), brushing in trees, extra people, and an unseen carriage, probably for a postcard.

Master pharmacist Victor Brillant at his pharmacy, c.1935. Courtesy of Avigdor Brillant.

Sigmund Schwarzer rides shotgun on a carriage ride with his family, c.1930. Courtesy of Mitchell Schwarzer. Left to right, Unknown driver, Sigmund, his cousin Gerda, his sister Danuta, his aunt Edzia (Gerda's mother), and his mother Sophie.

Sigmund Schwarzer (right) with an unknown schoolmate, 1938. Courtesy of Mitchell Schwarzer.

Back Cover:
Area map from Karte des westlichen Russlands, 1916. Public domain. Source: Topographic Maps of Eastern Europe, easteuropetopo.org. Held by Geography and Map Division, Library of Congress.

Srul Prinz and his second wife, c.1910. Courtesy of Lauren Shulsky Orenstein.

Friends on an outing, probably spring 1929. Courtesy of Susan Adelman. Front center is Mollie (Malka) Bank; to her left, her childhood friend from Sieniawa, Miss Ehrenwald.

Brothers Jan and Edmond Brillant at chess, c.1932. Courtesy of Avigdor Brillant.

GeoPolitical Information

Jarosław, Poland is located at: 50°01' N 22°41' E and 171 miles SSE of Warszawa

	Town	District	Province	Country
Before WWI (c. 1900):	Jarosław	Jarosław	Galicia	Austrian Empire
Between the wars (c. 1930):	Jarosław	Jarosław	Lwów	Poland
After WWII (c. 1950):	Jarosław			Poland
Today (c. 2000):	Jarosław			Poland

Alternate Names for the Town:
Jarosław [Pol], Yaroslav [Yid], Jaroslau [Ger], Jaroslav, Yereslev, Yareslov

Nearby Jewish Communities:

Radymno 8 miles SE
Skołoszów 8 miles SE
Przeworsk 9 miles WNW
Kosienice 9 miles S
Pruchnik 10 miles SW
Sieniawa 11 miles NNW
Kańczuga 12 miles WSW
Grodzisko Dolne 14 miles NW
Siedleczka 14 miles WSW
Krzywcza 16 miles SSW
Cieplice 16 miles N
Markowa 16 miles W
Przemyśl 17 miles SSE
Krasiczyn 17 miles S
Cewków 18 miles NNE
Oleszyce 19 miles NE
Dubiecko 19 miles SW
Żołynia 19 miles WNW
Dzików Stary 20 miles NE
Jawornik Polski 20 miles WSW
Łańcut 20 miles W
Wielkie Oczy 21 miles E
Leżajsk 21 miles NW

Krakovets, Ukraine 22 miles E
Zabratówka 22 miles W
Kuryłówka 22 miles NNW
Ułazów 22 miles NE
Lubaczów 22 miles ENE
Nyzhankovychi, Ukraine 24 miles SSE
Dynów 24 miles SW
Tarnogród 24 miles N
Cieszanów 25 miles NE
Bircza 25 miles SSW
Husakiv, Ukraine 25 miles SE
Rybotycze 25 miles S
Mostyska, Ukraine 26 miles SE
Łukowa 27 miles NNE
Nahachiv, Ukraine 27 miles E
Wola Żarczycka 27 miles NW
Błażowa 28 miles WSW
Nove Misto, Ukraine 29 miles SSE
Tyczyn 29 miles W
Ulucz 29 miles SW
Sokołów Małopolski 29 miles WNW
Tvirzha, Ukraine 29 miles ESE
Krzeszów 30 miles NNW

Jewish Population: 4,820 (in 1890), 6,577 (in 1921)

Map of Poland with **Jarosław** indicated

TABLE OF CONTENTS

Jaroslaw Book: a Memorial to Our Town... (Jaroslaw, Poland)

50°01' / 22°41'

Translation of:
Sefer Yaroslav: gal-'ed le-zekher 'irenu...

Edited by: Yitzhak Alperowitz

Published in Tel Aviv 1978

————

Acknowledgments

Project Coordinator:

Susan Rosin

**Our sincere appreciation to Yad Vashem
for the submission of the necrology for placement on the JewishGen web site
and to Sondra Ettlinger for extracting the pictures from the original book,
enabling their addition to the project.**

This is a translation from: *Sefer Yaroslav: gal-'ed le-zekher 'irenu...*
(Jaroslaw book: a memorial to our town...),

ו ע ד ת   ה ס פ ר

משה (מונדיק) העבנשטרייט   משה קלעכהיים

דב (ברק) פרוכטמן   רייסקה (שושנה) קוסטמן   אשר גרף

The Book Committee

Top row L – R: Moshe (Mundek) Hebenstreit, Moshe Kalchheim

Bottom row L – R: Dov (Berek) Fruchtman, Reiska (Shoshana) Kostman, Asher Graff

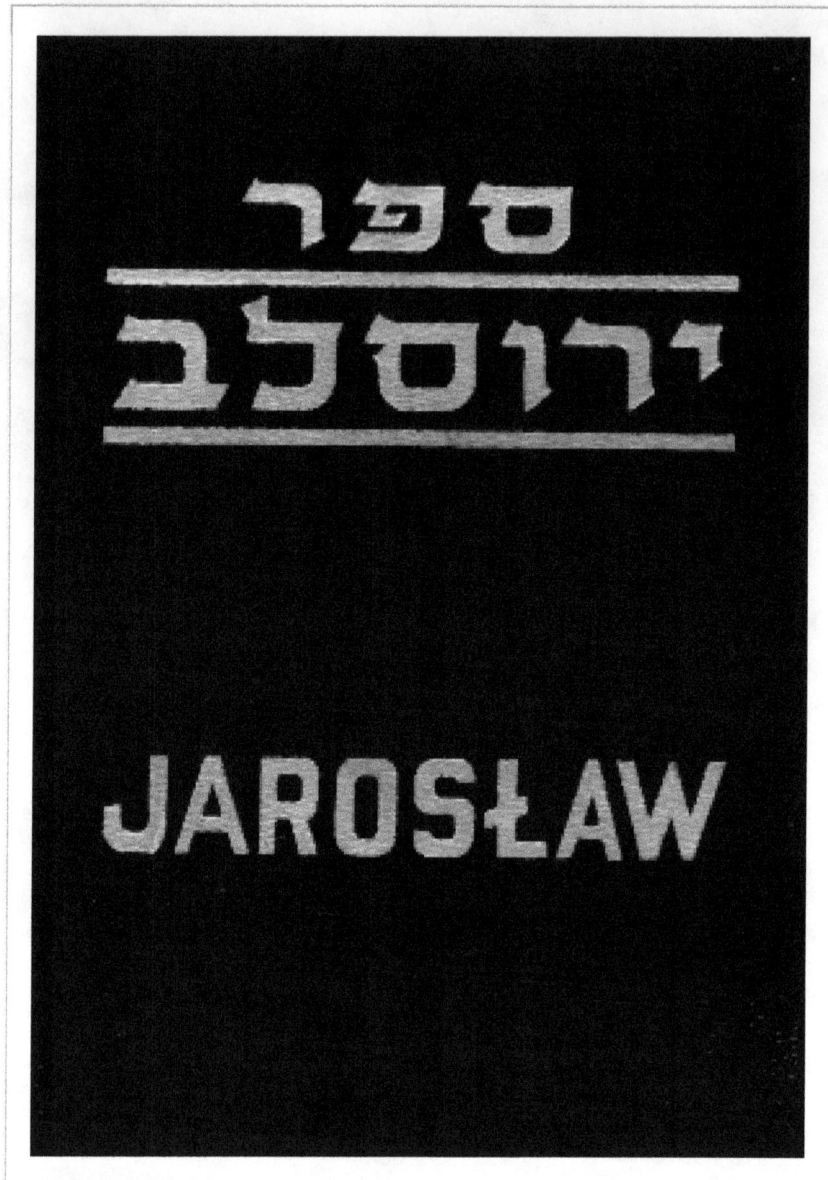

Mapa miasta Jarosławia
z wyszczególnieniem instytucji żydowskich do wrześn

מפת עיר יארוסלאב
בן גיל | אלתר ונלים 38 בהיג. עולאכ סוף 1939

STA JAROSŁAWIA
tucji żydowskich do września 1939

מפת עיר יא

1....Główna bożnica
2....Beit hamidrasz
3....Beit haszchita
4....Cheder (Hersz Meir)
5....Talmud Tora
6....Kchot klojz
7....Beit kneset
8....Beit sefer „TARBUT"
9....Beit am (Freblówka)
10....Jad charuzim
11....Biblioteka Tarbut
12....Bnei Zion
13....Beit jetomim
14....Dror
15....Żydowska Gmina Wyznaniowa

1. Main Synagogue
2. Beit Midrash
3. Slaughter House
4. Heder of Hersz Meir
5. Talmud Tora
6. Kchot Kloiz
7. Synagogue Yehoshua Moritz
8. "Tarbut" School
9. Beit Am (Preschool)
10. "Yad Harutzim"
11. "Tarbut" Library
12. Bnei Zion
13. Stirzower Orphanage
14. Dror
15. Jewish Kehila

[Page 7]

על
בהר ציון ירושלים ת"ו
לזכר חורבן קהלת
ירוסלב
(גליציה)
שהושמדו
ע"י קלגסי הנאצים ימ"ש
בשנת השואה תרצ"ט-תש"ה
ת.נ.צ.ב.ה.
ארגון יוצאי ירוסלב
בישראל ובתפוצות

י ז כ ו ר

קהילת ירוסלב איננה.

עלה הכורת על קהילת הקודש שלנו.

על-ידי מצבת-ניר זו, ששמה "ספר הזכרון", עומדים
אולמי-יגון, השרידים שנשארו לפליטה, ומעלים את זכר
נשמותיהם של יקיריהם, מחוללים בגוף וטהורים ברוח, אל
מנוחתם האחרונה, או שפוזרו עצמותיהם בדרכים-לא-דרכים
על אדמות פולין ורוסיה עקובות-הדמים, מאכל לחית-השדה
ועוף-השמים, ולא ידע איש את קבורתם.

שרידי קהילת ירוסלב

[Page 11]

O, Lord who art full of compassion…

"Is it nothing to you, all ye that pass by? Behold, and see if there be any sorrow like unto my sorrow, which is done unto me, wherewith the LORD hath afflicted me in the day of his fierce anger."

The Lamentations of Jeremiah 1:12

[Page 12]

Foreword

The Editorial Board of the Jaroslaw Memorial Book

Translated by Selwyn Rose

In awe and compassion, we present this Memorial Book of the Jaroslaw community to the survivors of the town in Israel and abroad. This Memorial book is about one of the oldest and most magnificent communities in Poland to be annihilated by the Nazi terror.

Generations distant and recent look out at us from the pages of this book; generations of Jews, masters of varied talents: rabbis, great *Torah* scholars, intellectuals and leaders of the Zionist movements and the wider public whose light shone forth for centuries in the community of Jaroslaw and beyond.

Jaroslaw was a dynamic and effervescent town full of life. Within it flourished loyal Jews, scholars, businessmen and simple people who grew up with a deep love for Zion.

Jewish Jaroslaw! You were our town and mother, a town within which was formed and cast a mode of life and a special way of life out of which burst the desire and ambition to present an example of excellence and a spiritual center of the region. Your citizens shaped your character, injecting western culture and the modern life of those times. You were a city of industry and commerce, *Torah* and education. A proud generation grew within you, a self–confident generation full of understanding, a generation imbued with ambition towards nationalism and humanitarianism.

That wonderful structure was destroyed and laid to waste.

From within the pages of this book, emerge forgotten images and "yesterday" is resurrected. We have described the lifestyle of the residents. We tell of the values on which they were educated and have tried to give a picture of prayer–houses, educational establishments, youth movements and political parties. We have tried to erect and recreate chapters from the life of the town, the material, the spiritual, and the creative.

We do not pretend to say that we have succeeded in illustrating the whole canvas of Jewish life in Jaroslaw, the individual's life–events and deeds. They did not come to full expressions, either because no one could tell about them or because of the scope of the book. At the same time, we ensured that the book would include and illustrate all the layers of Jewish Jaroslaw – its movements and social streams from the beginnings of the community's existence until its destruction. We also ensured that all documents, lists, registrations and surveys were authenticated to every possible extent.

Nevertheless, in spite of our greatest efforts we failed to find documentation for several personalities and institutions, organizations and societies that had occupied a significant standing within the Jewish community of Jaroslaw. May the positives atone for the negatives.

In this book, a special place is devoted to extensive articles on special and unforgettable periods in the life of the Jaroslaw community, as well as short lists of the survivors of the Jaroslaw community who put on paper their longings for a continuance of their destroyed families and the exterminated community.

May this book be an Eternal Flame of remembrance to the pure martyred souls.

Tel–Aviv 1977

[Page 14]

From the Organization
Jaroslaw Organization in Israel

Translated by Susan Rosin

This memorial book is late in coming to print. Many communities were able to memorialize their destroyed towns in monuments and in books. We were concerned that if we do not make this effort to publish a book, we will lose our last chance to memorialize our town, and there will be no trace to one of the more magnificent Poland's communities. Jews lived in our town for at least 600 years, the Synod of the Four Lands was located in our town. There were famous scholars and leaders, and at times the Jews of our town represented the entire Polish Jewry.

The work on this book was not easy. The material for the book was collected thanks to the efforts and persistence of many. Originally, we turned to our town's people and asked them to provide us with articles, memoirs, and journals.

Admittedly, there was little response. People rationalized their refusals due to forgetfulness, others promised to write and did not do so. Among the hundreds, only a few submitted material that was determined to be suitable for the memorial book of our town. The materials were written in Polish, English and Yiddish. Therefore there was an effort to translate it correctly and faithfully into Hebrew.

The truth is that the few memoirs were written with deep love and respect for our beautiful town. From the written material it can be seen that our town's people had great memories of their childhood in our town and proudly wrote about their town.

The Jaroslaw book mainly looks at the Jewish life of our town in the last 50 – 60 years. There is not much information about the Jewish life before the First World War and describes very little of the life during World War Two under the Nazi occupation.

Jaroslaw Jews were expelled from the town across the San River during the first weeks of the occupation. When Poland was occupied, the San River was the border between the German and Soviet zones.

[Page 15]

Since the expulsion, the fate of Jaroslaw Jewry can be described as individuals and not as a community. Their fate was the same as those in the different towns and villages where our town's people found temporary refuge.

Therefore, the book does not describe memoirs from the Nazi occupation era. Mainly it describes events during the short period before the expulsion, and later the fate of those that found themselves in various areas of the Soviet Union and with the anti-Nazi partisans.

May this book serve as a holy testimony to what was once Jewish Jaroslaw. May this book be a memorial to the glorious community of Jaroslaw. May the next generations find some of the Jewish reality, its beauty, its splendor and its grace.

It is our pleasure to express our gratitude to the main contributors that made this effort possible:

Moshe (Mundek) Hebenstreit – Chairman of the Tel Aviv branch of the organization of former residents of Jaroslaw. He worked enthusiastically and tirelessly to make this book a reality. He collected the material for the book and organized it. He contributed many articles himself and actively participated in the meetings and consultations. His efforts throughout the years are a major contribution to the successful completion of the book.

Moshe Kalchheim – Who has a phenomenal memory; He remembers all details and events of the public life in our town and even everyday occurrences. He himself wrote many of the articles in the book. He dedicated much of his time to the effort to bring the book to print, and his comments and corrections can be seen throughout the pages of the book. Without his help, we would not be able to have the accuracy of the facts and events in our book.

Special thanks to Mr. Dov (Berek) Fruchtman for translating many articles and his help in bringing the book initiative to fruition. He too wrote articles and was instrumental in the actual publication of the book.

We should note with gratitude Reiska Kostman and Asher-Simcha Graff who dedicated time and efforts to bring the book initiative to a successful completion.

We remember the late Josef Narzisenfeld, who was one of the first people to initiate the book idea.

We are grateful to our town's native Rabbi Moshe Steinberg – Rabbi of Kiryat Yam for his generous consent to include in the book his comprehensive article about the history of Jaroslaw's Jews.

[Page 16]

The organization is grateful to Mr. Josef Plant and Mr. Avraham Kenigsberg for their efforts among the Haifa residents to bring the book to a successful completion.

And finally we are indebted to Mr. Yitzhak Alperowitz - the book editor - for his efforts and talents to bring the book to print in a nice and pleasant format.

Special thanks to all those – in Israel and abroad - that helped making the publication of this book possible.

May this book be a testament for eternal memory.

[Page 17]

Jaroslaw Through the Generations

[Page 18] Blank

[Page 19 – Hebrew][Page 51 – Yiddish]

The Beginnings of Jewish Settlement in Jaroslaw

by Rabbi Moshe Steinberg

Translated by Selwyn Rose

We have no trustworthy information concerning the birth of the town of Jaroslaw; when the first Jews settled there. In spite of the fact that it is one of the oldest towns in Poland - founded, according to estimates, by the Russian Prince Jaroslaw the Wise (1019-1054) – there is no document suggesting the existence of Jews in Jaroslaw until the second half of the 15th century and the first confirmed mention supporting the existence of a Jew or Jews in Jaroslaw is from the year 1464 and the supposition of Orlowycz that Jews were settled in Jaroslaw in the days of Casimir the Great, that is during the 14th century, should be completely and utterly disregarded because there is not a shred of viable evidence to support that statement.

The fact that in 1561 (one hundred years after 1464), there lived in Jaroslaw just two Jews, Avraham and David, proves that the development of a Jewish community in Jaroslaw was exceedingly slow. That, and more besides: Rabbi Meir ben Gedaliah of Lublin, who resided at the time in Jaroslaw, is known to have taken part in the Council of the Four Lands (1608), and he declares in his book that the participants in the Council were obliged to bring a Scroll of the Law from nearby Przemyśl because there was not one available in the entire town. Here is clear proof that at the beginning of the 17th century, there was not yet a quorum of Jews in Jaroslaw.

The main obstruction to the development of Jewish settlement in Jaroslaw was the operation of the "*de non tolerandis Judaeis*"[1] that the townspeople received from the town's Princess Zofia Tarnowska in 1571, according to which "there will not be more than one Jewish house in Jaroslaw and at the very most two." The right not to tolerate Jews within its walls was claimed by towns like Warsaw, Lublin and others on the basis of the same Privilege of "*de non tolerandis Judaeis*" and they succeeded in exiling the Jews from their towns. But the difference with Jaroslaw was simply that here the two Jews were permitted to remain. One may assume that Tarnowska considered the prevailing situation and allowed the two Jews, Avraham and David, who already dwelt in the town at the same time, to continue to live in Jaroslaw. And all the owners of Jaroslaw after Zofia Tarnowska honored the *status quo*. Thus, according to the law it was always permissible for two Jews to reside in Jaroslaw.

Of interest, is that in that same year of 1571, Tarnowska brought the Jesuits to Jaroslaw and presented them with the village of Pawłosiów as a holding. It is very possible, therefore, that……the anti-Jewish law was enacted by her under pressure and at the express demands of the Jesuits. Indeed, it is in the opinion of Willus Adam that Piotr Scarga, her loyal friend, influenced Tarnowska in this direction suggesting the founding of the Jesuit monastery in Jaroslaw and as a condition of its development enacting the ban – hence the "Privilege".

[Page 20]

For many years, the city of Jaroslaw enjoyed this right and it was not violated, even in the slightest degree because the townspeople and the town's leading citizens were on constant guard against any infraction. In 1573 the Jew Avraham passed away and his wife Ziklia sold their house which stood between the house of Vasilko and the house belonging to the Jew David on Kozia Ulica "*Platea Caprima*", to a woman called Anna making the place available for another Jew – in accordance with the law of 1571 – and Moshe settled in Jaroslaw in 1574 and purchased the property from Ivan Shmiwitz.

Understandably, the law generated hostility towards the Jews and therefore the Council of the Four Lands passed a resolution forbidding decisively that their meetings should be held in Jaroslaw as it was considered a perilous locality. When, in spite of that decision, the Council convened in Jaroslaw, they expressed their regrets and renewed the prohibition on 13th *Tishrei* 5432 (1672), at the sitting of the Council in Jaroslaw itself, in the following words: "We remember our sins today in that we were reconciled with the mediators and tempters to convene in that place of danger and corruption – Jaroslaw, for many reasons and it is well that those who came before us forbad the meetings there. We wonder about those earlier ones we heard whispering their enticements for us to come here, and we should have owed it to ourselves that we abide by the boycott, which had been established by the officers and the leading elements in of earlier Councils. It is well we accepted the boycott of the aforementioned elders not to convene in the city, the place of danger mentioned above but about ten kilometers from Jaroslaw and at the Kremnitz meeting in 5432 the Council of the Four Lands will decide where we will convene and how many weeks before the Jaroslaw Fair. And there we will not convene for any reason in the world and any such meeting will hold no validity as explained in the previous pages that do not contradict regulations that exist as if they came out of our mouths today. The 24 officers acting on the advice of the Most High Lord, Thursday 13th of Tishrei 1572 in the Holy Committee here in Jaroslaw."

Having no option, the Jews were forced to comply with the existing law and settled in the suburbs on the edge of town – specifically the Russian suburb (Pełkinie), and there in a later period a synagogue and a "*Beit Ha-Ḥaim*"[2] were built. But gradually, with the passage of time the Jews for all that, managed to infiltrate the walls of the town and "the law", thus by the year1613, there were already living five Jews in Jaroslaw: Moshe, Hirsch, Baruch "the Licensee", Wolf and Levi, all of whom appeared as "Jaroslaw residents".

[Page 21]

The open infraction of the law encouraged the Jews to settle in Jaroslaw and the Jewish settlement increased and expanded. In truth, in 1630, the owner of the town at the time, Princess Anna Ostrogzka and in 1676 by King Jan III Sobieski made respective efforts to prevent the development of Jewish settlement in Jaroslaw and to that end renewed the edict of the Privilege 1571, but unsuccessfully, as it had become obsolete.

The Jewish community in Jaroslaw began to grow slowly and more firmly until it became an established fact.

B. The Development of the Jewish Community

Jaroslaw was a known commercial town holding a well-publicised Fair three times a year to which came people from all over the country as well as from abroad. Her streets and markets overflowed with Jews and non-Jews alike who came for the trade Fairs and filled the available accommodation for the period of the Fairs. There is not the shadow of a doubt that many of the Jews who came to the Jaroslaw Fairs wished in their hearts that they, too, in fact dwelt in that commercial town but standing in the way of that desire was the anti-Jewish law of 1571 and for nearly forty years no one was able to violate the *staus quo*.

Nevertheless when, at the beginning of the 17th Century they did manage to breach the difficulties presented by the above law and Jaroslaw was no longer limited to "two Jewish houses", Jews wishing to settle in the town began to flow ceaselessly and their numbers grew. In the thirties of the 17th Century there was already a population worthy of being called a community. In 1638 the reality of the situation called for the organization and recognition of the community and the Court of Władysław IV granted a "Privilege" that acknowledged the Jews of Przemyśl as a section of the population of the town.

[Page 22]

In accordance with that Royal decree all the surrounding towns close to Przemyśl including Jaroslaw, were obliged to obey the following instructions:

To recognize Przemyśl as their "big sister".
To bury their dead there.

To hold services in the Przemyśl synagogue.
To pay taxes.
To purchase there the *etrogim*[3]
Every licensee will pay 3 gulden for the benefit of the Rabbis.
Any legal appeal is to be addressed to the rabbinical authority of Przemyśl.

It is worth pointing out that in no way was Jaroslaw exceptional since, in accordance with the accepted norms, the defense of every large community spread over the smaller ones and as one of the central communities, they were obliged to accept the authority. And if every individual community chose, in general, between 22-34 community representatives, everyone would number just eight representatives.

And regarding the burial of the dead in Przemyśl, the renewed Privilege changed nothing because even before 1638, the Jews of Jaroslaw buried their dead in Przemyśl since they had no local cemetery. Thus explained Rabbi Joel Sirkis in one of his replies because in 1625, a fire broke out in Jaroslaw at the time of one of the Fairs and one of the Jews named Ya'acov Ashkenazi of Poznań was burnt to death and buried in Przemyśl since there was no cemetery in Jaroslaw. That Privilege was possible only by official authorization of the existing law.

There is certainly no need to emphasize that the Privilege by-law above obliging prayers to be held in Przemyśl, is completely illogical or unfair and totally unacceptable and is not worthy of further discussion.

During the same period, in the following decade after the 1638 event, the Cossacks, headed by Khmelnitsky invaded Polish territory and in every place they trod they left behind them destruction and suffering to property and people. The terrible devastating year of 1647 shocked all humanity bringing calamitous misery not only to the Polish people but first and foremost inhuman atrocities and suffering to the Jews because in their wild behavior and Satanic, bloody depredations three-hundred thousand Jews were martyred – men women and children.

The 1647 storm did not ignore Jaroslaw. The wild Cossacks destroyed the churches and monasteries, beating and abusing the Christian residents, and lost no time in setting fire to the whole town and only extorted money saved the town from being totally destroyed. Nevertheless it seems that on this occasion the Jewish population came out unscathed with no loss of life.

[Page 23]

Legend has it that with the awareness of the danger hovering over their heads from the Cossacks, the Jews fled the town before the start of the marauding gangs and when their anger had passed, they returned to their homes on 9th *Sivan* and fixed that day as a day of rejoicing calling it "Jaroslaw's 'Good-day'"

The establishment and numerical growth of Jaroslaw eventually drove the villagers out of their minds. The tension intensified, arguments and fights broke out between the townspeople and the Jews and Jaroslaw Jewish life became bitter until finally open violence broke out and became serious in 1686. The situation was very dangerous and only the intervention of the Queen, Maria Kazimiera managed to contain what was, in fact, a cold war. The Queen sent Cardinal Stanislaw as her personal representative with the aim of reaching a settlement giving him explicit instructions to settle the arguments between the two sides.

But usually the townspeople were supported by the town owners, the clergy and some of the kings of Poland like Jan III Sobieski, who tried to block the expansion of the Jewish settlement in Jaroslaw. For example, in 1664 the town's authorities published a law forbidding the renting of apartments to Jews and in future to exile them and not give them any work. A similar law was published in 1687 by the town owner Józef Karol Lubomirski, demanding "*Intra rigorum iurium*"[4] and to throw the Jews out of the town because "…some weeks after the Fair the Jews were still living in the town" and all those aiding them should be punished to the extreme limit of the law.

After a year passed, Lubomirski renewed the above order. And a final time in 1704, Ludwika Lubomirska renewed the Privilege of 1751.

From every aspect, we see that until the beginning of the 18th Century the Jewish population of Jaroslaw lived in an unstable and insecure atmosphere because of the occasional renewal of the anti-Jewish sentiments implicitly embodied in the laws that there should be "no more than two Jewish homes" in Jaroslaw placing them unavoidably under "the sword of Damocles". But nevertheless, in spite of the ongoing conflict and the will to exist, the Jewish population continued to increase in number and strength and especially after the economic downturn of the town, the Jews found themselves in command of the town's economy and they increased evermore.

[Page 24]

The common danger experienced by the Jewish population of Jaroslaw that was engendered by the anti-Jewish acts of 1571, pushed them instinctively to draw together in one place since it was a natural response to the hostile surroundings and living together provided a common defense to whatever was coming. Thus was born, towards the end of the 17th Century, the Jewish street in the north-western corner of the town (today, the neighborhood of the Great Synagogue), in other words – the ghetto. Nevertheless, there was a basic difference between the concept of the ghetto as it was created in many European towns of the late middle-ages at the instigation of the Christian communities who forced the Jews to live in them and prohibited them from leaving them, as against the Jewish street in Jaroslaw which was a direct creation of the Jews themselves in choosing to live close together as a form of self defense.

Indeed, as the framework of the Jewish settlement expanded and in accordance with their growing number, deaths within their ranks became more common and the community began to think in terms of creating their own cemetery because the carrying of the dead to distant Przemyśl was becoming burdensome and intolerable, even on occasion leading in some cases of disrespect to the departed. There isn't a shadow of doubt that the general opinion of the Jews of Przemyśl themselves objected strongly to the idea from many aspects but especially budgetary considerations because they would lose the benefit of all the burial fees that were being paid to them for burial services. But the Council of the Four Lands that convened in Jaroslaw in 1700 decided in favor and authorized the creation of a cemetery in Jaroslaw. From then the project began to go forward to a planning stage.

In compliance with the law "*De non tolerandis Judaeis*", the cemetery was built outside the city walls in the Russian quarter beyond the Pełkinie Gate. It was in clear defiance of the Privilege of 1638 that was given to the Jews of Przemyśl according to which they were obliged to bury their dead in Przemyśl and also the first step towards the freeing of the community from the authority and regime of the central community of the town.

The purchase of the land cost the Jewish community several thousand Polish gulden in addition to which they were obliged to pay the heads of the Jaroslaw clergy every year on St Martin's day the sum of seven gulden. If it happened that the sum was not available to time, they were compelled to pay an annual interest of 120 gulden. The negotiations on behalf of the Jews were delegated to three Jews, Mordecai, Joel and Zalman Jacobowitz.

[Page 25]

At the same time that the cemetery was being established the burial fees were also fixed. The maximum was sixty gulden and anyone who expressed the wish to be buried in another town was charged thirty gulden. In the event that a poverty-stricken person died during the Fair and it was difficult to determine his place of residence, money was collected from shop-keepers and the compassionate to purchase the burial shrouds. Here we must mention that four members of the Council of the Four Lands, Rabbi Naphtali Cohen of Poznań, Rabbi Shaul and Mr. Zachariah Mendel of Krakow, Mr. Menaḥem Mendel of Lvov consecrated the cemetery ground and they also fixed the above-mentioned burial fees.

Among the distinguished people buried in the cemetery who were not residents of Jaroslaw were Rabbi Meir of Husakiv, the father of Rabbi Yitzhak Levi of Bardichev known as the Holy One of Barditchev. Even Rabbi Meir was connected with Jaroslaw because his son Levi Yitzhak studied there during his youth and was known as the "Jaroslaw prodigy". For all that, it is not known for certain how he came to be buried in Jaroslaw and not in Husakiv, where he was born, or in Przemyśl where he served as the town Rabbi.

During that same period, the 1690's, the Chair of the Chief Rabbi of Jaroslaw was occupied by Rabbi Yeshiayhu, the son of Rabbi Natan Netta of Krakow who, by all accounts was the first Rabbi of Jaroslaw. It seems in those days there was another "Jaroslaw" under the authority of the central government of Przemyśl so there was some uncertainty concerning the Privilege of 1638 – about the Rabbi of Przemyśl. Indeed Jaroslaw was not his last stop because from there he received the Rabbanut of the town of Kowale in Wohlinia and one can assume that already in 1700 he was no longer in Jaroslaw for otherwise he would certainly have taken part in the consecration of the cemetery as the local Rabbi together with the four mentioned above.

From the same period there is preserved from the synagogue the prayer book from 1695 as used by the Jews of Jaroslaw, composed by Josef Kahana. The prayer book, made of parchment, has on nearly every page, hand-drawn various artistic illustrations. Among the prayers were: Reception of the Sabbath, the Angels' praises for King Jan III Sobieski, the prayer for rain, lamentations in memory of those victims of the Cossacks from 1647, and an edited version of the "O Lord who art full of compassion" prayer in memory of the martyrs of Nemyrov (Niemirów, Nemirova) and Tul'chyn (Tulczyn), who fell in 1647,.

That prayer book is therefore an accurate and confirmed, incontrovertible source that at the end of the 17th Century there was a synagogue in Jaroslaw. Nevertheless, because of the lack of historical sources, we know nothing of its architectural design or the materials from which it was constructed but it is certain beyond doubt that because of the law of 1571 they were forced to erect it outside the city walls as was the case with the cemetery.

Part of the town center, market place and municipality

[Page 26]

Although what Orlowycz tells us that "in the Russian suburb beyond the Pełkinie gate in 1675 the Jews had two synagogues" is simply not acceptable and must be seen as an absurd exaggeration, for in the second half of the 17th Century there were simply not enough Jews in Jaroslaw as to justify two synagogues.

Here we have a Jewish street, a separate cemetery, Rabbi and synagogue – all going to prove conspicuously how deeply entrenched were the roots of the Jewish community of Jaroslaw. From the start of the 18th Century, the community was already a significant element and by then an important factor, with which, not only the city, its rulers and Christian residents, but also the central authority in Przemyśl had to take into consideration. Thus, the Jews of Jaroslaw began the march to independence and in the not too distant future, it would become an independent community in its own right.

Translator's Footnotes:

1. Intolerance of Jews. Cities that held the old Privilege *de non tolerandis Judaeis* were not obligated to admit Jews.
2. Literally "House of Life" but here used euphemistically for a cemetery.
3. A member of the citrus family of fruits used during the Festival of Tabernacles (*Succoth*)
4. To introduce the full rigor of the law.

———

C. The Independent Community and its Rabbis

Translated by Selwyn Rose

There was a significant turning-point in the history of the Jewish community in Jaroslaw in 1774. It was the beginning of a very important period. That same year the Jewish community of Jaroslaw became totally independent of its "big sister" the central authority located in Przemyśl, and became a separate and independent one. There were, however, attempts by the community of Przemyśl to change things back to the *status quo ante* and at the request of Przemyśl, King August III renewed the Privilege of 1638; but it was simply a voice calling in the wilderness because the independence of the Jaroslaw community was already an established fact.

[Page 27]

In the second half of the 18th Century, the number of Jews continued to grow and according to the statistics of 1765, the number of Jewish residents in Jaroslaw was recorded as 1,884. Together with the increase in numbers, the boundaries of the Jewish settlement grew and from 1785, the surrounding villages were also part of it.

At the head of the community stood six community Elders but in practice all the business of the community was handled by just three of them known as "*Reginars*" who received their salaries from the community coffers. The functions of the three of them were significantly restricted and upon them was the task of preparing a list of all those paying tax and fixing the amount of tax that each person had to pay. The Elders were elected for a period of three years and at the end of each session, new elections were held. During the second half of the 19th Century, the *Reginars* decided to forgo their salaries and fulfilled their duties voluntarily.

The first Rabbi of the independent community was Rabbi Moshe Yehoshua Horowitz.

Before we continue to write all the names of the Rabbis who came after him, we should note at this point all the others known to us, who officiated as Rabbis of the town in order, in the period between the first Rabbi of Jaroslaw Rabbi Yeshaya Bar Natan Netta (see above in section 'B') and Rabbi Moshe Yehoshua Halevi Horowitz above:

Rabbi Ya'acov Ashkenazi, the brother of Naphtali Hertz Ashkenazi, Head of the Rabbinical Court of Lvov.

Rabbi Arieh Leibush Halevi Horowitz, the brother of the above Rabbi Moshe Yehoshua.

Rabbi Zaḥaria Mendel Frankel the son of Rabbi Meir Frankel Head of the Rabbinical Court of Międzyrzec (Mezeritz, Mezritch). He was the son-in-law of the above Rabbi Arieh Leibush and the student of Rabbi Noam Elimeleḥ of Leżajsk (Lizhensk), the author of *"Ha-Noam Elimeleḥ"*. There are many who say that the book "The Ways of Justice" attributed to Rabbi Mendel of Łużki (Luzhki) is, in fact by Rabbi Zaḥaria.

Rabbi Ya'acov Ḥaim Halperin was the son of Mr. Avraham of Lublin, member of the Council of the Four Lands. Already as a young child, he was recognized as being exceptionally gifted and married the daughter of Rabbi Avraham Yitzhak Ḥazak, known as the Physician of Jaroslaw. He was a gifted doctor and sought by many of the great and noble of Poland, extremely wealthy and a member of the Council of the Four Lands. After his wedding, his father-in-law sent him to Prague to the *Yeshiva* of the *Gaon* Rabbi Yohanan Eybeschütz and counted among the greatest of his pupils and while still young in years was installed as Rabbi of Jaroslaw. Not long after he was installed as Rabbi of his hometown Lublin.

[Page 28]

Ḥaya, the wife of his youth, died 15th Iyar 5512 (29th April 1752), in Lublin and on the first day of the month of Elul 5529, (3rd September 1769), Rabbi Ya'acov Ḥaim Halperin died and was buried with honor in Lublin.

His son, Rabbi Yitzhak Halperin, was the Rabbi of Tarnow, his daughter Zippora was the wife of Rabbi Yosef Hochgelernter, the author of *"Mishnat Ḥaḥamim"* a commentary on the *Rambam*, and his second daughter was the wife of Rabbi Avraham Ha-Cohen of Zamość (Zamoshtch), the author of *"Beit Avraham - Questions and Responsa"*.

Rabbi Ya'acov Ḥaim Halperin was the descendant of the *Gaon* Moshe Halperin of Brześć Litewski (Brisk, Brest-Litovsk).

It is appropriate to point out here, that the Halperin Family was known in Jaroslaw because at the end of the 17th Century the two brothers. Mordecai and Rabbi Joel Halperin lived there. They were the sons of Rabbi Yitzhak Isaac Halperin, Head of the Rabbinical Court of Tykocin.

After Rabbi Moshe Yehoshua Halevi Horowitz left Jaroslaw, the son-in-law of Rabbi Zaḥaria Mendel Frankel, the earlier Rabbi of Jaroslaw, was appointed Rabbi of Jaroslaw, Rabbi Yehuda Leib Heller was the son of Rabbi Ze'ev Wolf of Dobrzyń (Dobrin), and the grandson of the Rabbi Yom Tov Lipman Heller, author of *"Tosafot Yom Tov"*.[1]

In a dramatic scenario, the second son-in-law of Rabbi Zaḥaria Mendel Frankel, Rabbi Naphtali Hertz "Ḥariff" (sharp) was appointed Rabbi of Jaroslaw from among the wise members of the Brody *Kloiz*. At the end of the 18th Century, when the question of the Rabbinate of Jaroslaw arose, the heads of the community offered the position to the above Rabbi but because of his advanced age, he declined the offer. And because Rabbi Ya'acov Meshulam Orenstein, the author of "*Yeshuot Ya'acov*"[2] the son-in-law of Rabbi Tzvi Hirsch Wahl, was in town he was chosen and installed as the Rabbi. Nevertheless, the wife of Rabbi Naphtali Hertz continuously agitated her husband for having declined the honor and when this became known to Rabbi Orenstein, he returned the formal document since he was reluctant to show opposition to his uncle, thus he was again installed as Rabbi of Jaroslaw.

Rabbi Naphtali Hertz Ḥarif approved of the book "*Shem Shmuel*" a work of commentaries on the *Torah*, by Rabbi Shmuel Salir, Rav and Head of the Rabbinic Court of Lvóv (Lviv Lwów), published by the author's son Rabbi Natan Hecht of Jaroslaw. Old and blessed in years, Rabbi Naphtali Hertz passed away in 1819.

During his incumbency as the Rabbi of the town, the Great Synagogue was erected, and is still standing until today. On 6th *Tammuz* 1810 a building committee was created for the synagogue headed by Rabbi Naphtali Hertz Ḥarif and already by 15th *Av* 1811 they had the pleasure of celebrating its completion.

To state the obvious, the synagogue was built within the town itself and not outside its walls, as were the first synagogue and cemetery compelled to do in order to comply with the anti-Jewish edict of 1571 then in force.

[Page 29]

Regarding the building materials used in constructing the synagogue, Orlowycz had his own ideas. In 1807, the church steeple collapsed during a prayer service and more than twenty people were killed. The Austrian authorities ordered the entire building to be razed and as a sign of support for the Jews transferred the rubble to the Jewish authorities to use in the construction of the synagogue. That proposition has, of course, to be discounted with full vigor since it goes against any possibility of complying with *Halaḥa*.[3]

In the meantime, the Jewish settlement continued to grow and according to the statistics of 1813, there were 2,355 Jews representing 25% of the total population.

Starting in 1845, the Jewish community was headed by Dr. Mauritz Frankel. He was energetic and courageous, talented and progressive and during the 37 years of his leadership, he was at first a "*Reginar*" and later the elected chairman of the Jaroslaw community, fighting for its advancement and giving a helping hand to the *Haskala* movement. At no time, however, was Jaroslaw in any way a bastion of *Haskala* like Lvóv, Brody and Tarnopol in Galicia and Odessa, Kovno and Vilna and Warsaw then in Russia. Nevertheless the movement did find its way into town and struck roots, due mainly to the tireless efforts of Dr. Frankel on behalf of the town which became almost totally "*Haskala*"

It is quite possible that the *Haskala* movement in Jaroslaw prepared the ground for Yitzhak Arter, the student of the apostate Yosef Thaler. Arter came from the village of Chojnice (Khoynitsy), in the region of Przemyśl. Until 1814, he was a teacher in Jaroslaw and as such gave his soul to the movement. His activism was continued by the poet Aryeh Leib Kinderfreund who was born in Zamość and moved to Jaroslaw in that year and from there to Brody. Taking his advice, Arter tried to obtain a post as teacher at Josef Perle's school in Tarnopol but when that failed, he moved to Lvov. Here he met fierce opposition from the Rabbi of Lvóv, Rabbi Ya'acov Meshulam Ornstein the author of "*Yeshuot Ya'acov*" and published a boycott dissociating himself from him, declaring him as mistaken, in error, a deceiver, detractor and inciter. The Austrian government even became involved and compelled the Rabbi to cancel the boycott. Nevertheless, Arter found no means of sustenance in the hostile atmosphere and was forced to leave Lvóv and move to Brody where he quickly made a name for himself as a distinguished writer and a leading *Haskala* proponent in Galicia.

Among those born in Jaroslaw who were predominant *Haskala* stalwarts was Wolf Weiler (born in 1819). But unlike most of the *Haskala* followers, he didn't break his ties with the

[Page 30]

academic world, because the study of *Torah* was his hobby and as an ex-student of a *Yeshiva* he had published a number of articles on the *Torah* under the name Benjamin Ze'ev Aharon, in which were found sharp and knowledgeable comments.

And if, with the beginning of the 19th Century the *Haskala* movement began its first steps in Jaroslaw and succeeded by the second half of the Century to conquer the community, thanks to the efforts of Dr. Frenkel, the *Hassidim* and scholarliness had made their mark on the town. Among the founding personalities of the *Hassidim* in Jaroslaw were Rabbi Zaharia Mendel Frenkel, the Rabbi of Jaroslaw, the student of Rabbi Elimeleh of Leżajsk (Lizhensk), author of "*Noam Elimelech*", and above all, the Rav Rabbi Shimon Marilys known as Rabbi Shimon the Jaroslawi, the author of the book "*Shimon on the Torah*". He was the student of the "Seer of Lublin", and also travelled to visit Rabbi Shalom Rokah of Belz and other righteous men of his time and wrote in his book on the verse "Justice. Justice thou shalt seek", in the book of Judges: "and thus I strove to travel to the righteous ones even in my old age."[a]He passed away on the first day of Succoth, 1850 (Z"L) and was interred with honor in Jaroslaw in a special mausoleum next to the mausoleum on his left bearing his son Rabbi Bonam Mendel and to his right his son-in-law Rabbi Kehat Halperin, in one corner the wife of Rabbi Bonam Mendel and in another corner the wife of Rabbi Kehat, Mrs. Sheyndl Reisel. The others of his offspring, the continuation of the dynasty were Rabbi David, Eliezer and Rabbi Yisrael. The first of them died of natural causes about two years before the outbreak of World War Two and was brought to a burial in the family vault.

A native-born resident of Jaroslaw who became famous as a *Gaon* and righteous person was Rabbi Aryeh Leibish Lipshitz Head of the Rabbinical Courts of Korosteszów (Korshev), Ścinawa, Wyżnica (Vizhnitz) and Brzesko (Briegel). He was born in 1766 to his father, Rabbi Haim Lipshitz and when he was ten-years old was already recognized as a scholar of the Babylonian and Jerusalem *Talmuds* and considered a child wonder and referred to as Rabbi Leibish "the Sharp". He was the student of the author of "*Ktzot Ha-Hoshen*" Rabbi Aryeh Lev Ha-Cohen, an authoritative work and a friend of the author of "*Yeshuot Ya'acov*".

He authored two books "Questions and Responsa" as Aryeh Devi Ila'i and several learned works on the Tractate of *Ketuvot* from the *Gemara* his *Hassidut* Rabbi was "The Seer of Lublin" who was his son-in-law from the second marriage of Rabbi Moshe Teitelbaum, the author of "*Yismah Moshe*".[4] When his son-in-law was accepted as the Rabbi of Ujhely (Ihel), he filled his place as Rabbi of Ścinawa from where he moved to Wyżnica (Vizhnitz) and later to Brzesko (Briegel) where he died and was buried with honor. He died on 17 *Tevet* 1845. His daughter was the wife of Rabbi Yehezkiel Shraga Halberstein of Ścinawa.

[Page 31]

A conspicuous personality in the Jaroslaw gallery of *Hassidim* was Rabbi Mendel Hassid (died 1824). According to his will, he wrote that all who would come and pray over his grave on Sabbath Eves would have their dearest wishes fulfilled and consequently masses of people would come and prostrate themselves on his grave.

In conclusion we must mention that a few years before the Holocaust Grand Rabbi Yehoshua Rokeach of Jaroslaw, son of Rabbi Issachar Dov of Belz came to settle in town. For many years Rabbi Elimeleh Lam a direct descendant of Rabbi Elimeleh of Leżajsk, known to all as the "Rabbi of the Land of Israel" because he had lived there for a time. He had the habit of wearing three sets of phylacteries for Rashi, Rabbi Ya'acov ben Meir and a representative group known by the acronym SHaDaR[5].

It is thanks to the activities of these men, Jaroslaw claimed an honored position in the world of *Hassidut* and it is no surprise that they were considered as being God-fearing and reverenced. But in addition to that, Jaroslaw was – and had always been a place of *Torah* and an indication of such was that the Rabbi Meir of Hýskov considered it wise to send his son the author of "*Kedushat Levi*" to study *Torah* in Jaroslaw. There were three elements directing Jaroslaw in the path of learning: A) The Council of the Four Lands made it their meeting-place and the town therefore hosted the great *Gaonim* of the era, B) The Chief Rabbis of Jaroslaw were among "the greats" of *Torah* learning, C) The personality of the author of "*Yeshuot Ya'acov*" who resided there at the time in the Hill of Talpiot.[6] Among the regular visitors, who gathered in Jaroslaw were Rabbi Aharon Moshe Tobias the author of "*To'efet Ram*", who later officiated as Rabbi of Śniatyń and Ia°i (Yassi) Rabbi of Tarnogród (Tarnogrud) and approved of by Rabbi Eliezer Horowitz the author of "*Noam Megadim*".

Referring to his time in Jaroslaw in his memoirs, Rabbi Ya'acov Meshulam Ornstein the author of "*Yeshuot Ya'acov*", praised the Jews of Jaroslaw in general, and its students in particular, as masters of the *Torah* and scholars.

And although from the middle of the nineteenth century there was a turning point in the fashion and essence of Jaroslaw, a considerable part of it turned its back on *Ḥassidism* and *Torah* study, slowly severing its ties with the old world and in the streets of Jewish Jaroslaw began a new spirit of education and progress. And as a result of that there was an increase of assimilation and about twenty years after its beginning, it returned to its former glory and there were again many *Torah* scholars, *Ḥassidim* and functionaries.

With the end of the First World War, Jaroslaw began a vibrant revival of national and religious life and the impact of the revival penetrated deep into the hearts of the youth, and from then the *Aliyah* began. In the beginning there were mainly individuals, but over time the *Aliyah* grew and encompassed wider circles and hardly ceased until the Holocaust.

[Page 32]

The city square and the City Hall

[Page 33]

When in 1772 the first division of Poland occurred and Austria acquired Galicia, on the 18th February 1788 a military order under which everyone, irrespective of ethnic or religious background, was obliged to serve in the army. From one point of view, the Jews could consider it a significant advantage because it meant that the Austrian government would be publicly and implicitly recognizing the Jews but on the other hand, the Jews were unable to come to terms with the edict because military service then was terrible in their eyes. They therefore were much relieved when, in 1827, when the above law was corrected and it became possible for those who were unable to fulfill their obligation for personal reasons could send someone in their place on payment of a certain sum of money. In all the towns of Galicia, special committees were created with the aim of raising enough money by contributions that made it possible even for the poor, to pay for someone to replace him in the army.

On the 9th *Tevet*, 1834 such a committee was brought into being in Jaroslaw with seven members from among respected members of the community, headed by Rabbi Shimon. When in 1854 Rabbi Yitzhak Ya'acov Horowitz the Rabbi of Cieszńow was installed as Rabbi of the town, he became head of that committee. Rabbi Horowitz was the son of Rabbi Arieh, Head of the Rabbinical Court of Trembowla (Trembovla) and he occupied the Rabbi's chair until the day of his death 24th *Tevet* 1864.

About three years after his death, Rabbi Shmuel Waldberg was chosen as the town Rabbi. He had been the Rabbi of Żółkiew (Zholkeva) for ten years but because of arguments that had broken out between him and the community, he left Żółkiew and moved to Jaroslaw to officiate as town Rabbi in 1867. But the relationships between him and the community of Jaroslaw were also not satisfactory and an open dispute broke out reaching such proportions that in 1871 the community dismissed him and only thanks to the intervention of Rabbi Lowenstein of Lvóv was the feud finally settled. In spite of that, the relationship of the community with Rabbi Waldberg remained cool.

Rabbi Waldberg authored five books: "*Omrei Da'at*", "*Ateret Shoshanim*", "*Davar B'ito*", "*Darkei Ha-Shinu'im*" and "*Divrei Shmuel*" a book commenting on the order of the alphabet. He died in 1906 when he was 77 years old.

His brother, Moshe Waldberg was one of the big bankers in Bucharest and among the initiators of the trade agreement between the Austrian-Hungarian Empire and Rumania in 1875. As a result of that on 12th June 1875, he was raised to the Nobility and 16th May, 1884 became a Baron. He died in 1901 and almost immediately upon his death his son converted to Christianity.

[Page 34]

In the meantime, shockwaves had stunned the Jewish community because on the 25th March 1869 gangs of Jaroslaw ruffians had spontaneously descended upon the Jewish community in an anti-Semitic rage, robbing and looting Jewish stores and stalls, smashing the windows of Jewish homes and the home of Adolph Julius Strisower was particularly damaged. And in addition, many among the Jewish population suffered injuries. The rioting bullies exploited the hostile attitude of the local authorities towards the Jews and succeeded in their depredations from the 25th March until the 5th April (with a few small pauses) without any reaction from the authorities. Only through the efforts of the Lvóv Regional representative and thanks to the impassioned plea of a Jew who pleaded with the army in Jaroslaw to intervene in the desperate situation that had developed, did the pogrom come to a halt.

As evidence strengthening our claim that the hatred of Jews was in the hearts of the Jaroslaw authorities, we present the following facts:

When the representatives of the community, Hirsch Barihal and Sandor Gavel appeared before the Regional officer named Halbyk asking his help and that he should act against the hooligans, he replied in vulgar and brutal language: "Clear off out of here!"

According to the advice of the mayor at the time, the Municipality decided to forbid Jews to take part in any form of public auctions.

But exactly as recorded in the Bible: "But the more the Egyptians oppressed them, the more the Israelites multiplied and spread and the more alarmed the Egyptians became."[7] – The census of 1872 shows that the Jewish population of Jaroslaw then numbered more than 4,500. Three hundred children attended non-Jewish schools and the community maintained a teacher for Hebrew, and sustained him at their expense. Also maintained was a Jewish hospital with thirty beds financed from the income of the bath-house. A significant element of the hospital's budget was from different donations, legacies and estates.

A most important date in the history of the Jewish community of Jaroslaw was 1876. In that year, the system of the "*Reginar*" ceased to exist and for the first time elections were held, in which sixteen members were chosen. The rule of the few was replaced by the democratically elected representatives. Even so, the right to vote was still restricted to those who paid taxes and even though there was still not a general election it a great step forward in the direction of democratization of the community. The elections took place on 5th October, 1876, and the number of voters entitled to vote, together with the surrounding villagers was 268. It is worthwhile noting that women too, if they paid taxes, had the right to vote but only by appointing a male power of attorney. Dr. Frankel was elected Chairman and his deputy the attorney Dr. Emil Gottlieb.

[Page 35]

In 1880, the town of Redimno (Redem) that up until now had been considered an extension of the community of Jaroslaw was granted freedom and independence. In 1883, Dr. Frenkel left Jaroslaw and moved to Lvov where he died two years later at the age of 77. His place as chairman was filled by his deputy Dr. Gottlieb who remained in that post until the end of that session on 31st December 1885. The cooperation between the elected members was not good and when Dr. Friedwald resigned together with five other members Dr. Gottlieb was forced to hold new elections for six new members.

In 1885 the doctor Ya'acov Raff was elected as Chairman and in the four years of his Chairmanship he earned for himself the general support and respect of the community and thus on his retirement in 1889, he was unanimously elected as honorary president of the Community.

His successor was Heinrich Strisower who was elected Chairman 27th November 1889. During his time in office, the new Study House was built on the site of the old one. On the site of the *Talmud Torah* a school with two classes was erected, named for Baron Hirsch, an old people's home financed from the estate of Chairman Adolph Strisower's father while the chairman himself contributed 1,000 Gulden, paving the road to the cemetery and building there a waiting room. In addition, it was decided to refurbish the Great Synagogue, build a slaughter-house for poultry and a bath-house in the town because the previous one stood in an inconvenient location and was deemed to be unfit for use. A special committee was formed, headed by the Chairman's brother, Julius Strisower. The committee's task was to manage the building of the bath-house. In the meantime, the Chairman Heinrich Strisower passed away in 1905 after he had managed the community's affairs for 15 years. Heinrich Strisower's period in office was seen as a period of construction and creativity. And it is appropriate that if, until now the *lingua franca* of the community had been German, it was decided in a committee meeting in February 1902 that henceforth the official language of the community shall be Polish.

After him, on 18th January 1906 Dr. Avraham Friedwald was elected as Chairman and his deputy Julius Strisower who was the living spirit of the community. The first actions taken by the new administration were restricted and only the earlier, planned buildings were executed; thus the bath-house, the slaughter-house and the Great Synagogue were raised.

[Page 36]

And now, after the post of town Rabbi had remained vacant for a number of years, the community approached the election of a Rabbi on 7th January, 1914. The main candidates at the time were: Rabbi Leibush Mendel Landau, the disciple of Rabbi Yitzhak Schmelkes of Lvóv and Rabbi Meir Horowitz from Buczacz (Betshotsh). Because neither of the two candidates received the required two-thirds of the votes, neither one was accepted and installed.

With the outbreak of World War One in 1914, the committee decided to institute a special fund to the sum of 300 Kroner, to assist all the needy and poverty-stricken families (with no discrimination of religion) whose head of family had been mobilized into the army, and to the Polish National fund the sum of 200 Kroner.

Immediately with the cessation of hostilities, on June 19th 1918 (*sic*)[8] anti-Semitic rioting broke out in Jaroslaw and among other damage windows in the bath-house and the Great Synagogue were smashed. In the light of the serious situation with its anti-Semitic background, the National Jewish Council organized representatives from all the Jewish parties with the objective of protecting the rights and interests of the Jews – political, national and economic. The National Council saw itself as the only representative of the Jews and turned to the committee and demanded that it resign and transfer power to the National Council in all matters concerning the Jewish population. Taking into consideration the critical situation, the committee agreed to broaden its framework and named some additional new members from outside the present committee – and the situation became calmer.

In May 1919, Dr. Friedwald resigned as Chairman of the committee and of all public activities he preferred the *Talmud Torah* of which he had been Chairman for many years. As an old man, Dr. Friedwald passed away on the 6th January 1937.

On the 6th May 1919, Julius Strisower, honored as "Advisor to the Emperor" was installed as Chairman in his place. When Julius Strisower took the reins of power in the Jaroslaw community, he was already well-known as the previous deputy chairman and involved in the life of the community as a founder in 1917 of the orphanage in Jaroslaw, manager of the town's savings fund and as deputy mayor. The first act of the newly appointed Chairman was his war against the profiteering of basic needs and he was active in the field of philanthropy and among other things, he was head of the Jaroslaw branch committee of help for Polish Jews. Among his tasks was to assist all those in need who suffered as a result of the war.

[Page 37]

When life returned more or less to normal, and the situation stabilized, the time came to elect a Rabbi for the town since the post had been vacant for fifteen years. At a joint session of the committee and the residents on 25th May 1921, the father of the author of these few lines Rabbi Yitzhak Steinberg (Z"L), of Halicz (Helitch) was installed as the town's Rabbi. He also acted as Head of the Rabbinical Court until the outbreak of World War Two – until the destruction. The Rabbi Yitzhak Steinberg, the son of Rabbi Shemaiah Steinberg Head of the Rabbinical Court of Przemyśl, the son of Rabbi Avraham Menaḥem Mendel Steinberg, Head of the Rabbinical Court of Brody, the author of "Questions and Responses – Abraham's Play", was the last Rabbi of Jewish Jaroslaw.

In April 1924 Rabbi Steinberg was elected as Head of the Rabbinical Court in Radom but after a while he resigned his position because of the many internecine arguments and feuds that existed there for many years and also because the pressures brought upon him by the community of Jaroslaw not to accept the post in Radom. On 3rd May 1926 after speaking in the Great Synagogue in honor of a national festival beginning that day, in a spontaneous meeting of the respected leaders of the congregation they demanded of the congregation to make every effort to persuade Rabbi Steinberg to resign his new post in Radom. In consideration of their pleas, he relinquished the seat in Radom.

The Court of Rabbi Steinberg was at first comprised of two *Dayanim*[9]: Rabbi Pinḥas Hemerling and Rabbi Benjamin Moshe Goldman. As this latter Rabbi aged, a third *Dayan* Rabbi David Diller was appointed in his place.

Apart from Rabbi Steinberg's normal duties as town Rabbi, he also preached *Torah* and instituted study classes in his home for the youth and *Yeshiva* students. He was the manager of the *Talmud Torah* that in its day was a most important educational foundation in town where several hundred children learned. In 1923 the *Talmud Torah* became a small *Yeshiva* that was headed by Rabbi Mordecai Ḥaim Hertzberg of Pistyń (Pistin), the author of "*Tamḥin D'oraita*"[10].

In 1928, the charitable organization "*Gemilat Ḥassidim*" was created in Jaroslaw headed by Julius Strisower but a few years later Rabbi Steinberg was appointed Chairman. The charity did much to fulfill the needs of the impoverished especially the small traders and stall-holders who received loans at no interest. Because of this help, they were able to manage and save their small businesses from total collapse.

A most praiseworthy and blessed element of Rabbi Steinberg's activities was his dedication to helping the Jewish soldiers serving in Jaroslaw. Thanks to his efforts the military authorities in Jaroslaw compelled all the Jewish soldiers to attend prayers on *Shabbat* and Festivals in the Great Synagogue as an organized group. He also founded a special fund to ensure that religious Jewish soldiers were provided with Kosher food during their military service and with the approach of Passover stood at the head of "Operation Pessaḥ" with the target of ensuring that a special kitchen was organized to supply them with special Passover food for the whole week of the festival. The Passover meal opening the festival for the soldiers was conducted with the participation of Rabbi Steinberg and the Cantor Meshulam Lam.

[Page 38]

With the outbreak of World War Two, the Rabbi left Jaroslaw moving to eastern Galicia and from there was exiled to the Ural forests of Russia. He had many adventures during his years of exile especially in Samarkand in Uzbekistan. The wanderings from place to place, the conditions in which he lived, hunger, changes of climate, it all had a negative effect upon him including the death of his son – the writer's brother, Benjamin Ze'ev – who died in Samarkand at a young age. At the age of seventeen, he was licensed as a teacher and left behind him the manuscript of "Commentaries on the 'Tur Shulḥan Aruḥ' of Maimonides".

After the Holocaust, Rabbi Steinberg was installed as the Rabbi of Brussels, the capital of Belgium and in 1951 immigrated to Israel where he became Head of the Rabbinical Court of the Tel-Aviv area and lastly as the Rabbi of the "*Yeshuran*" synagogue, in Tel-Aviv. During the Holocaust all his writings, on all the aspects of the *Torah* were lost among them his manuscript of "*Sha'arei Yitzhak*" – "The Gates of Isaac" – a treatise on the "*Mezuzah*". He died 27th Heshvan 1966 and was buried with honor in Tel-Aviv.

On 1st April 1925, a ceremonial meeting took place in the Council's meeting room, celebrating the consecration of the Hebrew University on Mount Scopus, Jerusalem. At the suggestion of Dr. Schorr, it was decided to institute a stipend for a Jaroslaw-born student of little means enabling him to study at the Hebrew University and to send a congratulatory letter in Hebrew and Polish to the Rector of the University.

In 1927, celebrating the tenth anniversary of the Orphanage Home, the institution was renamed in honor of its founder, "The Julius Strisower Orphanage Home" because of the indisputable fact that he dedicated so much effort to its creation and he was as much a true surrogate father to the orphans. Even after they matured and left the home, he interested himself in their progress, welfare and education with heartfelt devotion.

In 1928 new elections were held in Jaroslaw for the community council and on the basis of the new constitution twenty members were elected apart from the local sitting Rabbi. Julius Strisower was again elected Chairman and his Deputy, Dr. Mauritz Ettinger; as Chairman of the Council the attorney Dr. Maximilian Segal was elected while his deputy was Eliezer Berish Goldman, an estate holder.

[Page 39]

With the ending of that term, all parties in Jaroslaw agreed to prevent at all costs, election wars and a wall-to-wall front was created including economic non-party circles. The agreement found approval in the eyes of the whole town and without an election, the elected members of the community took control in 1934.

The last Jewish community leaders of Jaroslaw

Sitting from R to L: A. Reich, A. Rager, Rabbi Yitzhak Steinberg, L. Diller
Standing from R. to L: Sh. Licht, M. Hass, Piskosh, Sh. Lang, A. Glass, N. Tanzer, L. Metzger

At the head of the management stood the attorney, Dr. Shmuel Schorr, the brother of the Senator Professor Rabbi Moshe Schorr of Warsaw. As a man who stood far away from the stormy world of politics and Party and as a supporter of rebirth, he was considered to be the right man in the right place and Eliezer Berish Goldman was elected as the deputy Chairman. Max Selig was elected as chairman of the council as representative of the Zionist Organization. Shimon Spiegel, the owner of a silk-screens factory and Chairman of the Artisans and Traders' Bank of Jaroslaw and representative of "Mizrahi" was his elected deputy and after his immigration to Palestine, his place as deputy was taken by Adolph Rager as representative of the Craftsmen's Association.

From its very beginning the management of the community under Dr. Schorr ran into serious financial difficulties springing principally from a reduction in incomes because of the notorious Pristor Law. Nevertheless, the congregation participated in the maintenance of the institutions by subsidies, and the old people's home was maintained by the congregation alone, at its expense. Two community buildings, each of two storeys, were used by the congregation only. In one of them were the offices of the congregation, the "*Gemilat Hassidim*" (Charity for the Poor), and the meeting room. In the second building was the old people's home "Taz" of ambulatory residents, managed by Dr. Mauritz Shafetz who for some years, had been the head of the Zionist Federation in Jaroslaw; The offices of the Rabbanut were in the same building.

[Page 40]

The full complement of both the management and the community Council until the outbreak of World War Two was as follows:

Sr. Shmuel Schorr (Chairman), Eliezer Berish Goldman (Deputy Chairman of management), Committee members of the management: Moshe Hess, Leib Metzger, Max Folkman, Elimeleḥ Reich, Dr Wilhelm Schwarzer, Mendel Schlafrig and Rabbi Yitzhak Steinberg.

Max Selick (Chairman of the Council), Adolph Rager (Deputy Chairman). Members of the Council: Yona Everett, Mordecai Orenbach, Avraham Glat, Shimon Licht, Yeshaya Lang, Dr. Mauritz Meister, Eliyahu Sandik, Haim Aharon Zilbiger, Adolph Fechter and Aharon Rosenfeld.

These were the names of the last committee members of Jaroslaw before the destruction.

Original Footnote:

a.   He used to say that the virtue of longevity was to lessen the burden on the Holy One, blessed be He, for if we do so what will he say if the Holy One says to him "Come up to me in heaven and you will see that everything is in order and that there are no problems" – therefore he who wishes to live long will not visit and will not burden the Holy One. Rabbi Shimon's father was strongly critical of, and looked unfavorably upon, his son's strong attraction to the B'ESHT and according to legend compelled his son, before his death, shall not grant him the title of "Cohen" and not recite the *Kaddish* prayer since he knew that he would recite the section of *"Veyatzmaḥ purqaneh viqarev"* (And may his salvation blossom and his anointed be near), instead of the accepted pure Ashkenazi version. After his death he regretted with great sadness about it and when the author of *"Divrei Ḥaim"* came on the customary condolence visit he ordered him to recite the *Kaddish* with the added *"Veyatzmaḥ purqaneh viqarev"* because now his father was *"b'alma dakushta"* [From the *Zohar*, meaning the "World of truth" a pseudonym for Heaven – trans.] and knows the truth and *"Veyatzmaḥ purqaneh viqarev"* needs to be said.

Translator's Footnotes:

1.   A commentary on the *Mishnah*.
2.   A commentary on the equally learned and erudite "Shulḥan Aruḥ"
3.   The overall basic framework of Jewish day-to-day law.
4.   Considered one of the classic homiletic works of *Ḥassidism, "Questions and responsa"*.
5.   See https://en.wikipedia.org/wiki/Meshulach for a full description.
6.   A synonym for King David derived from the Song of Solomon 4:4
7.   See Exodus 1:12
8.   I am unable to determine why this date is given. Although the later stages of the war did show signs of disagreement and reluctance to continue with the conflict among some of the fringe coalitions on both sides, it is certainly-well known that the official cease-fire and signing of the armistice occurred at 11:00 a.m. 11th November 1918.
9.   A Dayan is a specially qualified, respected and highly learned Rabbi who sits in a Rabbinical Court judging cases in accordance with Jewish law.
10. A religious work on the *Torah*.

[Page 41]

Chevra Kadisha in Jaroslaw

by Rabbi Moshe Steinberg

Translated by Susan Rosin

The very first Jewish organization established in our town was the "Chevra Kadisha", which predated the establishment of the hospital. During that time, the main function of the organization was to transport the deceased for burial in the Jewish cemetery of Przemyśl (Pshemishl). After the establishment of the Jewish cemetery in Jaroslaw, the organization extended its activities to include philanthropy.

Charity for the town's poor as well as for the visiting-poor was always part of the organization's budget. Each year a large sum was distributed before Passover in the form of "Ma'ot Chitim" (This special Passover fund, originally intended to provide the poor with matzah, is known as ma'ot chitim, "the wheat fund"). The town's rabbi received 10 golden per year: 8 golden for two sermons and additional 2 golden from the annually (during Chol Hamoed Pesach) elected management. Starting in 1714, the organization provided yearly subsidy to maintain the "Hekdesh" which served as a hospital and homeless shelter. The subsidy amount was 20 golden per year and it was paid in four installments: The first day of Iyar, Yom Kippur eve, Hanukkah and Chol Hamoed Pesach. The community contributed another 25 golden as an annual subsidy[1].

Originally there was a "Bikur Cholim" (visiting the sick) organization. Due to budgetary difficulties, Bikur Cholim and Chevra Kadisha merged in 1756. Since that time, the Chevra Kadisha acted also as a Bikur Cholim charity, and assigned special amount for this purpose. From that time on, any new member of Chevra Kadisha had to be a member of Bikur Cholim as well.

The Chevra Kadisha was well organized and operated according to rules and regulations that were well documented. The management was comprised as follows:

5 Heads of households, 6 Gabai'im (beadles), 6 Accountants, 3 Permanent members, 5 Regulators.
The numbers of the management members changed from time to time.

[Page 42]

The members of Chevra Kadisha were always from among the distinguished in town. To be a member was considered a great honor.

The discipline within the society was very strict and any offending member was punished severely. For instance, one of the members slighted the society. It was decided to excommunicate him. Only because of his family, his punishment was changed to lashes. The punishment was carried out in the cemetery, and he had also to go three times to synagogue to beg for forgiveness in public. Normally a punishment would be removal of the member permanently and recording the offender in the society's book.

The "Chesed Ve'Emet" organization served its members only, whereas Chevra Kadisha was a general organization providing services to all. The main function of Chesed Ve'Emet was to assist members during the Shivaa, or during illness when a member was unable to work and provide for his family. In addition, the society arranged for funerals for their members. In the 1930's the society completed the construction of their building that also included the synagogue "Chesed Ve'Emet".

Another ancient society, but of a different type was "Shomrim laboker" (those who await the morning). The members recited "Shomrim" every day at dawn, and in the evening after the prayers they would study a chapter of mishnayot. It is worth noting that until 1788 the organization had a leader who gave sermons on Saturdays and holidays. The last such leader was the rabbi from Sędziszów.

In 1810 the society approached the synagogue building committee in Jaroslaw. They committed 400 golden to the effort as well as one third of the Monday and Thursday collections. For their contribution, they were to receive a room on the first floor to serve as the Shomrim Laboker synagogue.

Translator's Footnote:

1. Based on the budget of the Synod of Four Lands from 1726, it appears that the "Hekdesh" in Jaroslaw received 60 golden. See Halperin, the Synod of Four lands, page 503.

[Page 43]

The Council of Four Lands

by Rabbi M. Steinberg

Translated by Susan Rosin

Jaroslaw was blessed with being the location of the Council of Four Lands meetings. Due to that fact, the town is important in the history of the Jewish people and specifically in the history of Polish Jewry. This supreme institution of Polish Jewry opened a spectacular page in the history of Jewish Jaroslaw. Truth to be told we need to separate the history of the council and the history of Jaroslaw Jewry. The council's discussions were mainly about general, country-wide Jewish issues. However the fact that this town was selected as a meeting place of the council in addition to Lublin, shows the importance and standing of Jaroslaw among the most important towns in history of Jewish Poland. During the meetings of the council, the town hosted the spiritual representatives and leaders of Poland's Jewry. Jews looked-up to this judicial and legislative body in Jaroslaw as it instructed them in matters of education, religion, public and economical life. Many of the issues of the time found their resolutions in our town.

The Jewish population in town was scarce when the council first started meeting in Jaroslaw. In time, the number of Jews in town increased and they were witnesses of this historic institution. It stands to reason that the great and important leaders influenced the local population in positive ways.

Meeting of that sort were held in many countries such as France (in the 12th century), Germany, Castile, and Moravia. The difference is that these meeting were of a local character, whereas the coouncil dealt with general Jewish issues not limited to a certain country. The implications of their decisions can be felt up to this day.

There are some speculations about the origins and reasons for the establishment of the council. The most common opinion is that the establishment of the council is attributed to the Lublin rabbi Mordechai Jaffe (1532 – 1612).

[Page 44]

Every year multitudes of Jews came to the Lublin fair. Disagreements and quarrels were a common occurrence. As the rabbi, Jaffe had to mediate and even judge. During the fair, many rabbis, leaders and heads of Yeshivas used to come to Lublin as well. They normally discussed important general issues affecting the Jewish population. In order to make these spontaneous and infrequent meetings into a permanent institution, rabbi Jaffe initiated the Council of the Four lands.

Another theory on the establishment of the Council is due to the meetings from time to time of leaders of the large Jewish communities. In these meetings they discussed issues pertaining to a certain region and sometimes the entire Polish Jewry. Representatives of the communities appeared before the king to discuss Jewish rights and privileges as well as the hostile attitudes of the local authorities and the church. The relationships between the kehila (Jewish community) branches and the main kehila were discussed during these meetings. There was an opportunity to exchange ideas about religion and tradition during these meetings because kehila rabbis participated. And that is how the Council of the Four Lands came into being.

Another theory – and the most plausible – is that the Council was established as a direct result of the "poll tax" that was imposed on the Jews by the Polish Sejm. Due to the lack of organization, the government itself was unable to collect the tax and the communities were tasked with the collection and distribution of the tax. The common interest of the government and the communities required therefore to establish a responsible supreme institution with authority to deal with this issue. And so, in the year 1580, the Council of the Four Lands was established. It has to be noted that during ancient times and then in the middle-ages, the authorities did not deal with individual Jews, but with the Jewish public as a whole. The obligation to collect the tax and meet the quota was the responsibility of the Jewish communities.

At the beginning the Council was comprised of five countries: Greater Poland, Lesser Poland[1], Russia, Lithuania and Volhynia. Sometimes only three participated, and it was called the Council of Three Lands. In 1623, Lithuania withdrew and established its own council. From that time on it was called the Council of the Four lands (Congressus Judaicus).

The main function of the council was to deal with financial issues and that is where most of its time was spent. From time to time there was a need to change the tax distribution between the communities and the district.

[Page 45]

The total original amount of the "poll tax" was 18,000 golden. In time, it was increased and reached to more than twenty thousand golden. Because the council meetings included rabbis, head of yeshivas, Torah scholars, and spiritual leaders, it is only natural that the council discussed all matters of importance to the Polish Jewry as well as Jews around the world.

The measures and decision of council became laws, and communities that did not comply were punished and fined. The council was a kind of a "kingdom within a kingdom" and was the symbol of the unification of Polish Jewry. It is assumed that the number of members was 70, the same as the number of members of the Great Sanhedrin. Of course this number was symbolic, as not all members were worthy and besides the location of the Sanhedrin can only be in Eretz Israel.

The council was headed by members elected "Parnas"[2]. Other elected officials were treasurers, secretaries, and lobbyists who represented the council externally. The "Parnas" was a "secular Jew" whereas the treasurers and secretaries were rabbis. The "Parnas" and the administrative staff were involved throughout the year and received their salaries from the council's coffers. The rest of the members were involved only during the council meetings and therefore received their symbolic salaries from the communities or the district that elected them. The members of the council were highly regarded.

It appears that the council met for the first time in Jaroslaw in 1591. Since 1680 and until its abolishment, the council no longer met in Lublin, but only in Jaroslaw that became its permanent meeting location. In the 18th century, the council met sometimes in other towns (that belonged to the treasury secretary), such as Ryczywół (Ritchvol), Pilica (Piltz), Konstantynów (Kostentin) and others.

The language spoken during the meetings was Yiddish, as well as the announcements for the public. However the regulations, resolutions and judgments were written in Hebrew.

According to a regulation from 1594, "No books will be printed without the permission of rabbis and champions". Various authors arrived in Jaroslaw to obtain the council's approval[3] or the approval of a great rabbi.

[Page 46]

In the years 1587 and 1590 a regulation by the council in Lublin determined that no man should be appointed for money. This regulation was renewed during the council meeting in Jaroslaw in the year 1640.

In the middle of the 17th century there was a great danger to the Jewish population due to the Sabbatai Tzvi movement. The council in Lublin announced "A great and terrible excommunication by blowing the shofar and extinguishing candles on the criminals and thoughtless" who follow the Shabbtai Tzvi movement. In the year 1672, the council in Jaroslaw sent out an announcement in Yiddish to the public to this effect.

[Page 47]

These excommunication announcements were apparently not effective, so that in 1731 the council in Jaroslaw placed an ultimatum that if people will not repent, they will be punished with severe excommunication.

The famous controversy between rabbi Jonathan Eibeschitz and rabbi Jacob Emden[4] regarding amulets was a divisive matter among the Jewish population and was on the agenda for a long time. The matter was finally closed during the council meeting in Jaroslaw on the second day of Heshvan 5414[5]. The meeting was chaired by Avraham Halperin from Lublin (the father of the Jaroslaw rabbi Yaakov Chaim Halperin). The judgement determined that "No voice of blame will be heard against the famous genius in his generation rabbi Jonathan" and all the opposing libel writings were burnt in front of the public.

Reading of the bible was not easy for the multitudes and women due to the lack of knowledge of the Hebrew language. So, in order to read and enjoy the holy book, the council in Jaroslaw allowed on the 24th of Elul 5437 (1677) to print the bible in an Ashkenazi – Jewish translation by the printer Joseph Athias[6] from Amsterdam.

Among the many actions of the council and important problems that found their resolutions by the council, we need to note that the council never ignored the plight of the poor and those needing help. They were always cognizant of the needs of the poor and there was always an item in the budget for this purpose.

[Page 48]

After the Polish-Turkish war of 1672, many communities were destroyed, people lost all their possessions and many were captured and imprisoned. As the council was unable to help all the unfortunate financially, they wrote to both the Sephardic and Ashkenazi communities in Amsterdam requesting assistance for the victims of that war and to do whatever is possible for the captive redemption commandment[7].

The council was involved in supporting the poor in Eretz Israel. Each of the four lands had a specifically appointed representative whose function was to collect funds for the poor in the holy land. A special proclamation in the year 5387 (1627) for Eretz Israel poor: "Awake and remember the poor in Eretz Israel; Please bring all donations to the fair in Jaroslaw - those collected by rabbi Nechemia and all other donations".

During the Jaroslaw council meeting in the year 5499 (1739) "appointed collectors in every district and every town" to collect donations for Eretz Israel poor.

The council in Jaroslaw devoted much time in an effort to settle conflicts between various communities. In 5452 (1692) the council declared that small towns and villages that do not have their own synagogues and are in a two miles proximity to a main community will have to be under that community's authority in matters relating to business and taxation.

The rabbis participating in the council were involved in halachic matters. The most famous was the "Vienna Get"[8] which attracted the rabbinical world at the time because of the dispute between two very well know rabbis – rabbi Yehoshua Falk[9] and the "Maharam"[10]. The council in Jaroslaw determined that rabbi Falk was right and the divorce stood.

The council devoted most of its time to financial issues. Since the middle of the 18th century, the council's debts grew. The increasing debts were the main topic of discussion and were always part of the agenda until the council was abolished. The first time the council discussed the financial issues in Jaroslaw was in 1687 and because of the seriousness of the situation, the council's "Parnas" Naftali Zeligowitcz was forced to take a loan of 20,000 golden from Jaroslaw's Jesuits.

[Page 49]

The serious financial situation caused the council to meet less frequently. In 1711, when the council met, they were told by one of the senior members that the minister of the treasury is not interested in the meeting, and thus this subject was not discussed.

When the deficit grew from year to year, the council met in 1739 to seriously discuss the matter. However this meeting ended without any real resolution. Only in 1753, the council in Jaroslaw was able to reach a satisfactory solution.

We need to note here that the council discussed internal issues of our town. In 1700, the council approved the community request to establish a separate cemetery.

As there are many questions if the establishment of the council was connected to the poll tax, there is no dispute of the fact that its abolishment was due to it. In the Polish Sejm many argued for collecting the tax directly without the involvement of the council. A resolution passed on June 1st, 1764 (1st of Sivan, 5524) to abolish the council, to conduct a census of all the Jews and collect a tax of two golden per year from every person.

The resolution read:

"It is well known that the Jews collect taxes based on various arrangements. As such, they collect more than the amount established in the 1717 statute in the amount of 220,000 golden. They use the rest of the amount for their benefits and private expenditure. The state can easily collect a higher amount from the Jews. Therefore we cancel the tax as it was determined in 1624 and establish a new system of taxation for all Jews and Karaits in the villages, the towns and under the rule of nobles and the church: After payment of the amount owed for this year (1764), the taxes will be collected as following: After settling the debt for 1764, each one of the Jews and Karaits will pay two golden per person per year starting from the year of birth without exceptions.

[Page 50]

And because the poll tax established in the 1717 statute is now canceled, the various assemblies, apportionments or other kinds of injunctions, levies or compulsions relating to the Jews are prohibited in the towns, cities and villages as of January 2nd, 1765. Non-compliance can carry up to 6,000 golden fine and or confiscation of property.

And that is how this magnificent institution that existed close to 200 years ceased to exist. During its existence it instructed, educated, corrected, judged and represented Polish Jewry and it left behind an illustrious chapter in the history of Polish Jewry and specifically Jewish Jarosław.

Translator's Footnotes:

1. Lesser Poland, often known by its Polish name Małopolska (Latin: Polonia Minor), is a historical region situated in southern and south-eastern Poland. Its capital and largest city is Kraków. Throughout centuries, Lesser

Poland developed a separate culture featuring diverse architecture, folk costumes, dances, cuisine, traditions and a rare Lesser Polish dialect.

2. "Parnas" refers to a civil leader of the Jewish community.

3. For example: a general agreement of the council in Jaroslaw (J. Halperin, Notebook of the council of four lands, page 15) As we gather here in the town in the year 363 (1603) we agreed to give permission to print the assay by the genius rabbi Yaakov Ben Elyakim, the books that were written by the renowned teacher and rabbi, rabbi Isaac Abarbanel. He wrote the books Sefer Zebach Pesac? (Passover Offering), Nachlat Avot (Inheritance of the Fathers). And his books are very detailed and very long, preventing many from reading them. Until came the genius above and copied these two books in a language that is shorter and understood by all. And because the above always produces correct material we allowed him to print the books.

4. Jacob Emden, also known as Ya'avetz (June 4, 1697 – April 19, 1776); Jonathan Eibeschitz (1690 – 1764)

5. Heshvan 2nd, 5414 was October 23rd, 1653

6. Joseph Athias was a printer and publisher; born in Spain, probably in Cordova, at the beginning of the seventeenth century; died at Amsterdam, May 12, 1700

7. Pidyon Shvuyim (Hebrew: פִּדְיוֹן שְׁבוּיִים, literally: Redemption of Captives) is a religious duty in Judaism to bring about the release of a fellow Jew captured by slave dealers or robbers, or imprisoned unjustly by the authorities. The release of the prisoner is typically secured by a ransom paid by the Jewish community. It is considered an important commandment in Jewish law.

8. In 1611, a 16-year-old boy from Lviv, Yitzhak Walpish became ill, and relatives of his wife, Bat Sheva, from Vienna - who feared that he would die, asked him to give a divorce to his wife, on condition that if he did not die, he would return and marry her again. The divorce was arranged by rabbi of Vienna Manoach Hendel and one of the greatest arbiters of the generation, rabbi Yehushua Fleck Katz. The divorce itself was not enshrined in the condition, but was given unconditionally, with the promise that the boy would marry the woman if he recovers and was given regardless of the divorce.
The husband recovered, but after a sudden fight with his wife's relatives, they informed him that they will not allow him to marry Bat Sheva again. The husband, who was left without a wife and without assets (his house had already been given as a gift to his ex-wife), turned to the Maharam of Lublin the Lvov rabbi, and he ruled that because the husband recovered the divorce was not a divorce, since the condition that guaranteed its existence (the death of the husband) was not met. Therefore, the Maharam ruled that the wife was still married to her husband, and in order to divorce him, she needed a new get.

9. Yehoshua Ben Alexander HaCohen Falk (1555 – 29 March 1614) was a Polish Halakhist and Talmudist, best known as the author of the Beit Yisrael commentary on the Arba'ah Turim as well as Sefer Me'irat Enayim (ע"מס) on Shulkhan Arukh.

10. Meir of Lublin or Meir ben Gedalia (1558 – 1616) was a Polish rabbi, Talmudist and Posek ("decisor of Jewish law"). He is well known for his commentary on the Talmud, Meir Einai Chachamim. He is also referred to as Maharam (Hebrew acronym: "Our Teacher, Rabbi Meir").

The three houses of the "Large Porch" in the City Hall Plaza

The "Small Porch"

[Page 81 - Yiddish] [Page 76 - Hebrew]

The City of Jaroslaw and Its History

by Mundek Hebenstreit

Translated from the Yiddish by Pamela Russ

[ ] translator's remarks

Jaroslaw belongs to the oldest cities in Poland, which has a long history of over 800 years, including 500 years of Jewish activity and the period of the assemblies of the "*Vaad Arba Artzot*" [the Council of Four Lands; the central body of Jewish authority in Poland; 16ᵗʰ century to 1764], which would also take place in Jaroslaw.

I remember that more than once, with great amazement, we saw the historical houses on the marketplace, with their added on porches, or we visited the deep and curious cellars of our houses, and thought about when and in what sort of situation they were built, but we never received exact answers. Actually, for us Jews, this problem was not so essential. We were then living with the thought of how to solve our own burning Jewish problem: how to first free the Jewish nation from exile by getting to the Land of Israel (Zionists), or to liberate the world from capitalism and at the same time also solve the Jewish problem (a group of Marxists), or simply: wait for the Messiah (a group of religious Orthodox Jews).

Hala Targowa ["Market Hall"]

[Page 82]

Now, when we live in our independent Jewish country and are writing a Yizkor Book about the life of Jaroslaw Jews, I feel it necessary to emphasize that in spite of the fact that about the history of the Jews in the city there has already been an article written by HaRav Moshe Shteinberg, it is appropriate to bring forth some general historical information about Jaroslaw itself.

*

The destiny of Jaroslaw was crystalized in the 12th and 13th centuries, under the influence of the Polish-Russian revolution in Przemysl border areas. The actual name of the settlement was connected to the name of the Russian duke Jaroslaw, who, while absorbing these areas into his duchy, had to call the settlement by his own name. But these are only conjectures that have no real historical substantiation.

In the year 1340, before the times of King Kazimierz [Casimir] the Great, Jaroslaw went permanently under the Polish rule.

The political relationship, similar to the economic relationship, stabilized. The number of residents of the city grew under the impact of the migration of a large number of settlers from other places of Lesser Poland and Szlonsk. During that time, Jaroslaw received local rights, such as the cities of Radzymin and Pruchnik did. This well-planned action of Casimir the Great continued into the times of the rule of Ludwik Wegierski (1372-1378). Jaroslaw has him to thank that it was the second, according to the order, to be granted local privileges, based on the "Magdeburg rule." This gave the city great municipal rights and possibility to run the city and the economy. With this "new " Jaroslaw, in the year 1387, Queen Jadwiga took over the "held" of the entire Przemysl ground, and gave the city of

Jaroslaw as possession to the feudal lord Jan Tarnowski, and later, according to the order, the city remained the property of the Odrowazi, Kostkis, and Ostrogs.

[Page 83]

At the end of the Middle Ages, Jaroslaw was already a large Jewish settlement that was built up with wooden and brick buildings. A large, successful cultural and economic development took place in the times of the 16th and half of the 17th centuries. The Jaroslaw fairs – known to those inside and outside the country, brought fame to the city.

These fairs that took place during the summers and lasted for three weeks, attracted a great number of merchants not only from Poland, but also from Germany, England, Moscow, Persia, Italy, and Spain. A large number of Jewish merchants would also come to these fairs, and at the same time, the *Vaad Arba Artzot* [the "Council of Four Lands"] would assemble as well. At this point, it is important to note that Jaroslaw of that time was located on a segment of the market square and the nearby streets. The area was surrounded by a defense wall, and according to the orders of the ruler of Jaroslaw – Zofia Tarnowska (at the end of the 16th century), the Jews were forbidden from living inside the city. Only a small number of Jews lived on the other side of the defense wall and in the area of Pelkinie.

At the cusp of the 16th and 17th centuries, there were already 3,000 residents. For the summer fairs, around 30,000 merchants would come to Jaroslaw.

The buildings on the market square are basically maintained to this day, and they were mostly used for business. Wide, comfortable entrance hallways through which large merchandise wagons could fit, the huge inner halls, which were called "*wiata*" [like carports, canopied for the wagons], were covered over the top [canopied] with glass, and this enabled them to bring the merchandise over in terrible weather conditions, and the premises for the stores and stalls were in the outside frontline arcades. For selling large volumes of merchandise, there were some city deep cellars. A significant number of Italians settled in the city. The large buildings of the past, which belonged to the Italians Attavanti and Arsetti, houses with small porches, are still maintained to this day. In the 16th century, Jaroslaw already possessed a water line. The water ran through wooden oak wheels that were found in the south of the city to the market square. This was a time of blossoming and good standing for the city.

[Page 84]

Beginning in the mid-17th century, a slow but consistent downslide of the evolution of the city. This process of stagnation was a result of the long and constant wars of the Cossacks; Sweden, Turkey, and the Tatar attacks. And at the same time, businesses decreased – the merchants who used to come to the Jaroslaw fairs. The attacks of Chmielnicki's Cossacks (1649) marked particularly the city people, and especially the Jews of the surrounding areas. In the year 1656, the Swedish invasions were no less painful for the city. And particularly, the invasion of the month of March, when the Swedish soldiers, under the rule of King Karl Gustav, invaded Jaroslaw. The two-week Swedish occupation of the city affected the total liquidation of everything that was of value. After Jaroslaw, there were conflicts between the Swedish soldiers and the units of Czarniecki, which were described by Sienkiewicz in his magnificent work "*Potop*" ["Deluge"; Henry Sienkiewicz, published 1886]. But the Swedes had hardly left Jaroslaw, when soon the units of *Rakoczy* [Hungarian noble family, warred against King Casimir of Poland; allied with the Swedes] marched in and destroyed almost everything. This period of unrest, which began in the second half of the 17th century, stretched to the very end of that century.

[Page 85]

In the year 1772, the Austrian military forces invaded the city, and for about 150 years they ruled, and the city was in their possession. As Jaroslaw was under their rule, many changes took place. New borders separated the city from Poland, with which the city was physically connected. The former trade business that took place during the large fairs were prohibited with only markets of small volume that would take place during the week in the nearby surroundings. In particular, the Jewish residents painfully felt the restrictions, as they, at the beginning of the 17th century, settled in larger numbers in Jaroslaw, taking up trade only.

In the second half of the 19th century, Jaroslaw was proclaimed as a free city and became the capital city of the district (1854).

Another new thing in the city area was in 1860, the new train line on the Krakow-Przemysl track, that cut through Jaroslaw. After it was connected into the transportation network, the city quickly revived.

In the years 1867-1914, many significant changes took place in the city, which appeared in the regulations of places and streets. Gaslights were also established (1900), the former suburbs were built up, and the population grew, which in the year 1910 already numbered 23,400.

The Jewish population, which at some point was forbidden from living in the center of the city, slowly and by degrees, took over all the houses in the area, that means: Grodzka, Opolska, Sobieskiego, Spetka, Lubelskie, and understandably, in the first line in the main square. During this period of building, the Poles settled in the suburbs, and particularly in the Krakow quarter of town.

[Page 86]

For interest sake, I would like to add that some buildings in the market square, which had an interesting historical piece, were inhabited by Jews, and they [the buildings] were also the property of wealthier Jews. For example, there was House #2, the quarters of the Kaiser Jusef II (1773). House #6 was the quarters of the Swedish ruler Karol Gustav X, during the time when he stayed with his Swedish army in Jaroslaw. Building #12 belonged to Queen Maria Sobjeska, and Building #15 near the main square was the sitting place of the committee of the National Guard during the time of the "Spring of Nations" (1848). The rich building with the so-called small porch, was built in the year 1750 by the Italian Arsetti.

The First World War in the years 1914-1918, created a lot of destruction in the city, which was a result of the bitter slaughters between the Russian-Austrian armies in the front lines of the San. The city passed from hand to hand. As a result of the unceasing military requisitions, the city population suffered from a lack of important foodstuffs.

In October 1918, after 146 years of captivity, Jaroslaw once again became an integral part of Poland. In the first years after the war, the city grew in population numbers, and quickly evolved. In the years 1924-1928, Jaroslaw acquired electricity and a large "trade center" was built. Trade grew very quickly, as did small industry and banking. These were in the first line of earnings for the Jewish residents, in whose hands there was about 80% of the various ventures of the city. It is important to underline that there was no real large industry in Jaroslaw, and few industrial projects, such as the tie factory (Salik-Reif), cake factory (Gurgul), the mills (Glosberg, Korn), eggs export (Sobel Margolis, Horn) and the bacon shop and brickyards did not make a great influence on the business of the city which had a trade and work character.

[Page 87]

There were not many factories in the city. There were many military units in the city, which actually were not proportional to the size of a small city as Jaroslaw.

In the city, there were also a large number of middle schools, and in one of the schools, the school of [learning the] building [profession], there were students from other cities in the Lemberg administrative district. In Jaroslaw, there were two weekly publications: "*Przeglad Jaroslawski*" ["Jaroslaw Digest"], editor Shifman, and the "*Tygodnik Jaroslawski*" ["Jaroslaw Weekly"], editor Margiel.

In the 30s, the city was witness to many unrests caused by the peasants. These happened during the time of the "Green Week" [*Zielone Swiatki*"; Slavic "Pentecost"], and in August 1937, when 20,000 farmers, within a few days, blocked up Jaroslaw.

At the beginning of September 1939, Jaroslaw already felt the storm of the oncoming World War II. The city and the surroundings were heavily bombed by the German aircrafts. Soon the war operations came close to Jaroslaw, in which, after a brief battle, the enemy units invaded the city. This was on a Shabbat, September 10, 1939.

A great danger hung over the city's Jewish population, which was expelled from the city, and the Jews from the surrounding areas were murdered in the nearby places of death, such as: Pelkinie, Belzec, Komaczow.

With the expulsion of the Jews from the city, at the time of Sukkot 1939, the glorious history of the Jews of Jaroslaw came to an end.

The passage of the "Small Porch" with City Hall in the background

[Page 89]

Excerpt from a Polish newspaper in Jaroslav, 1956

Na jarosławskim rynku zawaliły się dwie zabytkowe kamieniczki

W nocy z 12 na 13 bm. potężny huk obudził mieszkańców domów położonych w jarosławskim rynku. Spowodowało go zawalenie się dwóch średniowiecznych domów oznaczonych nr. 12 i 14.

następnie runęła przytykająca do niego połowa sąsiedniego domu nr 12. Zawalone mury osunęły się w podziemia. W miejscu katastrofy powstał dół.

Katastrofa nie pociągnęła za sobą

Rynek w Jarosławiu, miejsce katastrofy oznaczone krzyżykami

Jak już niejednokrotnie wspominaliśmy pod rynkiem jarosławskim ciągną się olbrzymie, sięgające od 5—8 pięter wgłąb, podziemia, które powodują coraz większe obniżanie się powierzchni rynku. Woda zaskórna, która dostała się tam z powodu braku konserwacji w latach wojennych, podmywa fundamenty budowli tak, iż zawalenie grozi kilkunastu domom. Niektóre groźnie się zarysowały. W związku z tym wiele domów opróżniono.

Krytycznej nocy zawalił się doszczętnie najperw dom nr. 14, a

ofiar w ludziach, gdyż jeden z domów był pusty, a w drugim znajdowały się biura gminy. Władze bezpieczeństwa i straż pożarna odcieły dostęp do miejsc zagrożonych oraz zabezpieczyły urządzenia biur.

Katastrofa jest sygnałem alarmowym i ostatnim ostrzeżniem, iż prace nad zasypaniem podziemi i zakryciem ich płytami żelbetonowymi muszą się rozpocząć bezzwłocznie. Oba zawalone domy należały do średniowiecznego tzw. „Podcienia wielkiego" i posiadały cenne zabytkowe sklepienia oraz kryte, oszklone wiaty. (Grot)

[Page 90]

אלי, אלי נפשי, בכי

קינה עפ"י "אלי ציון"

אלי, אלי, נפשי, בכי
וזעקי, בת־ישראל,
מספד שאי והתיפחי,
אבלה האש בישראל.

על טבח־עם, אשר הוכן,
יסורי שכול, אשדות דמים,
זקן גם טף לא רוחם,
על עקדה קרבן תמים.

על עוללים, גמולי חלב
המרוטשים לפי צורים
ועל דמם, אשר הוזב
בראש חוצות לעין הורים.

על הקהלות השוממות
ועל חרבן מקדשי אל,
יקודי להב שלהבות
ערי פאר בישראל.

עלי דורות, אשר נגדעו,
דמי אבות על דמי בנים,
בגיא אושביץ תמו גועו
במוקדות הכבשנים.

עלי כלואים, הגורי שק
הנמקים ברבבותיהם,
בטרבלינקי ומידנק
ואין מלקט עצמותיהם.

עלי קרונות, צפופי אדם,
אשר רופדו גפרית וסיד,
ציחי־צמא, בכלות נפשם,
צעקו מים ואין מושיט.

עלי בנות, אשר עולפו,
רעיות בנפשן שלחו ידן,
צ"ג הטהורות יחדו נספו
ולא חולל תום כבודן.

עלי קפואים בשדות שלגים,
ילדים רכים בחיק אמהות
ועל קדושים השואגים
קבורי חיים מתוך בורות.

עלי גווילים המחוללים
בידי נאצים מנאצי אל,
טרופים, קרועים ומגאלים
בין אשפתות ואין גואל.

על צדיקים ענוי עולם
נדיבי עם, הוגי תורה,
בתאי רעל נחנק קולם,
נפלה, כבתה המנורה.

עלי נוער פרחי העם,
חלוצי־קרב, כפירי מרי,
מול זדונים שופכי הדם,
השתלהבו רשפי חרי.

עלי קדוש השם ועם
ועל נקמת דם טהורים
בתעצומות מסרו נפשם
לחמו נפלו הגבורים.

ראה, אלהים, עורי צפד,
נפל לבי, שונאי קמים.
הקשיבה שוועי, חישה מפלט,
הצילה נפשי מאנשי דמים.

הקינה מאת י. ל. ביאלר מנצילי השואה.
פורסמה לראשונה ע"י הרבנות הראשית וועד הקהלות בפולין בשנת תש"ח.

This elegy was written by the late Holocaust survivor Yehuda Leib Bialer (1896-1977) in 1945, after his return to Warsaw at the end of the war. It is written with the same poetic meter of Eili Tzion, and can be sung to the same haunting melody. It mentions the death camps of Auschwitz, Treblinka and Majdanek. It notes the crowded railway cars, the victims buried alive in pits, the desecration of the holy books, the gas chambers, the deaths of the righteous sages, the youth who mounted resistance, and the Kiddush Hashem.

Lament, lament, my Soul Weeps

My G-d, my G-d, my soul weeps
And cry out, daughter of Israel,
Raise a cry and a lament
For a fire has consumed in Israel.

On the slaughter of the nation, which was prepared,
Tribulations of bereavement, a flood of blood,
Elderly and children without mercy,
A pure sacrifice upon the altar.

For the babes, weaned from breast,
Split upon the rocks
And for their blood that flowed
In public, before the eyes of their parents.

For the destroyed communities,
And for the destruction of the sanctuaries of G-d
Gone up in fiery flames
The cities of the glory of Israel.

Woe about the generations that were cut off,
The blood of fathers with the blood of children,
In the valley of Auschwitz they were cut off and perished
In the smoke of the chimneys.

Woe about the prisoners, dressed in sackcloth
Wasting away in their myriads,
In Treblinka and Majdanek
With no refuge for their bones.

Woe about the train cars, cramped with people,
Spread with sulfur and pitch,
Those parched with thirst, as their souls departed,
Shouted for water, but nobody gave.

Woe about the daughters who swooned
Women to whose souls the hand struck out
In their cotton robes they perished together
Without any concern for the desecration of their honor.

Woe about those frozen on the snowy fields,
Young children in the bosom of their mothers
And on the martyrs who shout out
Buried alive in pits.

Woe about the scrolls that were desecrated
By the Nazis who blasphemed G-d,
Shredded, torn and sullied
In the dung heaps, with nobody to rescue them.

Woe about the youth, the flower of the nation
Girded for battle, ready to rise up,
Against the murderous evildoers,
They shot at them with flashes of anger.

Woe about the martyrdom to G-d and the nation
And the revenge of the blood of the martyrs
With strength they gave up their souls
The fought and fell the deaths of the brave.

See, oh G-d, arise oh shriveled one,
My heart falls, my enemies rise.
Hear my prayer, hasten with a refuge
Save my soul from the men of blood.

[Page 91]

Jaroslaw
As it Lives in Our Memory

[Page 92] Blank

[Page 93]

The beginnings of the Zionist Movements in Jaroslaw

by Moshe Kalchheim

Translated by Selwyn Rose

The data we have suggests that the Zionist movement in Jaroslaw started to organize at the beginning of the 80's of the 19th century, at the time of the "*Hovevei Zion*" movement in Russia and Austria, that is to say, before the appearance of Dr. Theodore Herzl on the Zionist "stage".

In 1889, on the initiative of Dr. Reuven Bierer, the "Jewish National Academic Society" – "*Kadima*" was founded and among the 54 members of the Society were the student Emil Blumenfeld and Dr. Salo Rosberger of Jaroslaw. "*Kadima*", was therefore the first Zionist organization created in Jaroslaw.

In 1892 Dr. Nathan Birnbaum – one of the leading figures of "*Hovevei Zion*" of the period - visited Jaroslaw, with the intention of reorganizing all the Zionist organizations under the name "Settlement of the Land of Israel", the target of which would be the collection of money and donations for advancing the establishment of settlements in Palestine.

In 1894, Jaroslaw already had an active branch named "Settlement of the Land of Israel" called "*Zion*", and at a national conference in Lvóv that took place on 30th and 31st of August that year, Shimon Brenner, the representative of Jaroslaw, reported on Zionist activities in our town.

The conference also instituted a new body called "The Political Society of Galician Jews", directed towards "Zionist education of the Jewish populace, work for all Jewish needs, especially political and economic, safeguarding the rights of Jews as citizens of the country and State and as members of the towns and communities."

Dr. Emil Blumenfeld of Jaroslaw was elected as president of the Society. The fourth conference of the Galician Jews that convened on 25th October 1896 in Lvóv, elected Dr. Salo Rosberger as a member of the central committee of Galician Zionism.

Another central personality in Zionist life in Galicia was Rabbi Leibish Mendel Landau who during the Nineties of the 19th Century was the town's Rabbi. He was born in 1861 in a small village near Jaroslaw and from the beginnings of Zionist activities, he joined the movement and was active in disseminating the Zionist ideology in Galicia. The Rabbi of Belz[1] was openly hostile to the movement because of its Zionist activities and several times tended strongly to frustrate and indeed sabotage the Rabbi's attempts at being elected as the community Rabbi (as was the case in Kolomyia) and also his attempts to become Rabbi of Jaroslaw were obstructed by the fierce resistance of the Belz Rabbi who, by informing the authorities of their activities, hoped to have his candidacy invalidated.

[Page 94]

The local Jaroslaw Zionist Committee in 1927

**Standing R to L: Hirsch Hariton, Rivka Ludmir, Diamont, L. Matzner, Mrs. Potascher,
Raphael Gatzhow, Weissler, A Tanzer, Shalom Stolbach, Attorney A Reszler, Moshe Beitler
Sitting from R to L: Dr. Yitzhak Rabinowitz, Dr. Moshe (Mauritz) Shafetz (Chairman). Izzio Leon,
Elimeleḥ Reich, Dr. Freizman
Sitting below: Manar, Izzio Horowitch, Devora Wolfsztejn, Jacek Zelinkowski**

In the book by Dr. N. M. Gelber, "A History of the Zionist Movement in Galicia", we find the following passage:

"In 1891 a "reading room" reflecting a national character was established here (in Jaroslaw – MK). Although two members of the Viennese "Kadima" – The lawyer Dr. Emil Blumenfeld and Dr. Salo Rosberger as well as the publisher of "The Treasure of Literature" Shaltiel Isaac Graber who was one of the veteran members of the National Movement lived in Jaroslaw; they were not inclined to found a Zionist Society... "The first Zionist Society was founded in 1894. Representatives of the National Committee in Lvóv came in January; The Chief Rabbi, Leibush-Mendel Landau, David Schreiber and Shimon Rantzer and their assistants Dr. Blumenfeld and Dr. Rosberger convened a meeting on the 8th January inviting the intellectual circles of the community. After an opening address by Dr. Blumenthal, Schreiber spoke about the conditions of the Jewish people in the countries of the Diaspora and pointed out the damage that assimilation was bringing upon the Jews as a united front based on historic traditions..."

[Page 95]

In the debate, Dr. Landau[2] attempted to prove that through emancipation, the Jewish question would be solved and the Jews should become assimilated with the Polish people. To that Dr. Rabbi Landau, Dr. Rosberger, Rantzer and David Schreiber gave the answer. Their words made a deep impression on the gathering that decided to create a committee to establish the "Zion" society. Dr. Blumenthal, the Community head, Heinrich Strisower, Natan Kutzman, Clement Maschler, Shaltiel Isaac Grauer, Attorney Shmuel Nebenzahl, B. Pomeranz, Ḥaim Kaufmann, Dr. Rosberger and Leon Hayil were elected.

On 25ᵗʰ November 1894 a local branch of the "Settlement of the Land of Israel" – "*Zion*" was established. 150 new members joined the Society following the meeting, addressed by Rabbi Leibush-Mendel Landau, Dr. Gershon Zipper and Dr. Rosberger, where they called for support of the settlement project. Dr. Blumenthal was elected President and Dr. Salo Rosberger -Vice-President, Yitzhak Wausza (apparently Gausza – M.K.) - Treasurer, Shlomo Stitzel - secretary for development of the land, Shaltiel Isaac Grauer – Hebrew secretary and Yisrael Schusseim, Ya'acov Goldschmidt, David Kornman David Weinberg, Shmuel Brenner, Shaul Sternal, Shlomo Mandelberg, Yosef Kaufteil and Marcus Krieger.

[Page 96]

The first convention of the Movement took place in Lvóv and the second, as it happens, in Jaroslaw - (In 1902); it speaks significantly for the importance of that town that it was so.

The name of the Movement in Jaroslaw was "*Shaḥar*" – "The Dawn" and represented an integral part of the National Society as "The Zionist Academic Federation" with the aim of: "elevating the spiritual status of the Zionist youth by National-Zionist education and creating a permanent connection between the corporations and the individual Societies."

A special honor fell upon part of the Jaroslaw Zionists with the election by the National Council of Dr. Emil Blumenthal, the President of "*Zion*" as a delegate to the First Zionist Congress.

He was one among 23 delegates from Galicia who took part in the Congress and his photograph appears in the published photograph of the delegates of the First Zionist Congress.

In 1903, there were three Zionist societies in Jaroslaw:

> "Sons of Zion" headed by Dr Eberzohn;
> "Raḥel" headed by Mrs. Regina Dykess;
> "*Aḥvah*" headed by Heinrich Zumpf.

That same year in Jaroslaw, a counseling session took place among the members of the National Council concerning national work of the Zionist movement.

Regarding the youth movements, it is worth noting that they were composed of students and graduates of the various gymnasia throughout all the towns of Galicia. We do not have much detail about the size of the movement except that in 1913, at the time the Federation Council was convening in Przemyśl "*Shaḥar*" had 28 members five of whom spoke Hebrew, and was represented at the meeting by two of its members: Benno Ḥamiadas and Wilhelm Genisfal.

"*Shaḥar*" also had a youth movement – "Young Zion" close to and deeply interested in the question of Socialism and tended to follow the "*Poalei Zion*" then organizing in Galicia.

In 1911, "Young Zion" numbered 18 members in Jaroslaw of whom ten members were learning Hebrew.

* * *

Another aspect of Zionist life in Jaroslaw concerned the Hebrew teachers, who were organized in the Hebrew movement in Galicia. The Movement had its beginnings in 1893 with the foundation of the first Hebrew school in the town of Jaroslaw.

[Page 97]

The local Zionist Committee with a group of "Ḥalutzim Akiva" pioneers during their training in Jaroslaw

In 1906, the "Society of Hebrew Teachers in Austria" came into being with the aim "…to educate the young generation with a National-Hebrew spirit and to revive the Hebrew language." At the same time, there existed 21 schools and courses in Hebrew in Galicia and Bukovina, among them Jaroslaw, named: "Clear Speech" ("*Safa Brura*") with 66 students under the management of Mrs. Zippora Haber.

*

As we have said, there was a Socialist youth movement in Jaroslaw "Young Zion" but before them there existed a branch of a labor movement named "*Ivri*" that contained within it laborers and assistants to traders and businessmen. The "*Ivri*" Society represented an integral part of "The federation of Zionist Worker and Laborers in Galicia" and it numbered in 1903 one hundred and eighty members. From among its roots sprang one of the prominent leaders of "*Poalei Zion*" in Galicia, the engineer Anslem (Anschel) Reiss who already in 1910 was elected as representative at the ninth congress to the board of Management of the "*Poalei Zion*" in Austria and has continued as an active participant to the present day.

[Page 98]

Also elected to the same council was the second delegate of the movement in Jaroslaw, the well-known doctor, Adolph Hendl.

A group of Zionist workers

Sitting from L to R: ?, ?, I. Zelinkowski, Horowitz, Dora Wolfstein
Standing from L to R: ?, ?, Zelinkowski, Beitler, B. Schlissberg, S. Striks, S. Lieberman, ?, ?

* * *

From the details mentioned above about the beginnings of the Zionist Movement in Jaroslaw, we learn that the Jewish community in our town was significantly involved and active in the development of Zionist activity in Galicia and the town's public activists fulfilled a central role in the life of the Movement from its very beginnings until the last days of the existence of the Jewish community in the town.

Translator's Footnotes:

1. Although not specifically named in the text, the available chronology and other sources suggest that he was *Rebbe* Yehoshua Rokeach (1855-1891) of the Belz *Yeshiva* dynasty
2. Dr. Landau was a noted Assimilationist in Jaroslaw.

[Page 99]

Zionist Activities in Jaroslaw During the 1920's

by Asher Graff

Translated by Selwyn Rose

After the ratification of the British Mandate over the Land of Israel in San Remo, recognition of the importance of the idea of "Love of Zion" increased and the longing for the return to Zion took a more tangible form.

The "awakening" found expression in establishing and organizing Zionist institutions and organizations in their several forms, including cultural foundations whose nature and importance will be addressed in this article.

The activity included a large part of the Jewish public in Jaroslaw that expressed a readiness to act upon all the instructions of the Zionist Federation in West Galicia, based in Kraków. A large number of activists responded eagerly, contributing to the various National funds like: The Foundation Fund, the Jewish National Fund and many other active causes that the times demanded. During this period, various youth movements, each according to its particular program and political stream, also came into being. The pioneering youth movements also established themselves and in 1919, the first group of pioneers, numbering about twenty members, immigrated to Palestine.

Among the participants in that group were: the brothers Shalom and Shmuel Spiegel and Kurzman. Shalom Spiegel is now a Professor at *Yeshiva* University in New York and Shmuel Spiegel (Sam Spiegel) is the well-know film producer in America while Lusk (Ludwig) Kurzman is today known as Arieh Sharon, the well-known architect.

Simultaneous with the wide-spreading Zionist awakening, cultural activities, both Hebrew and national also struck deep roots. A branch of the "*Tarbut*" society arose and it is to their credit at that time, that a string of impressive cultural activities can be recorded. A library came into being that included books in Hebrew and other languages, and in time grew to become a cultural asset for the youth and adults.

The librarian, during these years was Sela Striks and it is due to her work and dedication that the library became what, in fact, it was – an institution of great value.

The cultural activities of that time included the involvement of many hundreds of the Jaroslaw youth requiring the local Zionist council that was comprised of delegates of almost all the Zionist organizations – to rent *Beit Sobell*, which contained about ten rooms and a meeting-hall of about one-hundred square meters. The *Beit Sobell* foundation concentrated within its activities hundreds of students studying Hebrew.

The management of the house, that gave it the name "*Beit Ha'am*" - "The People's House", opened courses for studying Hebrew, employed two full-time teachers: Devora Wachner and Rivka Ludmir and the veteran teacher Halimer on a part-time basis. The majority of the youth at that time, acquired the Hebrew language there.

[Page 100]

The local Zionist Committee

Sitting from R to L: Dr. Rager, X, X, Dr. Rosberger, Mrs. Morenberg, E Rich, S Spiegel
Standing R to L: S Graff, B. Licht, Mrs. S. Charitan, L. Melon, G. Zielinkowski

My late brother Joshua Graf conducted much work teaching the Hebrew language, with great dedication for years and with no thought of "winning a medal" until he immigrated to Israel in 1926.

During that same period a Hebrew-Polish school was founded and recognized by the Government. In the beginning, the school was situated in the Chopin School of Music building but after some time the school transferred to the building belonging to the Horn family.

[Page 101]

The school came into being thanks to the dedicated work and inspiration of Dr. Yitzhak Rabinowitz (Z"L) and the time he invested in its creation it succeeded and developed. A children's nursery was also created and employed two pre-school teachers.

The extensive and well-attended activities continued until near the end of the thirties. Following the economic crisis in Palestine, the disturbances caused by the Arabs in the country and the difficulties the Mandatory authorities created regarding immigration, the attendance and associated numbers began to gradually decline and the courses suffered from the lack of attendance. The numbers of youths that had frequented *"Beit Ha'am"* on Sabbath eves and enjoyed enthusiastically dancing the Hora, diminished more and more.

The "B'nei Zion" Management

Standing from R to L: Brat, Metzger, Ziga, Dobschitz, Schneebaum, Gertner, Wasserman, Olek Silberman
Sitting from R to L: Wintergrin, N. Rot, Simcha Graf, Sianka Nas, Siku Schleider

[Page 102]

The Management of "The People's House" was forced to evacuate the building because of financial and other difficulties. It goes without saying that the various Zionist and other organizations also reduced the extent of their activities.

At the same time, towards the end of the 1930s, two adolescent Zionist activists recognized that it was necessary to adapt the shape of national activity to the present situation as is and to establish a Zionist association that would centralize university students and also those culturally and socially able to find their place in it, giving them the opportunity to play their part in national action, thus was founded and created "*B'nei Zion*" association.

The "Tarbut" Management, 1926

Standing from R to L: S. Stulbach, R. Ludmer, S. Graff, D, Wachner, L. Metzger
Sitting from R to L: Schtulbach, I Rosenblit

[Page 103]

"WIZO"

Mrs. H. Halberstam

The womenfolk of the Zionist Movement in our town fulfilled an honored role.

From 1923, Mrs. Franya Pacher (Z"L), Mrs. Pohorilles (Z"L), Mrs. Lute Turnheim (today in Israel), and other women, known as Zionists organized themselves into a "Jewish Women's Circle". Mrs. Blumenfeld of Slowatzki Street headed the organization. The circle had official standing under the auspices of Ms. Meltzer from Lvóv; Mrs. Meltzer was a senator in the Polish parliament. She was invited to our town, to a general meeting and banquet in which nearly all the leaders of the Zionist Movement took part, among whom were Dr. Rabinowitz, Dr. Spatz, Dr. Schwarzer, Dr. Rager and others.

The organization directed its activities to cultural and Zionist topics. Meetings were held in members' homes and normally one of them would prepare a topic for conversation or debate: on education, culture or Zionism.

After the founding in London of the Federation of Women Zionists ("WIZO") in 1924, a delegation of the organization arrived in Jaroslaw. Mrs. Ada Maimon of Palestine also visited us as did Sabba Gottlieb of Kraków, now living in America.

Then there was a big meeting in the "*Yad Ḥarutzim*" meeting-hall and it was decided to join "WIZO". Our center was in Kraków. We began with mobilizing the women in "WIZO" whose membership numbered four hundred. Among the activists in the organization were thirty women members.

Mrs. Hurt, Mrs. Kurzman and Mrs. Storch were elected as a management.

The treasury was handled by Mrs. Rager and Mrs. Rabinowitz (today in Israel), Mrs. Ludmir (today residing in Israel), Mrs. Schlafrig and Mrs. Weinbaum who was for a period the secretary of the Management (today in Israel), Mrs. Franya Morenberg and Mrs. Ada Emmar.

"WIZO's" work program was far-reaching. The "WIZO" organization took part in every Zionist activity in town helping pioneers, the Foundation Fund of Israel, the Jewish National Fund and other activities.

The women of "WIZO" met on Wednesdays to debate issues of the day and the town. Our club functioned in collaboration with the local council. These meetings segued into social gatherings to listen, to learn, to see and to be seen.

[Page 104]

The women organized festivals. Like *Purim* and *Hanukah*, or displays of handicrafts and the proceeds transferred to "WIZO" in Palestine. We were visited by members from the Center in Kraków – Mrs. Maria Afte, the writer and Gusta Lindenbaum-Cohen, who complimented us on our work encouraging us with their words.

Our activities for the young members of "WIZO" won an honored part of our work – there were those young ladies, still students in school or who had learned a profession and were thinking of immigrating to Palestine.

Each Saturday afternoon, I met with them at the club (the home of Mrs. Schlafrig.). There, I gave lectures on the history of the Judaism, Zionism and the geography of the Land of Israel. With the help of Dr. Rabinowitz, we managed to collect sufficient sums that enabled some of them to make *Aliyah*.

"WIZO" earned a name for itself even among non-Zionists, as an active organization. In 1929, the winter was particularly severe in Poland and Mr. Strisower, who was the Deputy Mayor at the time asked for our help in opening an emergency kitchen for the needy. We managed the kitchen ourselves with financial help from the Municipality.

That same year, we were visited by Mrs. Pozner of the Jewish National Fund who came from Palestine. We managed to raise 100 Dollars in order to register the name of Poland in the Golden Book of the National Fund, celebrating the tenth year of its independence.

In 1930, with the help of Dr. Rabinowitz, a Hebrew school was founded in which the language of instruction was, nevertheless, Polish but the curriculum included Hebrew and other Jewish topics. We assisted in getting Jewish girls to attend the school and provided whatever else they needed.

In that school, we saw the beginning of the Hebrew education that we wanted to instill in our children and who knows what fruits would have been born of it, had it not been for this terrible last war.

The Second World War put an end to the work of "WIZO" as well, together with the deaths of hundreds of its members who perished in the Holocaust that came upon us at the hands of the murderous Germans.

[Page 105]

The "Mizrahi" Movement in Jaroslaw
(From its founding until the Thirties)

by Moishe Kalchheim, Jerusalem

Translated by Selwyn Rose

The "*Mizrahi*" movement in our town included the elderly, the young, pioneers and "*Ha-Shomer Ha-Dati*" (The "Religious Guard"). All of them were imbued with the great idealistic spirit: the building of the Land of Israel inspired by Religious Zionism. Even before "Hertzlian" Zionism, famous and well-known Rabbis - "Greats" of the *Torah*, and of "*Hovevei Zion*" – ("Lovers of Zion") belonged to the Movement.

Up until the First World War, there were only single men who belonged to *Mizrahi* in Jaroslaw. The Federation did not yet exist and these individuals had much influence.

One must recall the historical fact concerning the *Mizrahi* Movement. From 1867 Rabbi Shmuel Walberg was the Chief Rabbi of the town (he officiated for about ten years, before which he had been the Rabbi of Żółkiew (Zhovkva)). He was the author of five books: "*Imrei Da'at*", ("Words of Knowledge"), "*Ateret Shoshanim*" ("A Crown of Roses"), "*Devar B'ito*"("Timely Words"), "*Darkei Shinu`im*" ("The Ways of Change") and "*Divrei Shmuel*" ("Sayings of Shmuel"), an A to Z book of glosses and explanations; he died in 1906 at the age of seventy-seven.

The community leaders sought a town Rabbi in about 1910; several Rabbis appeared offering their services to the community together with their demands. The candidates were: Rabbi Leibush Mendel Landau, Rabbi Meir Horowitz of Kozats'ke, Rabbi Ziff of Lvóv, the Rabbi of Turka and others. The election committee numbered 16 community members and a further 16, holders voting rights through "Power of Attorney" of the electorate. (My father (Z"L), was among the electors).

By all accounts, Rabbi Leibush Mendel Landau should have had the greatest chance of being chosen but the *Hassidim* of Belz and Sieniawa (Shinova), objected fiercely to his election. The main cause of their objections stemmed from his dedication to Zionism and as one of the leaders of the "*Hovevei Zion*" movement in Galicia and a co-founder of the world *Mizrahi* movement. Rabbi Landau had also been a candidate for the Rabbi's seat in Kolomyia and there, too, the Belz *Hassidim* had thwarted his attempts at election. In the elections for community Rabbi in Jaroslaw, Rabbi Landau received more than twenty votes out of the 32 possible but one Belz *Hassid* craftily deposited two voting slips in place of one. At the count, there appeared 33 votes instead of 32. It seems likely that it was done with either the agreement or the actual participation of the town Marshal and as a result, the elections were declared invalid.

[Page 106]

It was during this period that the influence of *Mizrahi* found expression. Rabbi Gedaliah Schmelkes – the Rabbi of the town Przemyśl, engineered a propaganda war in favor of the friend of his student days and ideological opinions. Rabbi Natan Levine – the Rabbi of Rzeszów (Raysha), also supported him when the three of them were students of the *Gaon*, Rabbi Yitzhak Schmelkes of Lvóv. (The Rabbi Natan Levine was the son-in-law of Rabbi Schmelkes (Z"L)).

In 1920, Rabbi Landau was elected almost unanimously as the Rabbi of the town but nevertheless after a short while in office he passed away.

The awakening in the consolidation of the ranks the *Mizraḥi* in town began after the First World War. Significant influence and a deep impression was made upon us by the appearance of the delegate from the Warsaw central office, Rabbi Y. Rappoport of Jędrzejów (Yendzshev) who spoke with the utmost grace and laid the foundation for the framework of the Movement in Jaroslaw.

In 1920, the Religious Zionists began their activities in town. Among the veterans of the Movement were: Chairman Shimon Spiegel, Elimeleḥ Reich, Ḥaim-Aharon Zilbiger, Noah Lemm – son of the ADMOR[1] Elimeleḥ Lemm, Ben-Zion Dominitz, David Kramer, Shmuel Schleider, Asher Wegschel and others.

The youth circle elected a committee. The writer of these few lines was the Chairman and the first secretary was Ḥaim Licht who filled that position until his immigration to Palestine in 1924 together with Esther Wernberg, who married there. Another member of the committee was Mordecai Landman, the son-in-law of Julius Graff. During the first period, the young activists were Yehoshua-Herschel Graff, Simḥa Graff and Shalom Stelbach. They later left our Movement and joined the General Zionists.

During this first period, the activists were Eliezer Schiff and his brother Shalom. Eliezer immigrated to Palestine in 1922 and became the secretary of the General Federation and later worked as an insurance agent.

The meeting-place of the *Mizraḥi* was the Study-House and the *Mizraḥi* youth met there for lessons on the *Torah*. The lecturers were: on the *Talmud* – Moshe Lieber and Yeshayahu Lang. "*Hovot Halevavot*"[2] (Duties of the Heart), homiletics and legends based on the *Talmud* – Shimon Spiegel. The activists of the *Mizraḥi* Youth were: Haim Lemm, the brothers David and Yosef Halberstam (they perished in the Holocaust), Yosef and Yisrael Narzisenfeld, Hirsch Charit, Ben-Zion Licht (he died in Nahalal). Known to have acted at times as secretary were: Ze'ev Friedman and Shmuel Schleider (both of them in Israel).

Representing the local Zionist committee in the movement were the columnist, Shimon Spiegel and others. The Chairman of the "*Mizraḥi* Youth" following him was the writer Zisha Bak. Among the most active young members were: David Wisla, Moshe Bitler and Asher Kalchheim.

[Page 107]

Among the conspicuous intellectuals was Rabbi Ben-Zion Dominitz who later moved to live in Łódź. Among the delegates to the national committees of *Mizraḥi* in Lvóv and Kraków was the writer of these lines. Yesheyahu Lang was the delegate to the convention in Warsaw in 1923.

The Leaders of *Ḥaredi* Judaism were in opposition the Religious Zionists and especially the Belz *Ḥassidim* and others. The *Ḥassidim* of Czortków (Chortkov) were supportive of Zionism. Clearly, no one had predicted the terrible Holocaust that was to occur but those opposing Zionism were looking from within confined horizons with no view of the future. The assimilated in one camp and the *Ḥassidim* in the second camp found they were in a combined struggle against Zionism. It is necessary to emphasize "Zionism" and not "Religious Zionism" was exiled by the *Ḥassidim* of the Rabbi Shimon (Z"L) *Kloiz* and it was by chance that they caught Zisha Bak with the "Book of the Covenant" and banned him from the *Kloiz*. Zisha Bak was a participant in the "*Bat-Kol*" ("Divine Voice")[3] paper that was published by "The *Mizraḥi*" edited by Dr. Zeliger and was also associated with the weekly "*Ha-Mitzapeh*", edited by S.M. Lazar.

The *Kloiz* of Rabbi Shimon was burned in 1914 during the First World War. The congregation moved to join the *Kloiz* of Rabbi Kehat ("May he be remembered for his Righteousness"). My father (Z"L), purchased a seat in the *Kloiz* along the eastern wall and when Rabbi David Marilis, the son of Rabbi Shimon, came to live in town, I permitted him to occupy my father's place. During the time I was active in the *Mizraḥi*, when I came to the *Kloiz* to pray on *Shabbat*, Rabbi David suddenly stopped the service and declared a short break stating: "For as long as that *Mizraḥi* is within the walls of this *Kloiz*," because he represents a danger and preaches to our youth to turn to Zionism – may the Merciful One preserve us. The service stopped and I continued to pray alone in my place. The women in the women's section said to my mother: "Your son is very dangerous, he is taking our youngsters under the wings of the *Mizraḥi*," to which my mother replied: "I'm very proud of him – you should wish you all had sons like him." I could see that tempers were rising and when the service ended, I said to Rabbi David: "Look at the pleasure I gave you." (He was sitting in my father's seat.) This made him very angry. He jumped from his seat and decided to call me to order in the Rabbinical Court (*Beit Din*).

The following day I appeared before the *Beit-Din* in town. I brought proof of ownership and that all I had done was legal and honest. After debating the matter, a compromise was agreed upon: I will permit Rabbi David to continue to sit in my father's place on the condition that he no longer stops the prayers.

[Page 108]

The "human material" that joined the *Mizraḥi* Movement was comprised mostly of *Beit Midrash* students. They were tied by the very fibers of their being to Jewish tradition, to the culture of Israel and imbued with the ambition for redemption and the will to leave the Diaspora and settle in the Land of Israel. These members of the movement, who immigrated to Israel, were dedicated to their activities in the Mizrahi movement, or in the *Mizraḥi* executive committee.

The *Mizraḥi* Movement educated a generation towards immigration to the Land of Israel and those who achieved that ambition laid the foundation of *Mizraḥi* and the *Mizraḥi* Worker in the Land of Israel. Our friends and members from Jaroslaw helped, strengthened and were themselves foundation to Religious Zionism, its projects and educational institutions and of all its pioneering projects in the creation of the State of Israel.

Translator's Footnotes:

1. ADMOR: An acrostic for the Hebrew honorific referring to a highly esteemed Rabbi usually a dynastic patriarch "*AD*oneinu, *MO*reinu, *R*abbeinu," a phrase meaning "Our Master, Our Teacher, and Our Rabbi".
2. A philosophical treatise dating from the 11th century by Bahya ben Joseph ibn Pakuda. For a full explanation see: https://en.wikipedia.org/wiki/Chovot_HaLevavot
3. See: https://en.wikipedia.org/wiki/Voice_of_God

[Page 109]

The "Mizrachi" Organization in Jaroslaw Between the Two World Wars

by Shmuel Schleider

Translated by Pamela Russ

[ ] translator's remarks

The "Mizrachi" organization in our town, from the beginning of the 30s until the outbreak of the Second World War, was one of the very active and influential organizations in Jaroslaw. During that period, the organization claimed about 150 friends [members] and many sympathizers, all from the older generation. Aside from that, there was a youth organization in the "Mizrachi," called *Tzeirei Mizrachi* ["Youths of Mizrachi"]. The influence of the "Mizrachi" organization was so great in the city that there were four "Mizrachi" representatives in the community administration.

The "Mizrachi" in Jaroslaw was very active in the organizational area, and also in local politics. But the main emphasis was placed on the area of education.

The committee of that time included the following:

Shimon Shpiegel, Elimelech Reich, Chaim Aaron Zilbiger, Yosef Rosenblit, Mordechai Landman, Yeshiye Lang, Dovid Kremer, Shloime Schleider, Osher Wagshal, and Sholom Hirshfeld, all who put in a lot of strength and energy for the education of that generation. The committee also did a lot for the older generation: There were classes in *Gemara* [Talmud], *Midrash* [commentary], *Ein Yakov* [16th century text; commentary plus Talmud]. These lectures were given by Torah scholars.

The greatest emphasis was placed on the school "Yavneh," which was the pride of "Mizrachi." The director of "Yavneh" was *chaver* [friend/comrade] Dovid Kremer, who struggled, with great sacrifice, for the existence of the school "Yavneh."

"Yavneh" had about 100 students, who were divided into several classes, from the *alef beit* [ABC – elementary] to learning the *Gemara* with *Tosafot* [commentary]. They learned Hebrew and translations into Hebrew, which was not simple.

The teachers in "Yavneh" were:

The learned Mr. Khelemer, Moshe Rabin, and Yeshiya Lang. The financial situation of the school was very difficult and faced great challenges. But thanks to the energies and influence of *chaver* Dovid Kremer and his inexhaustible strength, they managed to normalize the existence of the "Yavneh" school.

[Page 110]

The "Mizrachi" organization in Jaroslaw conducted multi-branched cultural and social work. Prominent "Mizrachi" personalities from the central office would often visit the organization. Several times, HaRav Yehuda Leib Maimon (Fishman), of blessed memory, honored them with his visit to the "Mizrachi" organization in Jaroslaw, and during each of his visits to our town, he would stay for quite a few days. His visit to us would always turn into a holiday. We learned a lot from him, and gleaned much from his knowledge and wisdom.

From the Galician representatives, there were visitors several times, including the honorable Dr. Bernard Hoizner, Harav Naftali Halperin, and other important personalities. We would always use their visits for valuable consultations.

The "Mizrachi" organized a regular *minyan* [quorum] for the Shabbath prayers, where the atmosphere was warm and friendly. In the last four years, because of differing views, a second *minyan* was organized, which was called "Yavneh *minyan*."

In general, there was a tolerance and understanding among the "Mizrachi" representatives, and there was no place in the organization for sharply differing views.

In the last years before the outbreak of World War II, the head of "Mizrachi," *chaver* Shimon Shpiegel, and the *chaver* of the committee Mordechai Landman, immigrated to Israel. Their absence was strongly felt, but with the help of other devoted and active members, the work continued successfully.

Not long after the outbreak of World War II, the "Yavneh" *minyan*, with its own strength, commissioned that a Torah scroll be written for them so that they would not have to use a borrowed Torah scroll. The writing was supposed to be done on 48 sheets of parchment. Sadly, however, we did not get to the completion of the writing of the Torah scroll. The outbreak of World War II destroyed everything, along with all our hopes.

[Page 111]

Jaroslaw was a city with a beautiful Jewish community, and with valuable and important institutions. The city was rich with all kinds of political organizations and cultural institutions. There was a widely extended education network with honorable Jews, Torah scholars, and ordinary people. Everything was destroyed.

[Page 112]

"Hashomer Hatza'ir" - the Zionist Youth Movement

by Binjamin Gevishi (Yumek Feldmaus)

Translated by Selwyn Rose

The *"Hashomer"* movement began to develop in Jaroslaw, as in the rest of the towns in Galicia, after the First World War. The first seeds began to sprout even before hostilities ended. The Movement began its activities in the larger towns with large concentrations of Jews. But within a relatively short period of time "Federations" were created in towns like Jaroslaw. The *"Tze'irei Zion"* (Young Zionists), movement served as an ideological basis for our movement, a movement of young students that operated principally in the years 1912-1913. The idea of the *"Hashomer"* Movement (that was the name of the movement in its "infancy"), was brought with the youngsters returning after the war from Vienna, western Austria and other western countries. Jewish families had preferred to escape the threat of the Russians, penetrating from the east and become refugees in these countries.

Almost certainly among the founders of *Hashomer* in Jaroslaw were the families of Spiegel, Kurzman, Weinberg and others, whose names I cannot recall for I was only 10-years old at the time.

When I was introduced to the secret existence of the movement, I was in the first year of study at the technical gymnasium. My friends in the classics gymnasium, essentially older than I, awakened a strong desire in me to join them. And indeed, before the end of the first year's study I found myself belonging to the younger group. The Federation then numbered from 8-10 groups according to age, of 10 classes in the middle school. Every class was known by a Hebrew name taken from nature. For most of us, the name of our class was the first contact any of us had with a Hebrew word. Nearly every group was either only boys or only girls, who were in the minority. Only two older groups, students in the upper classes were co-ed and a few of them acted as "counselors" of the younger classes. The word "counselor" was, in fact, unknown to us and he was known to us as "group-leader" and we vocalized it fluently. At the head of the "battalion" was the "commander". From the days of my childhood I well-remember our leader was Lusk (Ludwig) Kurzman who later in Palestine became known as Arieh Sharon, one of the founders of Kibbutz Gan-Shmuel and a conspicuously well-known architect.

I remember well the admiration we, the youngsters, had for our leader, a young, blond tall man and how we listened to every word that came out of his mouth. We sometimes held meetings for the entire group in the private garden of his parents. We used the house of the Spiegel family as our local club-house. The first library of "Hashomer" managed by Monek Spiegel was also there.

[Page 113]

Some members of "Hashomer Hatza'ir

Standing R to L: Max Rager, Binjamin Gevishi (Feldmaus), Josef Silberman
Sitting: Monek Eichenfeld, Maio Silberman, Zigi Silberman

So what occupied our time, what was the ideological content of our lives in the Movement? I will try to explain in a few words the factors that influenced our founders, who had lived a few years in Western Europe. These adolescent youngsters came into contact with different Jewish and non-Jewish movements most of them with positive constructive ambitions. Among them, it is worth mentioning, was the Scout movement in the different countries, Jewish youth movements were *"Blau-Weiß"*, *"Wandervogel"*, *"Habonim"* and others. In the beginning, the *"Hashomer"* movement was a kind of synthesis of several movements, from which it adapted for itself the most positive and idealistic concepts combined with one great overall element: the aspiration for Jewish nationality. We of *"Hashomer"* aspired to educate ourselves as invigorated Jews, proud of our Jewishness, enlightened and with a great central vision – to go and build a new socialist Homeland in the ancient Land of Israel.

[Page 114]

Of course, for the children of the youngest groups it was far more fitting to undertake "Scouting" activities directed to turning them into strong people in mind and body with ennobling ideals, people always ready and obliged to help the weak and needy. Our "Ten Commandments" included the best of the ideas of the different youth movements. Following the above, the central theme of our activities was pure and simple scouting. The discipline was unequivocal since the very essence of our organization and being was voluntary and obligatory. The orders and instructions were given in Hebrew but only during group exercises and activities. After the activity our "group commander" was simply an older friend to each one of us; he advised us and was obliged to conduct himself as a living example, as an educator educating his pupils. We learned to love nature and live according to a healthy life-style. We were dissatisfied with the soft easy-going life-style that typified our family lives in our good Jewish homes. We learned to love the life of truth in both word and deed and many other fine elements. In addition to all this, there stood at the center of our practical program the study of the Hebrew language. I will dedicate more on that topic later in my memoir. For the moment a few more details about the name of our Movement. We knew from a very young age that we were Jewish scouts similar to the style founded by the Englishman Lord Baden-Powell. But later we learned to know that the name "*Hashomer*" was taken from an entirely different organization, an organization of young and courageous Jews entirely fearless, living and operating in a far, distant, legendary land – the Land of our Fathers. They willingly and with a burning desire organized themselves to protect the lives and property of the minority of Jewish farmers working the land their historic Homeland in their isolated settlements in a sea of hostile Arabs. We learned that these settlements were targets for wild gangs of robbers and thieves who would suddenly burst forth from the desert-like landscape surrounding the agricultural land. The members of "*Hashomer*" risked their lives taking upon themselves the dangerous task, replacing the traitorous Arab guards.

We thirstily absorbed all this knowledge about the Jewish settlements and the brave "*Hashomer*" members. Our counselors knew how to illustrate their conversation with stories and readings about the first groups who came to Israel and about organizations, especially the farmers who lived a communal life, owning no private property and sharing everything and by their combined strength turning the barren land and marshes into fruitfulness. We learned the basic geography of the country, its ancient history and some early ideas about the Zionist movements and settlements.

[Page 115]

In parallel to these educational studies and ideologies, our counselors also were concerned about our physical education. Of course, most of our activities required suitably large open areas for scouting exercises and games. Such areas were plentiful outside the town but we were not always welcome visitors. The most suitable place was a hilly area unfit for agriculture and almost completely exposed known to everyone as "*Wanduly*". It was really ideal for exercises and games. We held mass meetings there with programs nicely prepared by the local leadership. Sadly, we were occasionally the target of unruly gangs of older ruffians. They were very good at throwing stones while we were completely unprepared to defend ourselves. But it should be mentioned that we didn't give way to our enemies and stayed where we were in that place so suitable to all our physical needs. About a week later, on a free day we went there again and prepared special groups to guard our sensitive flanks. Our enemies made many attacks again and again but their boastfulness lessened somewhat in the face of our stubbornness. The hooligans had met a type of "*Yid*" unknown to them…

A group of "Hashomer Hazair"

Standing from right, first row: Schtulbach, M. Wald, D. Leidner

[Page 116]

Today when I look back at my memories and call them to mind, it seems to me that that was our first "Baptism of fire", when we were surrounded and outnumbered by enemies. As the years passed, history repeated itself. We were attacked by disorganized groups while we lived in tents and dilapidated cabins. Today, inhabiting our own land every so often we are again attacked by an enemy stronger and more numerous than we were. The "little" difference that existed now was that we were more than capable to strike back – and that angers the world...

Now is also the time and place to speak out – and not only in general terms, about our leaders and counselors of those times. The first among them, chronologically (at the time I joined them), was Bonek Distenfeld, a sturdy and active man. He devoted much effort to teach us to become sturdy and courageous. His responsibility also ensured that our ideological education received attention in his curriculum. Bonek himself was among the first group of immigrants to make *Aliyah*. In Palestine, he was one of the founding members of Kibbutz Beit Alpha – the first Kibbutz of *Hashomer Hatza'ir*. His entire life was rich and full of achievements. Bonek (Z"L) was the oldest veteran farm worker on his Kibbutz. He died a number of years ago after dedicating virtually all his life to improving cultivation and increasing the yields of the crops. He continued to adhere to the "Hashomer Hatzair" ideology.

I recall Leibek Eilberg (Z"L) was our second leader. He died young as the result of a road accident in Palestine while working as a senior inspector for the Mandatory Government. In Palestine, he changed his name to Arieh Lahav.

I recall him as being a leader and counselor who put the emphasis on the spiritual aspects of our education. He was a pleasant, courteous man. He, too, was in the first group of immigrants to go to Palestine nearly all of whom were in the seventh grade in the gymnasium. In the Diaspora, the ground "burned beneath their feet" and they didn't have the patience to complete the graduation year. In Palestine, Leibek (Z"L) (Arieh Lahav) was among the founders of Kibbutz Gan Shmuel. After a couple of years, he arrived in Jaroslaw (on the way to California) where he completed his matriculation. In California, he completed his studies in the Faculty of Agriculture and was appointed to a senior post in the Mandatory Government.

Among the first immigrants, I remember other leaders and counselors like Leibek Plesser, Gincha Horn, L. Kurzman – (Arieh Sharon in this country). I cannot recall other immigrants from that group because I was the youngest in the group and with the others, I had no real contact – they were then the oldest in the group. Concerning the first group generally speaking, I know that most of them became founders of Kibbutzim; worked building roads and draining swamps and did everything depicting the well-known song of the era: "We will be the first.Jaroslaw…

[Page 117]

After the immigration of the first group the very foundations of the group was weakened in our town. Although a new generation of counselors and leaders existed of intermediate ages time proved that they were not of the caliber to lead the "Federation". Leadership and counseling for the youth was particularly lacking. I recall that my group, in which I was a student, was lucky to have as counselor Monika Eichenwald (Z"L), who perished in the Nazi Holocaust. Monika was a gentle soul with few equals, conspicuously intellectual, a gracious instructor who never raised her voice. Today (after spending about 15 years as an educator), I came to understand it was in no way an easy matter for a young woman to be a leader of a group of young boys of the age of 13-14.

Monika taught us to read and appreciate the writings of world-famous authors. It seems to me that until today I can recall the inspiring atmosphere that spread around us while reading and debating the problems facing the world of the authors and their creations. During that same period, it was not sufficient just to educate the intellectual youth. Monika also was unable to remain a "*Hashomer*" teacher for reasons unknown to me. The situation was no better in other groups. The branch sank into failure and gradually disintegrated. In place of the involvement in spiritual and ideological pursuits different bodies were formed. Sports like football began to prevail and pervaded most of the age-groups in Jaroslaw and the remains of the "*Hashomer*" youth were included. Without actually deciding so, we became football teams. We didn't only kick a ball around during organized games but took every spare opportunity to do so. After some time many of us – in the past members of the Movement – began to feel a certain emptiness eating us up. The anti-Semitic gymnasium also had its positive effect on our spiritual needs. The hostile relationship towards the Jewish students had its influence.

On the initiative of the older students, we began to congregate in the winter evenings in a place aptly suitable for us. It was one of the side rooms in the building "*Yad Ḥarutzim*". There was someone who cared that the room would be heated, tea would be served and games like chess available. The group meetings in a pleasant location including the availability of mentally provoking games charmed most of those who came and the circle began to grow.

Thus, it was that the differences began to grow and become conspicuous between us and that part of the youth that was satisfied with their compulsory studies and spent their spare time wandering the main street nicknamed the "*Kurso*" where they had the opportunity for their first attempts in "the hunt" for "the fair sex".

[Page 118]

With all the positive aspects of the sort just depicted of the social and cultural activities, we were dissatisfied in the long run with the games of chess and tea-drinking "togetherness". As youngsters of 14, we sensed the need for some kind of ideological life – some spiritual content. Indeed, there were those among us, some with leadership qualities and were gifted intellectually. The most conspicuous among them in my memory is Zigi Zilberman (Z"L),

A group of the "Shomrit" of the Hashomer Ha'Tzair 1922

**Sitting from R to L: Miriam Narzisenfeld, Bianca Metzger, Fridka Neis,
Salka Liberman, Sianka Gerstenfeld, Ruth Kalechheim
Standing from R. to L: Sabina Mersel, Fanda Nes, Sianka Warenberg,
Dorka Kalechheim, Linka Salpeter, Salk Mahla, Fridka Rener**

the older brother of Olek Zilberman, (may he live a long life), a resident of the city of Haifa. Zigi initiated our transformation into a permanent fixed circle. He awoke within us the idea and interest of learning about the early history of our people, dispersed in our time throughout the entire world.

We were helped by two excellent books: Dubonow's History and the much harder one by Graetz[1] (originally in German), we read and prepared ourselves for conversations and analysis on the topic of the early world in general and the Jewish people of the time. Zigi knew how to add content to our conversation on "dry" themes thanks to his talents. He knew how to draw out knowledge from rare and serious books suited to our age at the time. He also knew how to arouse our interest in other sciences not included in the curriculum of the middle-school like early civilizations in the far-east: India, China, their early cultures, the early philosophies of those far distant lands. We also became interested in unconventional sciences like anthropology, the history of cultures, psychology and others.

[Page 119]

Thus, we existed for a certain period of time as a Zionist-intellectual group. Because there were a number of similar but different circles within the parent group the time came that we had to think how to define ourselves as an organization. As if it was obvious from the start, we melded with "*Hashomer Hatza'ir*". We began to make contact with the leadership in Lvóv and the other branches in Galicia.

Even before we rejoined "*Hashomer Hatza'ir*", we had recommended studying the basics of Hebrew. It is only fair to note that only a few among the young students had a traditional education and knowledge of the language from the sources. Generally speaking, there existed in town in "good homes" an atmosphere of the *Bourgeoisie* with a tendency to assimilation. With the strengthening of the Zionist movements, learning Hebrew became fashionable and many began to learn in courses organized by "*Tarbut*"[2]. The first teacher in the town I recall was an elderly man named Ḥelmer. But the excitement and enthusiasm didn't last long and was somewhat like a firework that fizzled out and many quickly dropped out. After some time learning in the old "*Beit Ha'am*" – the "home" of the youth groups – the teacher who understood well the youngsters' "soul" was Pella Engelberg. Pella awakened within us the fierce determination to struggle with the difficulties until we were able to read alone the home assignments. Until today, I recall the stubbornness that helped me to read Fierberg's "To Where". Our connections with the head office began to take place in Hebrew, like various letters and contracts, etc. In time conferences, regional and national were conducted in Hebrew. In that atmosphere, many of us began to study intensively alone. Thanks to our progress, it was possible for us to make connections with Kibbutzim in Palestine.

This article would be guilty of an omission if I failed to include a few lines on the topic of the "*Beit Ha'am*" in Jaroslaw. The building, which carried that honored title for some years, was a villa built in the style of the 19th Century. It was owned by the wealthy Sobell Family. The owners rented the building, which stood in the midst of a large orchard, to the local Zionist Committee. In the beginning, the expansive building was intended for the "*Tarbut*" as a home for courses in Hebrew and as a day-nursery but after a short while it became also a center for the Zionist Committees. If my memory serves me well, it was "*Hashomer Hatza'ir*" who was the first to receive the use of two or three rooms for their activities. Later they were joined by "*Heḥalutz*" who opened its club there and later still, the "*Akiva*" Movement. The presence of these clubs didn't conflict with the Hebrew courses being run by the teachers Pella Engelberg and Rivka Ludmir. "*Beit Ha'am*" was an effervescent youth center in the years 1924-1926. They were "golden years" of youth movements in Jaroslaw.

[Page 120]

I must add a few words about the constituents of our group under the leadership of Zigi Zilberman. After some time, a few young girls joined us who had previously been under the leadership of group leaders: Ḥanka Graff and Miss Lieberman. The change to a mixed status was very welcome. The addition brought new life and added years to the group and in time, almost all of us began to educate and counsel a new generation. In the meantime, Zigi and his generation in the gymnasium left and the onus fell on us of carrying our entire group into the future.

It is worth pointing out that the Jewish pupils in the Jaroslaw gymnasium were not studying in the most pleasant of atmospheres. As a basic illustration of my opinion on this, I can relate an event that occurred in two middle-schools in our hometown. 1925, or 1926 was an exceptional period of activity for the Zionist youth movements. Rumors of membership of Jewish youths to these movements apparently reached the ears of the managements of these two national institutions (the gymnasiums) and they decided to exploit the opportunity handed to them to attack us. The name "*Hashomer*" was at the time specifically known to teachers with Andak[3] sympathies. On a pre-determined date, all the Jewish pupils of the upper grades were invited to the administrative offices, each pupil separately, and interrogated with interwoven questions. At that time, there were several relatively young Zionist movements active in town like "*Akiva*", "*He-Ḥalutz Hatza'ir*", "*Gordonia*" and others. Then came a typical case of ironic fate. Because of belonging to "forbidden organizations", a considerable number of students of the seventh grade were expelled from the two gymnasiums. Their mistake was in their honesty because they admitted their "guilt". Among those expelled nearly all had joined "Young *Akiva*" only a year or even less before, while we, the "veterans" of "*Hashomer*" were ineligible under the method employed by the directorate. I remember that I managed to maintain an air of innocence. When asked by the manager with a threatening manner what the Jewish movement "*Hashomer*" was, I replied: "Aha! Yes, I know!

[Page 121]

It's a Hebrew word that means (in English) "gatekeeper" or "caretaker" – and I succeeded. I was sad and very sympathetic for those whose "sins" were so small and had been members of the Movements for such a short time. It was they who, unexpectedly fell prey and were expelled from the Gymnasium. But they were eventually returned to the institutions; they lost only one year's study.

During our adolescence, when we were approaching the end of high school, we sensed many significant changes in the world around us. In various levels of education also there began to operate in the youth circles, an underground Communist movement a movement that gnawed quite a bit at the Zionist movements of the youth. We realized we had to protect our fundamental ideals and ideology from this new foe, especially in places where young people were being attracted to it and joined the ranks of the movement.

In light of the situation and other various changes, the leadership of our movements began to act to strengthen and consolidate the ideological basis. In 1924 (with the Danzig Conference), the "*Hashomer Hatza'ir*" gained the status of a world movement. Institutions were elected whose task was to develop international connections in general and with the early Kibbutzim in Palestine in particular. A basic ideological program was defined and agreed upon that transferred our movement from its "romantic period" and turned it into an educational-political movement. It was decided in addition to all the specific principles, we were first and foremost a pioneering Zionist-Socialistic movement. It was also decided that our representatives be merged with "*Heḥalutz*" central in all countries; that and more besides. At the Lvóv conference in 1925, all graduated students were obliged to submit to a training course once they had completed their graduation or other course of studies. We organized training camps mainly in an agricultural setting where the object was to train them not only to physical work *per se*, but also to adopt the cooperative spirit in the fullest sense of the word. It was also decided that "higher studies" were in contrast to the principle of "pioneering fulfillment" and that any post-adolescent who attended university would find himself removed from the Movement.

The inclusive inter-movement decision stated: "All graduates for training and *Aliyah*" divided the candidates from the high schools into three groups according to their practical reactions to that command. Members of the first "camp" were those who saw their fulfillment as a final step in their membership of the Youth Movement – they turned their backs on higher learning and everything stemming from it. For them it was natural that they end their life in the Diaspora. Almost certainly, in that group, there were those who had serious personal doubts but they overcame them and went to the training camps of the leadership.

[Page 122]

The members of the second grouping, who were anchored to the "opposite pole" and were not be able to give up a career and a scientific profession etc., did their best to enroll in one of the colleges in Poland or abroad. Regarding the Movement, they disappeared "over the horizon".

There was also an "intermediate camp", the third such, of whom there were not a few who suffered many serious doubts and much soul-searching distress. They felt themselves pulled between two opposing forces because they could not forfeit continuing with the Movement but higher learning was also to them a major attraction. In the end each individual had to decide painfully to pursue one or other of the two directions, who with greater pain and who with less.

There were two instances known to me personally from this last group where a few of them began studying at one of the faculties, not always their original choice and couldn't come to terms with the atmosphere that permeated the place, especially the attitude towards the Jewish students. The anti-Semitism was quite open and often venomous and veteran members of the Movement (sometimes even leaders from the past) were not able to cope with the situation and continue to study. A few of them left the colleges and returned to the bosom of the Movement, most of them directly to the training camps. It must also be pointed out that these latter ones sometimes took that decisive step (leaving studies), because the move to study left them with an internal feeling of denying their ideologies.

A significant number of those who chose training also took personal steps preparing themselves for their *Aliyah*. The struggle of those in the queue waiting to immigrate was waged on several fronts both within the Movement and also among the delegates of the pioneering movements. The Zionist committees and "*Heḥalutz*" central distributed the few certificates that they received from the Mandatory Government of Palestine. There were bitter struggles at the time because it was the period of the "Peel Commission" and other restrictions.

In any event, the years 1929-1933 are recorded in history as a period of increased pioneering *Aliyah*, without eastern European Jewry sensing in any way the signs indicating the approaching Nazi Holocaust.

I hope that I will be able to justify my opening (a kind of "motto") if I point out and emphasize certain facts from the history of the Kibbutzim.

As is well-known, the Kibbutzim are the fruit created by the few ideological youth movements – the practical expression of fulfillment that was, as was said above, an indisputable "command".

There are in our country quite a few citizens who have absolutely no idea of the superhuman battle for existence most of the Kibbutzim faced in their first years. The struggle was so severe and prolonged that more than a few collapsed. We fought for our very existence in several senses of the word: in its simple physical sense, in the constant struggle against different gangs of ruffians and organized forces and for our economic existence as well…and more besides.

[Page 123]

The strength to survive and not to be broken morally, we drew from ideas we cultivated and developed as youngsters while in the Diaspora. During those early years, many Kibbutzim, the founders and also those they absorbed, found doubtful sources of courage and defense against the scorching heat and the pelting rain in tents and leaky huts and cabins. For years, the majority of the Kibbutz members had a standard of living that was significantly below that of the population in the newly founded State during the "rationing" period. Up until the founding of the State there were many bloody pogroms and the Kibbutzim, as small isolated communities far from Jewish centers, were in the gravest danger and paid a heavy price in the number of fallen.

Members of the Jaroslaw "Heḥalutz"

Bottom row sitting from R to L: M. Radar, Segal Rak, M. Marzel, Y. Konigsberg, Y. Kostman
Upper row center: Berik, Spindel

From the days of the War of Independence Kibbutzim like Yad Mordecai, Gat, the two Deganias and Tirat Tzvi became bywords in the Nation's collective consciousness. The fact that their members blocked the advance of the enemies' tanks with their own bodies, are well known and documented. Until today, all the border settlements and border Kibbutzim especially, are gates, walls and bastions of defense, defending our surrounded Homeland from attack. Nearly every Kibbutz paid a very heavy price when compared to the general population.

Translator's Footnotes:

1.   Heinrich Graetz was a noted Jewish historian of the 19th Century, credited with being the author of the most comprehensive Jewish history from its earliest days, See: https://en.wikipedia.org/wiki/Heinrich_Graetz

2.   *Tarbut* began to develop late in the 19th Century reaching a peak between the Wars; it was created initially to combat the traditional *Heder* education that taught only traditional Jewish themes while *Tarbut*, while it taught mainly in Hebrew was adamant in introducing secular programs. See: https://en.wikipedia.org/wiki/Tarbut

3.   A Polish Fascist political body of the first half of the 20th Century, particularly the inter-war period.

[Page 124]

"He-Halutz Hatza'ir"

By Leon Fast

Translated by Selwyn Rose

In my opinion the birth of the "*He-Ḥalutz*" movement in Jaroslaw is to be seen in the action of two young fellows (aged 16-17), named Lolek Haiter and Moshe Touzman-Wasserman, who, in 1919 went out on an unusual adventure: they hitch-hiked their way to Palestine, without money or passports. Their journey was very long and full of adventures by way of Germany, Belgium, Holland and France from where they took a boat to the Land of Israel.

A group of "Yehuda" pioneers
Standing from R to L: Binenstock, Donenhirsch, A. Fruchtman, Pokard
Sitting: Warschawer, N. Kornreich

[Page 125]

The "He-Ḥalutz" branch 1925

Standing from R to L, the upper row: Mersel, Kranz, Y. Rosenfeld, A. Rosenfeld, Wenig, Asłowicz, Z. Freifeld, Y. Distenfeld, Schacher

Lolek Haiter was counted among the workers at Pinḥas Rutenberg's hydro-electric generating plant at Aram-Naharayim[1] and after completing studies in Germany sponsored by the generating station, became one of the leading professional people there.

Touzman-Wasserman left Palestine in the twenties and immigrated to the United States. These two friends were among the first pioneers of the *Heḥalutz Hatza'ir* established at that time in Jaroslaw. The Movement at that time was composed mainly from the "Working Youth" group. *Hashomer Hatza'ir* of the time was mainly comprised of students both boys and girls. They did not have much in common with the "Working Youth" who saw immigration to Palestine as the defining element of their personal Zionism. The situation was made even more difficult after the immigration to Palestine of the first group of the leaders of *Hashomer Hatza'ir*. Among them were: Lusik Kutzman (today the architect Arieh Sharon, a resident of Tel-Aviv), Leib'ke Plesser, Polaner, Dampf, Zena Morenberg, Malka Reich, Bonik Distenfeld and myself. (That was in 1929).

[Page 126]

I worked with many of them draining swamps and together we contracted Malaria. Due to the illness, I had to return to Jaroslaw where, in 1925, I already found the "*Heḥalutz Hatza'ir*" Movement as an independent body, headed by Arieh Wenig (later Tamir). After his immigration to Palestine, I became head of the Movement in town.

The "*Heḥalutz Hatza'ir*" Movement at that time was a pioneering-scouting movement. In time, branches were created in nearby towns like Sieniawa (Shinova, Shenova), Radymno (Redem, Radimno), Pruchnik, Łańcut (Lantzut) and others. The Jaroslaw branch became the region's head branch.

Among the cultural activities of the branch, we learned Hebrew and the geography of Palestine and also devoted time to general studies in order to broaden the members' knowledge most of whom spoke Hebrew. An overwhelming majority of them were influenced by the general cultural atmosphere of the town, an atmosphere that was thirsty for reading and widening their horizons. Many of us worked with artisans and craftsmen and also studied agriculture, preparing for a pioneering life in Palestine and the hard toil of work on the land.

During that same period, a large group of members immigrated to Palestine under the leadership of Freifeld (the father of Professor Yirmiyahu Yovel), Schmeltzbach, Staffel, Rosenfeld and Marzel. They were absorbed into kibbutzim and working organizations and continued on that path to this day. They represented in Israel those of the second generation to realize the precepts of *Torah* and work, many of them are kibbutz members, professors, architects and teachers.

The Heḥalutz in training camp, among them some from Jaroslaw:
Shpindel (with the dog), Barik, Malka Shpindel (standing), Graf Simḥa and Ashe

[Page 126]

A group of "Heḥalutz" of Jaroslaw

**Standing R to L: Feiwel Donenhirsch, X, Ajzyk Fruchtman, Binenstock, Abraham Kenigsberg
Sitting: X, Siegel, Kostman**

Translator's Footnote:

1. On the river Jordan about 5 miles south of the Sea of Galilee, the remains of which are still to be seen see also: http://Jaroslaw.zionistarchives.org.il/en/datelist/Pages/Rutenberg.aspx

[Page 128]

The Hebrew Youth Society *"Akiva"* in Jaroslaw

by Moshe Kalchheim

Translated by Selwyn Rose

The Society of Hebrew Youth *"Akiva"* – or, as everyone called the Movement – *"Akiva"* was founded in the year 1932 after the division that occurred in the "Society of Jewish Youth" in Galicia.

The split took place in the summer-camp Baranowicze (Baranovich), near Przemyœl. When we returned from the camp the Jaroslaw branch and most of the senior leadership and pupils, left the "Youth" and founded *"Akiva"* with their clubhouse located on the grounds of the Aschenfeld sisters on Grodska Street.

Among those who left and founded "*Akiva*" were Yosef Zielenkowski, Fluser, Benek Krieger, Barak Winter, Mundek Kramer, Hosch Yackter, Itzik Lieberman, Akiva Katz, Shenker Rik, Rosa Lipper, Shulamit Kalimer and many more.

With the separation, the national leadership of the "*Akiva*" Movement transferred from its base from Kraków to Jaroslaw because the branch in that town was bigger and more important than the one in Kraków. Debates and discussions began on the ideological roadmap of the movement, which slowly acquired for itself a respectable place among the youth in western Galicia and from there it spread to eastern Galicia and Congress Poland.

The presence among us of the Movement's leaders (Dr. Idak (Yehuda) Orenstein, Marcel Zinger and others), added a personal dimension of importance to the branch and enriched our lives significantly during that period.

In a short period of time, the Jaroslaw branch of "*Akiva*" became the largest youth movement in town. Most of the members were students, mainly of the "Blue Gymnasium" (named for the color of the caps that the pupils wore), but also of the "Red Gymnasium" (for a similar reason) and the girls' gymnasium, but there were among them also clerks, sales people from shops and laborers, thus, in practice all layers of the Jewish population of Jaroslaw were represented in our movement and the relationship between them all was significant for its mutual affection and brotherly unity.

Our Movement encouraged combining both scouting and Jewish values. We were known in town for our celebration of *Erev Shabbat* and *Oneg Shabbat* organized by our branch for its members. On the eve of *Tish'a B'Av*[1] we allgathered together. We would sit on the floor to mark the mourning of the Destruction and after a "conversation" on the events of the day, we had a sing-along of Zionist songs continuing long into the night

[Page 129]

From Grodzka Street we moved to Zamkowa Street, almost out of town, an area where most of the residents were non-Jewish but after a short time, we returned to the center of town again, first of all to Opolski Street and from there to 2, Waska Street, where my family lived.

In 1934 I was head of the branch and the region and the membership of the Jaroslaw branch numbered several hundred youngsters both boys and girls.

Most of our counselors made Aliyah: Zielinowski, Fluser, Krieger, Katz, Rik and Lieberman. Every case of immigration to Palestine was a central event in the life of the branch and the farewell celebration that we organized for each immigrant left a lasting impression on the life of the Movement.

"The Society of Jewish Youth"

Standing from R to L: B Winter, M. Kremer, M. Halberthal, J. Zielenkowski, S. Schleider, Manes, and Gertner
Sitting from R to L: A Katz, D. Rubin, A. Fluser, X, X

[Page 130]

While I was head of the bureau, K. Katz, Shenke Rik, Regina Shpindel, Karol Gelernter, Y. Kluberg, L. Kudler, Benjamin Stecher and Mala Miller all immigrated to Palestine.

Chiefs of the Bureau who preceded me were: B. Krieger, Itzik Lieberman, Mundek Kramer, K. Katz and B. Winter. Together with me until the outbreak of the war, the leaders of the branch were S. Shpindel, R. Beck, Yosef Baliver, Yoel Glatt and Avrumk'e Zimmerman.

In 1934, the "*Akiva*" Movement organized a large anti-Nazi exhibition in its clubroom. Our accomplished artist member, Sh. Kalman, did excellent work. He was a graduate of the School of Engineering and a highly competent artist. He decorated the hall with excellent drawings, many of them black and white copies of the artistic works of Lilien (Ephraim Moses Lilien) that awoke admiration and surprise in all the visitors. I also recall the work of Benek Krieger, a portrait of Ahad Ha'am (Asher Ginzburg) created from microscopically small letters, taken from his critique "That is Not the Way."

A group of "Aḥvah" members of the Akiva Movement 1936

Standing from R to L: Janet Gerblich, Bunio Ringel, Heniek Mambach, Moshe Kalchheim (leader) and Heniek Frucht
Sitting: Heniek Eizenmayer, Heniek Ringel

[Page 131]

The focal point of the exhibition was large stained-glass presentations illustrating our struggle against Hitlerism in the history of the Jewish people.

The exhibition drew thousands of visitors and its echoes reached as far as the Zionist press in Poland. After two weeks, the exhibition was moved to some other towns like Przemyœel and Rzeszów (Raysha).

In 1936, a "Training Platoon" was established in Jaroslaw combining "*Akiva*" and "*Heḥalutz*", located outside town in my grandmother's house. It was a house constructed of wood standing in a garden in which our members prepared themselves for work in the "Land of Israel"…but in order to sustain themselves the trainees worked in different places in town like carpentries, factories and so on.

The "*Akiva*" Movement created for themselves "patrons" (a sort of "parents' association"), comprised of socially active Zionists in town whose function was to assist the Movement financially and to form a bridge between the youngsters and their elders. The head of the "patrons" at different times were: Dr. Rabinowitz, Dr. Rosenblatt, Dr. Reger and others and lastly, until the outbreak of war, Mr. Glazberg, the flour-mill owner and chairman of a charity fund located near the "Pioneers Memorial", living today in Israel.

The "*Akiva*" Movement in Jaroslaw also created a "patronage" that included within its ranks the parents of pupils of the Movement and its management was comprised of active Zionist residents of the town. The aim of the organization was to create a connection between the younger generation and the parents' generation. The "patrons" - accompanying the Movement in all its activities, taking part in their central events and being concerned also for the financial aspects connected with the maintenance of the branch.

The "Akiva" branch 1935

[Page 132]

The head of the "patrons" at different times were: Dr. Rabinowitz, Dr. Rosenblatt, Dr. Reger and others and lastly, until the outbreak of the Second World War – Y. Glazberg.

The *"Akiva"* Movement made a significant impression on its young pupils; it consisted of a combination between searching for a way of coming closer to Jewish sources by organizing bible study courses arranged by the head-office secretariat on a National level and to graduate, a boy or girl of the course was required to sit for an examination that was quite difficult and demanded serious and intensive study.

The bible study was not routine nor was it treated lightly: deep involvement was generated for everything we learned and with the years, the influence of the leaders of the Movement grew more and more so that an almost religious element seemed to be imparted on the Movement. With that as background, a crisis arose in 1936 when a group undergoing training in the town of Leopoldinov, close to Rava Russkaya (Rave), rebelled against the "religious enforcement" in the Movement and separated from it. Another splinter-group called the 'Seven Group", that immigrated to Palestine refused to join the *Beit Yehoshua* Kibbutz of the *"Akiva"* Movement, but settled in *Neve-Eitan* but in time left the Movement entirely and joined the Mapai.[2]

The division was felt even in the Jaroslaw branch of *"Akiva"*. A few members of the management left the branch and joined the "Seven Group" among them Mala Miller, Berko Winter and Regina Shpindel but mostly *"Akiva"* remained intact. In the meantime, some of the members made *Aliyah* and in Palestine joined the splinter group and went together with them to *Neve Eitan*, among them Shlomo Marzel, Akiva Katz and Shenke Rik. All of these, together with Mala Miller until today, are living in *Neve Eitan* in the Beit She'an Valley.

In 1939, when the Nazis entered Jaroslaw on Thursday 10th September there were about two hundred members. The clubhouse at the time was situated in court-yard of the Golowski cinema. On one of the days preceding the entry into town of the Germans, when it was clear to all of us that the end of Jewish and Zionist life in town had arrived, we all gathered in the big hall for a final meeting. Most of the members had already left town and only a small group appeared in the club in a depressed mood, broken in spirit, body and soul.

[Page 133]

We took down all the photographs – the handiwork of the artist – our friend Sh. Kolman, we packed them carefully and hid them in a hiding-place we had prepared in the building and covered them well ensuring that no strangers would ever find them. All the women who were present at the unusual event burst into bitter tears as our own eyes filled with tears…and a fervent prayer fell from our lips that G-d in heaven would grant us that we would live to return to this place dear to us all and to the life we loved here.

That was the last meeting of the "*Akiva-ites*" of Jaroslaw.

A group of youngsters from "Akiva"

Translator's Footnotes:

1. The 9th Day of the month of Av - a day of mourning commemorating the destruction of the Temple and many other tragedies that befell the Jewish People throughout history falling on the same day.
2. Israel's dominant Socialist wing for many years mainly lead by David Ben-Gurion.

[Translator's comment: I was unable to find any confirmatory reference to this work or the title's meaning. An entry in Even-Shoshan suggests a similarity to "Opus", an excellent literary work or masterpiece].

[Page 134]

The *"Akiva"* Movement in Jaroslaw

by Ben-Zion Krieger

Translated by Selwyn Rose

To write about Jaroslaw – that means returning some 50 years ago and scrutinizing a generation of life in the Zionist movement with all its events, hesitations and doubts, while at the center of the Movement, in which I took my first steps as a young student of 11 in the *"Akiva"* Youth Movement.

More than once, I held my pen trying to penetrate the mists and re-enter the beautiful days of the flourishing of the Zionist idea. During the time I was a high school student, little did I understand the purpose of the movement, and that the desire to return to Zion was but a dream.

To my sorrow, I was lacking the ability to recall the thoughts and memories looking back over 50 years until I attended a concert of the Israeli Symphony Orchestra, in the Haifa auditorium. Isaac Stern, the world famous violinist performed a concert of works by Mozart. The sounds of the music of Mozart took me all the way back the hall of *"Akiva"* – which was at the time "still in diapers" – where tens of members were sitting and listening, as one of the Movement's founders of the Jaroslaw branch, Ḥaim Shpringer was playing that same piece of music.

From that moment on, I loved music although I failed to understand the content of the concert. One thing was clear to me: I felt close to all those that absorbed the sounds and understood that I was a member of a large family destined to build a new life, an eternal life based on Jewish values.

And here begins my personal history, which is linked to the history of the Zionist movement in our city, including the Zionist youth movement "Akiva", which was founded in those days and included youth who either studied or were workers from all walks of life.

Its founders were academics from Kraków among them were Dr. Y. Freund (Z"L), Yehuda Orenstein, (may he be preserved for a long life), Yoel Dreiblatt and Moshe Zinger. The Movement quickly spread throughout western Galicia and its ideologies reached our town. I recall names like Yitzhak Horowitz, Z. Ludman,.Y. Margolis, Ḥaim Shpringer, David Rubin and others. They, students at the high school, headed the Movement and it was clear to them that Zionism must rise and develop into a movement that will provide the masses of Israel in the Diaspora, with armor against the anti-Semitism, aimed at the extermination of the Jewish people.

And indeed that is what happened; the match was struck and ignited the hearts and the ranks of the Zionist Movement grew, with youth movements that raised the flag of "Love of the People" the flag of General Zionism.

[Page 135]

I do not cry over Jaroslaw, a town in the Diaspora, over the daily realities of our lives, over the anti-Semitic Christians. My heart grieves and bleeds for the beautiful Jewish people who were and who no longer are, for the town that I loved, for in it I was educated and grew up and dreamed, in which I found my spiritual world. We loved our town, Jaroslaw, its centuries-long history of tradition of Jewish life.

From the age of eleven, my life and the lives of others became connected to "Akiva". With the passage of time, members gradually left. Some of them went on to serve the "progressive ideologies" of the "socialistic-Marxist" movements, others left because they could neither understand nor encompass the Zionist ideas to their satisfaction but many joined with me and we continued on to the end, until the fulfillment of the ideology that led us to the Land

of Israel, some to the kibbutzim of "Hashomer Hatza'ir" some to the "Betar" Movement and some to the General
Zionists.

Jaroslaw area group of the Federation of Jewish Youth

First row: Elke Kalchheim
Second row: Attorney Horowitz, Y. Zielinkowski, Simha Graff, Devora Hilfstein
Third row:Y. Shtricks, B. Shlisselburg, S. Lieberman

[Page 136]

The Jewish youth movement "*Akiva*" arose during what were in any case, hard days for the Zionist
movements. In those days, ways were being sought of realizing the Zionist ideology. There were those Zionists who
thought to base the movement on cosmopolitan or socialist thinking – and others who saw in the Zionist movement a
continuation of the eternal cultural and spiritual life of the Jewish people, that without the love of Jewish values
would bring about the collapse of the entire structure and gave up. A body without a soul. That group of youth
educated by the ideology of "Ahad Ha'am" and the love of Israel. With these ideas, we went out into the Jewish
street in order to "conquer" the youngsters.

We went through a period of hard divisions – but I admit that there were no differences of opinion amongst us
because the general Zionist youth ideology was clear and unequivocal and therefore there is sorrow for the time and
effort wasted.

The "*Akiva*" Movement was involved in all the efforts and activities of the Zionist movement in order to
introduce the wider public of our town to the Zionist ideas which were well-received and the number of friends of
the Movement grew from day to day.

The leadership of the Society of Jewish Youth 1932

Standing: Jozek Zielenkowski
Sitting from right to left: Mundek Kremer, Akiba Katz, Shlomo Mercel, Benek Krieger, A. Zimmerman, Moniak Halberthal

[Page 137]

The Jewish public was deeply concerned with the difficult fight for survival and was not open to the Zionist ideas. Students of the *Yeshivot*[1] rejected the Zionist idea of the "Return to Zion". Nevertheless, the youngsters and the town's activists who already had a taste of the poisonous anti-Semitism, began slowly to draw closer to the ranks of the Zionist movement and on more than one occasion, their halls were filled with both young and old who came to hear lectures from leaders of the Zionist movement and warning speeches that captured the attention but also provoked bitter arguments.

We cooperated with all the Zionist streams. We had meetings with other youth movements like "*Hashomer Hatza'ir*", "*Gordonia*", and "*Heḥalutz*", the revisionist movement and the ideological arguments were rich in content and everyone was convinced of the "rightness" of their several views.

I remember the big party we had celebrating the tenth anniversary of the founding of "*Akiva*". We went out to show the population of the town our strength in numbers and quality. Its organization of the excellent exhibition by its students, its conference of local members with the participation of the leaders of the General Zionist Movement led at the time by our friends, Mrs. F Mohrenberg, Dr. Rozenblitt and many other invitees. That same evening, we held a gala rally in the *Harutzim* meeting-hall, with folk-dancing and a display of art-work and lectures.

The ten years of our existence were proof that our direction was right. At this time, our first group of members from the Movement fulfilled their dream and made *Aliyah* to the Land of Israel.

But the heavens darkened and the Hitlerite beast threatened the very physical existence of our Jewish people.

Out of responsibility for the people, the entire movement – and among them the local branch of Jaroslaw, harnessed itself to warn everyone of the danger looming over us. Delegates from the Movement went out among the people and urged them to join the ranks of Zionism, to leave the Diaspora and save our existence and our souls. The Jaroslaw branch was significantly active in that field.

We were not a large group of zealots, who, with their exuberant enthusiasm were prepared to sacrifice all they had, everything dear to them. The fanatic belief and boundless dedication of the leadership of our branch, like Dov Winter, Shlomo Marcel, Akiva Katz (the last two are now in Neve Eitan), Y. Lieberman and their lead Yosef Zielenkowski – placed the Movement at the head of the warriors in our town and the region.

Who among us doesn't remember Saturday nights and our "*Oneg Shabbat*" when we sat together in our branch on Waska Street, close to each other in heart and soul, with songs of our faith and Jewish melodies echoed off the building's walls and our spiritual enthusiasm caused everyone to dance!? Yes – we were fanatics in our romantic mission and it was that which granted us strength for the beautiful future. It was our strength and spiritual fortitude.

[Page 138]

At the age of 16 we were still very young and naïve, but old enough to manage not only a branch of several hundred members, but also to take upon ourselves the entire region, from Jaroslaw to Rzeszów (Raysha), a county with wonderful, motivated youngsters, pioneers, students and workers, traders and academics.

Our attitude towards religion attracted traditional and also religious youth, who found in the "*Akiva*" branch their new home and in their counselors dedicated souls, because for us, Zionism was a kind of continuation of the life of the people of Israel, with its aspirations for the recreation of new Jewish values that correspond to our times. In that area Ahad Ha'am was a great help because his writings were for us a template and guide-book and represented a deep source from which we drew great inspiration.

A group of "Aḥdut"[2]

Sitting from R. to L.: Moshe Fierer, Benek Krieger, Izak Lieberman, Wilek Kluberg
Standing: Lonek Pokard, Chaskiel Fogel, Buch, Bunio Zimmerman, Josef Balibach, X, X, Benjamin Stecher

[Page 139]

Our life-style and Zionist activities awoke great interest among older Zionists and we found among them many intent listeners. Thus, it is fitting to mention the activities of the Movement's Dr. Schwartz, Dr. Rozenblitt, Mrs. F. Mohrenberg and many others who often visited us, danced with us and spent many hours in mutual conversation and ideological arguments.

The years flew by and we matured and finished school. Some of our friends went on to university to continue studying; some immigrated to Palestine to fulfill the Zionist ideal.

With the exodus of the elders, they were replaced with the younger members among us and so, after Y. Zielenkowski left for the Land of Israel, it fell upon the present writer of these few lines, to lead the Movement. In 1935, I too made *Aliyah* and the management of the Region was placed in the faithful hands of Moshe Kalchheim, at present the spokesman for the Jewish Agency in Israel.

We educated a wonderful generation of youth, a generation of youth with Jewish hearts, dedicated and faithful to its people. We will not get into the actual debate if our path, in light of the reality in the country, was right. One thing is certain and sure – all those who realized the right to live and to breathe the air of the Land of Israel, of the State of Israel, recall with great fondness those beautiful days in which they spent their time in the family circle of "*Akiva*", its meetings, its summer camps and conventions, nature outings, fruitful lectures and arguments on religion, orthodoxy, the existence of the People of Israel, with their eyes towards Zion and Jerusalem.

The youth movements that came into existence in our town Jaroslaw ignited a ray of light in the darkness that lay around. It is only sad that those same members who were unable to realize their dream and were unable to make their *Aliyah* because of the destructive policies of the Mandatory Government, that prevented thousands of Zionists to achieve that dream. To my great sorrow, they also were among the millions exterminated and destroyed by Israel's evil tyrant, Hitler - may his name be erased and perish from memory.

There was Polish Jewry and among them the Jews of Jaroslaw that are no more.

Translator's Footnotes:

1. Advanced academies of Jewish laws and precepts, usually leading to rabbinic ordination.
2. A Zionist Labor Party founded in 1919.

[Page 140]

The *"Zionist Youth"* Movement in Jaroslaw

by Ephraim (Philip) Baumgarten

Translated by Selwyn Rose

The Jaroslaw branch of the "Young Zionists" was created from a small kernel of "Young Zionists" and the organization "Mutual Aid", whose members were students of high schools in town.

The idea to establish this movement came from David Rubin (Z"L). Y. Zielenkowski, Chico Schleider and T. Plesser worked together with him on the project. He was the head of a small group of members of "Young Zionists" and worked to expand the framework of the Movement by adding students who were members of the "Mutual Aid" group who had no consolidated leaders.

Their first clubhouse was located on Pruchnicka Street, close to the railroad station. In the beginning, the clubhouse was shared by both movements of the Zionist youngsters, that of the "Young Zionists" and that of the *"Samopoc"* (mutual aid) and therefore each group gathered on different weekdays for their individual activities. That was in the early 1930's.

After some clarifications and conversations with the youngsters, David Rubin wished for them to join the Zionist youth movement and merge together with them. The operation was successful. The Zionist Youth Movement came into being and in time competed with the larger Zionist Youth movements like "Akiva".

The activities of the "Zionist Youth" continued to grow and expand. Its club first transferred to Rynek Street (the home of Dr. Kremer) and later to Trybulanska Street and finally, until the outbreak of war to Grodzka Street.

I recall important events in the life of the Movement.

I remember the visit of Dr. Mosensohn, the principal of the Tel-Aviv Hertzliya gymnasium to the youth club in 1933 was a highly treasured event.

The lecturer, who bore a resemblance to Herzl, stood alongside a photograph of the founder of the Zionist Federation and spoke about Zionism. I remember it was a Shabbat morning. His speech was in Hebrew and it was translated into Polish by one of our leading members. I can't remember who translated the speeches either Ephraim Steinbock or Moshe Halberthal. Both of them excelled in their knowledge of the language and were capable of offering faithful translations.

Another important event was a branch assembly in "Yad Harutzim" in which Yitzhak Steiger, at the time head of the world Zionist movement, took part.

[Page 141]

The preparations for this event took at least six months and caused a lot of tension among the members of the branch. Immigration to Palestine of members, after they had completed their training was a highlight in the life of the branch. I remember among them were our members Ḥaim Kremer and Shimon Pastor. Ḥaim Kremer is particularly worthy of mention because of his legacy and faithfulness to the movement and friends.

Immediately upon his arrival in Israel, he joined the Kibbutz and was sent to work together with Yitzhak Steiger. While he was in Haifa, he suffered a lot because of his association with the Federation of General Zionists and for a long time was without employment. Neither of these two is still alive. The "Young Zionists" Movement organized summer camps and members of our town's branch also took part. I recall my participation in a summer camp near the town of Krosno led by Yitzhak Golan, today a member of the Knesset, and a camp for Movement leaders in the Carpathians. Although the most beautiful period of all was the work camp at a farm near the town of Gorlice (Gorlitza) under the leadership of Agronomist Bauer. At the time there was a group working there in agricultural training for immigration to kibbutz life in Palestine. The time I spent there was one of the most impressive and beautiful periods of my life.

The "Zionist Youth" group of Jaroslaw

Second row from the top, standing from left to right: L Steinbock, M. Halberthal and the last on the left, A. Baumgarten
Among those in the center: Avraham Zimmerman
Sitting in the bottom row center: Peled

Our branch of the Movement in Jaroslaw organized a camp in a village for a few days. A great effort was put into the organization of the camp and its content. We rented two houses in the village intended as living-quarters for the group during the camp. When we arrived at the village and settled into the place, we were hindered by a gang of Polish hooligans who showered us with stones and forced us to shorten our stay there. We sadly had to cancel that program as it had been planned and were forced to return home the following morning.

[Page 142]

During the years I was head of the branch, we were visited by Dr. Israel Som of Lvov. It was a period of crisis for the branch after the founders of the branch in the city were forced to leave. Some immigrated to Israel and others went to training camps. The new branch leadership was staffed by young people who had no time to learn from the experience of the previous leadership.

It is fitting to compliment the earlier leaders: David Rubin, Moshe Halberthal, Avraham Zimmerman and Ephraim Steinbock.

Among the central operatives of the Movement's branch were: Yosef Ahrenthal, Ḥaim Kremer, Leon Sonnenblik and Shmuel Guttman. In addition to those mentioned there were other active members like Arieh Magram, Bluma Waltzer, Regina Friedberg, Oleg Hess, D. Lipper and Y. Wolf.

The branch published a newsletter containing articles written by members of the Movement.

The many contributions of our Movement did much to define the profile of our town's youth. It saved our youth from assimilation and "emptiness", brought us into closer contact with the love of our people and the Land of Israel and provided content in life.

When the war broke out, all the organizations and movements collapsed but the members of our Movement demonstrated a faith that in time the idealism of Zionism and the State of Israel will arise and exist. The members of the Movement, even in the most difficult of times of life, days of hunger and suffering, never forgot the Zionist education they had received in the Movement and drew from it strength and encouragement for the future...

[Page 143]

Betar[1]
(Jewish military training in Jaroslaw)

by Dov Narzisenfeld, USA

Translated by Selwyn Rose

When one sees in today's Israel the Israel Defense Forces and *Gadna*[2], it is difficult to believe that in the not long distant past, about 35 years ago, in exile in Poland, there were young Jewish dreamers who envisioned that in the not too distant future there would arise a Jewish State in which there would be a proud Jewish army.

Betar at summer camp
Sitting from the right: Engleberg, T, Ingbar, Dym
Standing in uniform: Enk Glat

During the period that Betar in Poland was experiencing many ups and downs, the movement existed in Jaroslaw with a strong influence on Jewish National life in the town. The Movement educated and introduced military training with actual military equipment: rifles and live ammunition, grenades and stones. Jaroslaw was the first town to achieve this under the leadership of the Jaroslaw Branch.

We must eternalize here, in the Memorial Book of Jaroslaw, one of the dreamers mentioned above, the leader and commander of Betar Jaroslaw at the time, Dr. Nahum Tanzer (or, as he was called - Nushek Tanzer), for it was he, with his boundless enthusiasm brought about that at the expense of the Polish government and military sources, and Polish officers

[Page 144]

as inspectors, trained Jewish boys and girls in the use of weapons and military discipline. It is with thanks to him and other young Jewish leaders, that several young Jewish organized groups, among them Betar, marched through the streets of Jaroslaw in military uniforms, with rifles on their shoulders and alongside the Polish eagle on their berets the Betar insignia. Thus, they marched three times a year, on the 3rd of May, the 11th of November and on Youth Sports Day. I am certain that even though the official Zionist bodies, the "playing games with guns" was a bit of a joke, many Jews secretly shed a tear, and quietly mumbled the prayer: "My only wish is that Jewish State with a real Jewish army would soon be established!" Many at the time sensed the coming of the Messiah. It was satisfying to see, a platoon of 50-70 proud young Jews dreamt, with Dr. Tanzer at their head, marching through the streets of Jaroslaw to the sound of a militsry band of the Third Polish Legion, with the knowledge they are fulfilling a mission, knowing that in the not too distant future those same youngsters (just slightly older), or their children following in their footsteps, will be marching through the streets of Tel-Aviv and Jerusalem in a Free Jewish State. And thus, it came to pass…only sadly many of those dreamers never came to realize their dream. Let us remember the six-million Holy Martyrs, among them one of the first victims: Dr. Nahum Tanzer.

The Betar Movement during the 1930's

[Page 145]

I must mention another personality from among the Jaroslaw young people of the 1930's, and that is the teacher and ideologue of the Jaroslaw Betar, Yosef Ingvar. He held Hebrew courses for beginners and advanced students and also courses in original interpretations of the Bible and his young pupils drank thirstily his words. The lessons were given to interested members in the Betar club-house or in his parents' home a private personal group (the "Hertzliya group that was well-known in Jaroslaw). I want to mention here the people of that group that survived: David Aizman, Ya'acov Prinz, Dov Nartzenfeld and Mendel Schleider. S. Weintraub and Yisrael Mueller are no longer alive and not long ago Michael Fleischer passed away. And who doesn't remember Yitzhak Ingvar (or as he was called "Isaac"), the musician who, with a mandolin in his hand he sang songs he had composed accompanying himself on the mandolin. He composed songs in Hebrew, Yiddish and Polish both the lyrics and the music. These melodies later became the general heritage of all without them knowing who the composer was.

That same Isaac Ingvar was also the founder (together with the musician P. Kartz) and organizer of the mandolin orchestra "*Zamir*" and later "*HaNigun*", numbering about 150 members. The orchestra was the pride of Jaroslaw for its unforgettable presentations in the "*Yad Harutzim*" hall. And we will also remember Yitzhak Ingvar – as the teacher of many young people who perished along with millions of Jews in the Holocaust.

May his soul be remembered for a blessing.

Translator's Footnotes:

1. The last Jewish fortress to hold out during the Bar Koḥba revolt in the second century C.E. and also an acronym for **Brit TRrumpeldor**, an early 20th Century Zionist hero; see: https://en.wikipedia.org/wiki/Joseph_Trumpeldor
2. GADNA : an acrostic in Hebrew for "Youth Battalions"

[Page 146]

Jewish Academic Youth in Jaroslaw
(Jewish Theater Life in Jaroslaw)

by Maximilian Meister

Translated by Selwyn Rose

The Jewish population of Jaroslaw, a suburban town in the Lvov region, numbered about 10,000 souls from a total population of 30,000 residents. The main occupations of the Jews were various branches of business and commerce and artisans. It is appropriate to mention that Jewish professionals in Jaroslaw were known for their high standard of professionalism and their work won for them the right to market their goods beyond the town's borders.

Thanks to the tolerant nature of the Austrian regime – under whose authority Jaroslaw remained until 1918 – the budding Jewish *intelligentsia* appeared, mainly comprised of doctors and lawyers and very few were engineers. Very few of these professionals were offered government posts. Among these few, it is worth mentioning the names of Dr, Leon Yarazowitz, who officiated as regional Judge; the engineer Gariski who was the railroad inspector, a few mail inspectors like Sphatt, Kurtzman and director of the Presidential Office of the sub-district court, Schmalzbach. It is also appropriate to mention the name of the long-serving Mayor of Jaroslaw and the Chairman of the Community Council, Julius Strisower – among the wealthy of town and one of the donors and founders of the Jewish orphanage.

The establishment of the independent State of Poland in 1918 was a turning point in the public life of the Jews. It was then that the Jewish youth began streaming to the high-schools in large numbers. In Jaroslaw there were two government gymnasia for the youth – a classic gymnasium in which Greek and Latin were part of the obligatory curriculum and a high-school that later became known as the Gymnasium of Natural Studies and Mathematics where the teaching language was French; the School of Engineering; the School of Commerce and Business where both boys and girls were taught and also a private gymnasium for girls. And a teachers' training college for girls.

Even Jewish parents of restricted means made strenuous efforts to provide secondary education for their children, especially to send their children to the classical Gymnasium at the end of which it was possible for them to continue on to the universities of Lvov and Krakow.

Even the "Numerus Clausus" in the higher educational institutions law failed to prevent the drive for academic learning and therefore many young Jews were forced to transfer to far distant colleges for studies in medicine, like Bratislava, Prague and Italy.

[Page 147]

In order to extend assistance to the youngsters studying in the universities a society "Academic Assistance", was established with the target of collecting money to finance and provide loans to the needy students. The Society followed a similar society in Lvov that stretched out a helping hand with financial assistance to the students. Initially, the association confined itself to fundraising and proceeds from holding annual New Year's Eve parties. However, the gathering of donations involved many difficulties, since all the Jewish associations - various charities and political organizations - followed this path. As a result, the income for the academic coffers was modest in the extreme and the help given to the young pupils was similarly reduced.

The turning point in the mobilization of cash began in about 1922, when the youth – graduates of the Gymnasiums – began to discover artistic talents.

It is worthwhile pointing out that there was a strong urge among the youth to acquire an education. The Jewish parents wanted their children learn to play the violin, the piano, clarinet and so on. The pleasant and comforting atmosphere of the classical Gymnasium was an added aid. In that Gymnasium were two orchestras – brass band and symphony. The best violinists and wind instrumentalists were Jewish and even the conductors of these orchestras were, for many years, Jews. Here is the place to mention names of a few conspicuous instrumentalists: K. Taubenfeld and his brother, Zigmund, who were conductors of the wind-instrument orchestra; H. Dorenfeld, H. Schlafrig-Shpringer, P. Mohrenberg, P. Karp were conductors of the symphony orchestra – Otto Schorr, an excellent violinist and his brother Yulek (Yulian), clarinetist; Y. Huttner (piccolo) and many others whose names, unfortunately, I can no longer remember.

It is interesting that an annual tradition existed to commemorate the memory of Yehuda Halevi. In the organization of this annual event, the students of the pre-graduation class invested much effort, receiving welfare assistance from the guardian of the Gymnasium orchestra, Professor Adamski. The program of the assembly was comprised of an opening speech in Polish, a recital of one of Yehuda Halevy's poems in Hebrew, a musical offering from the symphony orchestra created especially for the event where the members were only Jews and a skit, like the first act of the play "Uriel da Costa".

[Page 148]

But let us return to our academic youth. As stated above, in 1922, the students became active in supporting the "Academic Society of Self-Help". Among them were Julius Kessler, a law student and gifted poet; L. Metzger and Yuzek Teitel (Tarczewski), a law student and other gifted vocalist, who sang accompanied by a guitar; Y. Neuberg, a student at the Polytechnic and others.

It is worth noting, that while every single one of them had a specific political orientation with a particular party, within the framework of the Society they all functioned together as a team without any relevance to the political leanings that they may have held. They are the ones who ended up deciding to put an end to what was called in the simple language of the street as "begging", and to achieve financing by providing artistic performances for the Jewish public.

The first appearance was "The Jaroslaw Puppets", with lovely puppets designed by Y. Neuberg modeled on popular Jaroslaw personalities like, Julius Strisower the Chairman of the community and Deputy Mayor; Dr. Spatz, the doctor and Chairman of the Jaroslaw Histadrut Federation; Doctor Ludwig Blumenfeld, lawyer and active in the *Poalei Zion* movement and many others. Olek Kessler composed the comic script in which he exaggerated certain specific elements of these characters' profiles. L. Metzger and Y. Teitel imitated the characters' voices while operating the puppets' strings at the same time.

The play was a great success both in its production as well as financially and the "Yad Harutzim" hall was full to capacity. So the performance was repeated, although a few of the local dignitaries felt themselves somewhat hurt, they pinched their cheeks to provoke a blush and look tolerant in the face of the youthful antics.

The Orchestra of Jewish Students
Top row first from the left: Arnold
Second row sitting center: Dr. David Turnheim

The success of the production encouraged the initiative of the group and they decided to stage a full-scale show. Once again, Olek Kessler wrote an appropriate script for different skits performed with great humor by M. Sonnenstein, a pharmacy student and Y. Teitel and L. Metzger sang the melodies composed by Kessler. The production was a huge success and the revenues were also significant and its echoes reached Przemyśl, where they requested a performance. In order to increase the earnings from the performances the scenery constructed by Shionek Neuberg was sent by wagon that was provided free by Z. Ringel a pharmacy student. On the way to Przemyśl (36 km.), a heavy rainstorm completely destroyed the scenery that was constructed of painted packing paper. It is easy to picture the despair of the cast. One of the older members of the group who lived permanently in Katowice, the engineer Bratshpis, took the trouble to go all the way to Przemyśl in order to see the performance. When he saw the tragedy of the scenery he decided to work with Shionek and remake new scenery, (all he asked was a quarter of a liter of vodka). They immediately rolled their sleeves up and within only four hours, the eye beheld new scenery.

[Page 149]

One of the skits in the show was "The Illusions of a Condemned Man". The role was played by a handsome youth named N. Tanzer who sees through an opening in the scenery a platoon of soldiers coming to take him to the place of execution. The script created by A. Kessler, if my memory is correct, was spoken by L. Metzger. The scenery was made up of two sections, one secured by the engineer Bratshpis and the second by one of the cast. Because the engineer at the time was a little tipsy having had one too many shots of vodka, he lost his grip one of the scenery sections and it fell, sending impressive shock-waves throughout the hall. Although not scripted it was considered an addition to the performance and retained in future performances with great effect.

During the period when M. Meister, the law student, was Chairman of the "Academic Student Aid Society" for a number of years, there were two or three artistic performances each year which significantly improved the Society's balance. Although when the members and initiators of the group completed their studies in the universities and began to involve themselves in their various professions, their enthusiasm for their artistic performances began to wane. The students who came after them failed to exhibit the same enthusiasm in organizing and producing performances and resumed the old style of collecting funds. It was only in 1929, when the Academic Student Aid Society finally dissolved and no one tried to resuscitate it, a group of left-leaning youngsters decided to renew artistic productions.

[Page 150]

Only because the inter-party frictions were so conspicuous compared to the earlier period, it was decided that the Society should be chaired by the non-aligned Zigmund Taubenfeld, while the members of the committee were the left-leaning M. Gersten, P. Karp and the writer of these few lines. Within one year of its existence, three full productions were mounted one of which "O –Mona" was received with great acclaim and a repeat performance. These performances were also significantly successful financially and provided assistance to the students. The assistance took the form of loans of up to 150 Złoti for a trimester. The loans were repayable by monthly installments after the completion of studies over a period of 10 years.

It is appropriate to mention the names of two people who staged two productions without any personal recompense – the Postal Inspector Sphatt and the proprietor of the photographic studio Mr. Ziegler.

As a result of World War Two the youth found themselves dispersed to the four corners of the world. Many perished on the battlefield, and many found their death in the extermination camps and others still died a natural death or in the labor camps of Siberia. Many arrived in Israel and live there, while still others made their home in the different countries of the world.

After the Six-Day War and the break in diplomatic relations between Israel and Poland, a conference was held in the classical Gymnasium of Jaroslaw of the graduating class of the 1928-1929 school year. The only Jew in attendance was the writer of these few lines. The list of graduating students was read, and as expressed in the jokes at the time, Jews and Ukrainians constituted the national majority. In addition to the writer, there were only three other surviving students: O. Zilberman, B. Metzger, today living in Haifa and M. Keilitz who is a dentist in Bari, Italy.

These few memories are nothing but a miniscule offering of the total contribution of the Jewish youth to the cultural life of Jaroslaw.

[Page151]

Education and Culture Institutions

[Page 152] Blank

[Page 153]

The *"Yad Harutzim"* Hall

by Moshe Kalchheim

Translated by Selwyn Rose

One of the most magnificent essential institutions in our town of Jaroslaw was the *"Yad Harutzim"* hall on Mickiewicza Street at the foot of the hill. The *"Wiata Targowa"* was on top of that hill. It was a magnificent two-storied building containing several important institutions. It was an institution containing many cultural activities even though the town of Jaroslaw was not lacking societies, federations and foundations of many various types. Its official name was "The Federation of Master-craftsmen – the "Yad Harutzim" which was founded in 1901.

On the ground floor was a beautiful synagogue where prayers were held on weekdays, Sabbaths and festivals. The chief Cantor was Shlomo Mahler whose children live in Israel today. In that synagogue, Cantors from many towns in Poland and Galicia often performed recitals of liturgical and other pieces.

During the Days of Awe, the prayers were transferred to the large hall on the upper floor which was large enough to accommodate hundreds of seated men and women filling it from wall-to-wall and still some people had to stand during prayers. They did so willingly because the great attraction during those days was the Cantor Shmuel Shpindel with his choir, conducted by his eldest son Motek, who lives today in Tivon, Israel. I had the privilege to sing in that choir and even one year to be the soloist for the *"Untaneh Tokeff"* prayer. And if we are mentioning the Cantor Shmuel Shpindel, I want to say that he was a very interesting man, a baker by profession and distinctly Bohemian by nature, tall, handsome gray-haired and bearded. He had a well-developed sense of humor acceptable by all. Shpindel was a dedicated football fan; a match at the local stadium never took place when the prominent figure of Shmuel Shpindel was not seen among the spectators. He didn't particularly like his profession as a baker although his cakes were famed far and wide throughout the town. His function as a Cantor was a hobby and the public, as mentioned, rushed to hear him at the Yad Harutzim Hall and other venues in order to enjoy his performances in all their aspects.

Facing the synagogue were the offices of *"Kupat Gemilut Hassidim"*[1] and "The Artisans' Bank" of "Yad Harutzim Hall" which basically was the principal foundation of

[Page 154]

the Society. This bank gave loans to artisans and small businessmen on very convenient terms and was a central support for those of the Jewish population of limited means and a source of basic economic and professional support. The constructive assistance given by the bank in the shape of loans made it possible for borrowers to continue and broaden their activities. The management of the bank was comprised of representatives of all sections of the community: doctors, attorneys, industrialists and artisans – and noted citizens in town, who were all concerned with different incoming assets from various sources. If I am not mistaken, the bank received important and significant support from "The Joint"[2] in the United States.

The Hall of the "Yad Harutzim"

[Page 155]

The committee of "Yad Harutzim"

From right to left, first row above: Leon Schmalzbach, Feiwel Katz, Emil Tanzer, Pinkas Meister, Salomon Ehrlich, Izak Gaschge
The second row: Abraham Rotenberg, Mandel Weiszager, Leon Aschkenazi, Herman Rosenfeld, Szymon Mond, Leon Wycher
The third row: Jakob Baustein, Juda Berger, Salomon Mahler, Adolf Rager, Matis Springer, Jakob Fruchtman, Moses Zeller
In the center: Dr. Salo Rosberger.

[Page 156]

The second floor was taken up entirely by the large auditorium of generous proportions. There was room for nearly 300 seated people and a further 100 in the gallery. The stage was also large. In that hall, many meetings of the various parties and town institutions took place. The local Jewish theater group also found its home there and the amateur dramatic groups of different organizations, visiting dramatic ensembles of professional actors from Warsaw, Vilna, and Lvov and also from Palestine. We were fortunate enough to see "The Vilna Yiddish Concert-Theater", the actors Dzigan and Shumacher, Morris Schwartz, Ida Kamińska-Turkow, "The Broom"[3] from Tel-Aviv and other well-known Jewish actors and actresses who enriched the cultural lives of the Jewish community in unforgettable performances.

The large hall was also used as a gymnasium, fitted with all the necessary equipment such as wall-ladders, weights and so on, provided for the use of the various Jewish sports societies in town. In the building's cellar was the center for teaching "Hebrew in Hebrew" under the teacher Chelimer where both youngsters and adults learned the language. The windows of the school looked out upon a staircase that led to Mickiewicza Street and the "*Wiata Targowa*" and everyone that used them could hear on hot summer days, the sound of the Hebrew tongue – especially the lovely songs of Israel, that were being sung by the toddlers under the baton of their teacher Chelimer.

This, then, was the wonderful building of "*Yad Harutzim*" the main and important center of Jewish and Hebrew cultural life, art, sport and economic assistance and support to all layers of the Jewish population of Jaroslaw – without any consideration of status, ideology or political outlook. It served all those who wished to take a break from the daily routine and enjoy the satisfaction being provided to enhance and enrich the lives and content of the Jewish population.

Translator's Footnotes:

1. The broad spectrum charitable organization dedicated to providing comfort and aid, whether human or material, irrespective of personal standing, to all who need it.
2. See: https://Jaroslaw.thejoint.org.il/en/
3. Possibly a reference to Isaiah 14:23

[Page 157]

On the Schools I Studied in and the Teachers

by Dov (Berek) Fruchtman

Translated by Selwyn Rose

Because of a lack of a "*Tarbut*"[1] school within the educational structure of the large Polish towns, young Jewish students streamed into the various Polish middle-schools and gymnasiums in Jaroslaw, more than they did in comparison to other nearby towns. Our town was known as having schools and an army. The number of schools in Jaroslaw exceeded the number of schools in nearby larger towns like Przemyśl and Rzeszów. The school for "building studies" was the only one of its kind in the Lvov region and Jews and Poles came from afar to study there1. The school resembled a style of our own period for an practical engineering school.

Many graduates of that institution completed their studies at the Lvov Polytechnic and became engineers.

There were two gymnasia for boys in Jaroslaw; one was located on The 3rd of May Street and the second on Świętego Ducha.

During the 1930's the number of Jews in both of them amounted to a third of the total pupils but with the years, the number shrank for various reasons and the percentage of our brethren studying there at the end of the 'thirties had dwindled to some few tens only.

The beginning of the August Witkowski high-school was the Real-School during the Austro-Hungarian Empire. After the First World War, that school became a gymnasium and it remained in that format until the time of the reform of the Polish high-schools in 1936. Later, the school became an academic gymnasium with lyceum with two majors – applied mathematics and biology. The studies in the lyceum were after completion of four years in the gymnasium.

[Page 158]

I remember quite well my four years of study in that other gymnasium, a sign of recognition of their status was a red ribbon attached to their hat and a similar ribbon on the lapel of their coat. Because of this the institution became known as the "Red Gymnasium"[a] Later on, two years before the outbreak of war, and after the Polish educational reforms the gymnasium was known by the symbol "555" and that number was sewn on the left sleeve of every student.

The August Witkowski Gymnasium

Standing in the last row: First – M. Kornberg, Sixth – B. Fruchtman, Seventh – J Graf, Eighth – J. Kirschenbaum

The majority of the students were Jewish or Polish and very few were Ukrainian. I remember two of them. In my class, there was one Ukrainian as opposed to ten Jews.

The Jewish Teachers

There were only a small number of Jewish teachers in both of the famous gymnasia in Jaroslaw. Understandably, the teachers of religion were Jewish, like Distelfeld and Dreyfus.

But it is worth to note those of the Jewish teachers who were among the staff teaching general studies.

[Page 159]

One of the most famous was Professor Taube, a stalwart Pole, who taught Polish literature. No one could cast a shadow of doubt of his knowledge and excellence on the subject of Polish literature and the sources of the country's language, for if it were not so, how would it be possible to imagine that a Jewish teacher, of all things, would obtain the respected position as teacher in a Polish gymnasium during the period of significant anti-Semitism in Poland?

Professor Taube was a pleasant well-mannered man and although I was not one of his students in the first gymnasium, I remember his English lessons to pupils of both gymnasia during the afternoon hours in the framework of foreign language students.

The second teacher, was Jewish and a teacher in our gymnasium, Professor Bachmann who was the German teacher. His pupils did not reach the heights of excellence in the German language not because of the lack of his didactic ability but the difficulty of the Polish people to absorb the German language.

The August Witkowski Gymnasium

The Reali Gymnasium

[Page 160]

Next to the "Blue Gymnasium" was the gymnasium for girls, the classic gymnasium named in honor of Josef Pilsudski where the principal was the well-known Jewish sympathizer and adversary of open anti-Semitism in our town.

The Hebrew School in our Town

The Jewish school was established in 1930 or1931. Until then there had been no Jewish school in town. Hebrew was taught in the "*Yavneh*" school and other places in town also ran courses in the language.

The school was located in a two-story building on the junction of Wanska and Sowiaska Streets. For years, the school had been struggling with the authorities for recognition to prepare children for Government matriculation and for official status.

The Hebrew school bore no resemblance to the "*Tarbut*" schools in Poland that had achieved a rare status. The Hebrew language had been taught there as a foreign language as part of its curriculum with all the other subjects taught in the Polish language.

At its peak, the school had about one hundred pupils.

The new format of the school was co-educational where boys and girls studied together. A system that was not practiced in other Jewish schools, for one thing, even in Polish schools girls and boys learned separately. There were schools for boys alone and schools for girls alone.

I recall one of the more well-known teachers – Fella Engelberg, who taught Hebrew at the institution from the day of its foundation until the outbreak of war.

Original Footnote:

a. The nickname had no connection whatsoever with left wing politics of its teachers or its students as is supposed today.
On the contrary, the gymnasium was known for its anti-Semitic stand against the Jewish pupils compared to the other gymnasium.

Translator's Footnote:

1. The "*Tarbut*" schools thrived at the beginning of the 20th Century and between the Wars. They introduced education of a more secular nature compared the old traditional *Heder* religiously based education that had been usual. The lessons were taught in Hebrew.

[Page 161]

The *"Yavneh"* School

by Dov (Berek) Fruchtman

Translated by Selwyn Rose

The *"Yavneh"* school was located in a two-story building in the center of town facing the municipal registry building. It was the first Hebrew school of the *"Mizraḥi"* movement. The subjects taught in the institution were Talmud, The Bible and Hebrew.

Due to the efforts of the original founders, known *"Mizraḥi"* businessmen, (like: Shimon Spiegel, Elimeleḥ Reich, Haim Aharon Zilberger, Mordecai Landman, David Graff, Noah Lemm, Z. Reinhertz, David Kremer, Moshe Raff, Michael Silber, Tzvi Schlafrig, Yehoshua Begleibter), the teachers at the school were well-known educators.

Among the staff of teachers in the institute, I recall one by the name of Avraham Zuta. He was a well-built man with a short beard adorning his face. The Rabbi, our teacher of the *Gemara*, introduced difficult topics into our heads with a typical motion of his thumb. I remember to this very day the first page of the tractate *"Pessaḥim"*[1] beginning "On the eve of Passover, close to Minḥa time, a person may not eat until dark, so that he will be able to eat matzot that night with a hearty appetite. Even the poorest of Jews should not eat the meal of Passover until he reclines on his left side as free and wealthy people recline when they eat." Only a few among the pupils understood the nicety of the difference of opinion between Rabbi Yehuda and Rabbi Yossi. The second occasion when the Rabbi explained it, I searched the conclusions of the *Tanna`im*[2], and my face lit up with understanding and contentment. I discovered that it was possible for the issue to be explained either way.

The teacher Zuta habitually compelled his pupils to learn by heart complete pages of the *Gemara* and complete chapters of the *Torah*. Perhaps, thanks to him, I remember until today the complete first pages of several tractates and complete chapters of the *Torah*. And that brings to mind the saying: "Things learned in early childhood are remembered more easily than those learned later."[3]

Among the teachers of the institute was one who came to our town from the Vilna area. He would teach from the holy writings in Yiddish. To our surprise, his Yiddish was not the Yiddish that we knew and were used to in Galicia and in our everyday speech. Our 'A' suddenly became 'OO' and our 'EY' became a pure 'EH' and perhaps 'OI'. For some reason, this teacher, whose name was Yesheyahu Rabinovitz, provoked much giggling among the pupils, who found nicknames for him gathered from the Vilna dialect. Mr. Rabinovitz was well-mannered and pleasant. He had no beard and wore no ear-locks and appeared for lessons with a clean shaven face. It seemed to me that in those days, he was still single and the talk of the town labeled him a woman-chaser.

[Page 162]

I remember a few other teachers from the "*Yavneh*" school. One of them, Yesheyahu Lang, I got to know him well in Palestine. He was an excellent teacher and known as an active Zionist in town. For some time he was the principal of the school. I also remember with appreciative thoughts the teacher Rabin, with whom I studied *Gemara* privately, until the war broke out. He too, was among the "*Yavneh*" teachers in our town.

There was another school where the only scholar who taught there was the teacher Kelmar. I studied various courses under his tutelage for two years. The school was housed in one large room in the "*Yad Harutzim*" building. The windows of the room looked out on the nearby stairway that led to the "*Wiata Targowa*"

The studies in Kelmar's school took place during the afternoon hours in "corrected" Hebrew. In other words, Hebrew using the *Sephardi* pronunciation. The seats were occupied by students of various ages. Their knowledge of the language and not their age was the only criteria to be accepted to the courses.

The spoken language of Kelmar's family was Hebrew alone. All the family members had Hebrew names and spoke pure Hebrew. I remember from those days how we looked upon that in wonderment and envy on the members of the household of this famous teacher.

Kelmar the teacher had created in his home a way of life of as he imagined it would be in the land of Israel..

There were five children in the family and they all had Hebrew names: Haya, Shulamit, Arieh, Yocheved and Gideon.

Translator's Footnotes:

1. Pessaḥim is the third tractate (Chapter) of "Order of Festivals" of the *Talmud*.
2. The rabbinic sages whose views are recorded in the *Mishnah* from the first and second centuries C.E. The entire debate can be found here: https://Jaroslaw.sefaria.org.il/Pesachim.2a?lang=bi
3. A free translation of the original saying. See: https://Jaroslaw.thejc.com/judaism/jewish-words/girsa-dyankuta-1.8064

[Page 163]

The *"Tarbut"* Library

Dov (Berek) Fruchtman

Translated by Selwyn Rose

The official name of our town's library was "The Hebrew Library for Education and Culture - 'Tarbut', in Jaros³aw". In the beginning, the library was housed in the Community Center on Sanowa Street on the way to the River San. It was located in the house of the wealthy Jew Sobol.

The "Community Center", where the *"Tarbut"* library was located, existed before the First World War. The activities of all the Zionist movements in our town took place within its walls. In 1921, the *"Tarbut"* library was transferred to *"Yad Harutzim"* building and there it remained for 10 years. In 1931, the library expanded and grew and the place became too small to accommodate the treasure trove of books. It was then transferred to the home of Dr. Blumenfeld oin Kraszewski 6 and there it remained until the outbreak of World War Two.

The Librarian, Sala Striks

The *"Tarbut"* library was the largest among all the libraries in our town. Within it were books in four languages: Hebrew, Yiddish, Polish and German. At its peak, it contained close to 10,000 volumes.

[Page 164]

The Jewish youth in town were among the reading public. But the Polish people were also among the readers because only in the *"Tarbut"* library could the Polish *Intelligentsia* find the famous literary works of the world. The Polish *élite* preferred the *"Tarbut"* library over the large Meinhard library. The *"Tarbut"* library was a significant contributor in establishing the cultural image of the Jewish youth.

The central figure in the library was the institution's librarian Mrs. Sala Striks, (today Heftler), a resident of Tel-Aviv. She was not simply the librarian. She knew all the readers and they knew that she alone carried the burden of managing all activities of the library. She started her work in the library in 1921 and continued until the German invasion. Mrs. Striks knew all the readers and knew which books were suitable for that individual. If a reader selected a book beyond their understanding, Mrs. Striks would say: "This book is not for you" and would not recommend it to the reader knowing it was beyond their understanding.

The librarian remembered many of the (reference) numbers of the books and was rarely in need of the book's card.

One of the first managers of the library was Marcus Kurtzman (Z"L). The first chairman of the library was Dr. Rabinowitz and after his death, Dr. Erik Reszler followed by Bonek Metzger. But all the practical work, like acquisition of books, organizing and cataloging them and ensuring their maintenance from wear and tear, fell on the shoulders of the librarian, Sala.

After the Jews were deported by the Nazis, the library was abandoned.

[Page 168 - Yiddish] [Page 165 Hebrew]

The *cheders*[1] and the Teachers

by Moshe Kalchheim

Translated by Pamela Russ

The *cheder* of *Rebbe* Hersh–Mer, was one of the most popular ones in the city. It was located near the public school by the name of "Piotr Skarga," not far from the *Beis Midrash* and from the slaughterhouse. This was a proper house built from brick and wood, with a large yard. Many children from the city had completed this *cheder*.

The *Rebbe*, Hersh–Mer, with his idiosyncrasies, cast a fear on the children. By nature, he was not a bad person and not at all an angry person, but he was very particular and was a strong disciplinarian. There were *"belfers"* (assistants) for teaching Torah to his students.

I remember when I was a young boy about three years old as was done then, they "dragged" me to the *cheder* of *Rebbe* Hersh–Mer. Four boys appeared in our home, two of which grabbed me by the arms and two by the feet, and that's how they "carried" me through the large marketplace on Spitka Street to the *cheder*, totally disregarding my complaints.

In the *cheder* of *Rebbe* Hersh–Mer, the children learned aleph–beis [Hebrew alphabet] and when they already knew all that, the children started to learn the Hebrew prayers and *chumash* [the Hebrew Bible]. The *cheder* was a means of going from one stage of learning to a higher level, such as for example, to "Talmud Torah" [higher level Hebrew studies], even though they still learned the Hebrew prayers and *chumash*.

"Tall Shmuel"

At the edge of Sabieski Street, in the house where there was the *shul* called "*Hachnosas Orchim*" ["Guesthouse"] and the "Belz *shtiebel*" [informal synagogue of the Belz chassidic community] was the *cheder* of "Tall Shmuel." This was his nickname because of his height.

[Page 169]

In my memory, he is etched as an elderly, tall Jew with a white beard.

The *cheder* was in one of his rooms that also happened to serve as a dining room and bedroom. Over there, we also studied *chumash* and *Rashi* [commentary] and also *gemara* [Talmud]. He was a pleasant person, calm, compassionate, rarely spoke roughly with his voice and his students always behaved quietly and calmly. He never fell into a rage. He died at the beginning of the thirties.

"Talmud Torah"

As already mentioned above, the Talmud Torah in our city was an institution of higher learning. Approximately two hundred students studied there. The budget of the Talmud Torah was covered by the community. The parents who were unable to cover the cost of the tuition fees for their children were freed from this yoke of payment thanks to the community.

At the head of the Talmud Torah were select people who were responsible for various projects that were connected with sustaining the Talmud Torah, including maintaining the students.

In Talmud Torah, it was the best students of the city who studied there. Generally, a strong discipline governed. At the beginning of the thirties, in the Talmud Torah, a "*yeshiva*" was established, and in order that the *yeshiva* acquire a good reputation in that region, the staff brought in a Rosh *yeshiva* [dean, Torah scholar, director, all–inclusive] – an expert in Talmud, who prior to this, was a Rosh *yeshiva* in one of the smaller cities.

I studied in the *yeshiva* for one year along with the best students who excelled in their studies. I do not remember the name of the Rosh *yeshiva*, but his face is deeply etched in my memory. He was a Jew, an exceptional person, with a shining countenance. He was always very careful with his appearance and his manner of dress. His long white beard was always kempt, neatly combed, elegant. From under his black *yarmalke* [skullcap] his bottle–curled *peyos* [side locks] slid out onto his majestic face. He was an approachable, pleasant, refined Jew, with excellent characteristics, and had a beautiful, calm, melodious voice, with which he almost hypnotized the students. In that class there was an exceptionally pleasant atmosphere that evoked a special interest from the students as well as a great attentiveness to their studies.

[Page 170]

Along with me, the other students were Itzik Liberman (lives in Haifa), and the genius of the city, Dovid Eintratter, who later became one of the activists of *Tzeirei Agudas Yisrael* [the youth group Agudas Israel] in Jaroslaw, and was the head of the modern *shul* [synagogue] of the *Agudas Yisrael*. Among other boys in *yeshiva* with me, I remember Shmuel Kaufman and Aharon Brandt, now head of the *yeshiva* of the Belz *chassidim* in Jerusalem.

Of the teachers of the *Talmud Torah* [religious elementary school], I particularly remember Menachem Mendel and the teacher, Rebbe Schreiber, who taught us *chumash* [Bible], and *Rashi* [commentary], and also Rebbe Hershele Meller, whom I already mentioned.

Several Other Small *cheders*

Along with various recognized study institutions, there were scattered about other small, private *cheders*. In each of these *cheders*, there were about ten students. For example the *cheder* of Rebbe Yosef Yitzchok Shlatiner, was in a small house of two rooms on the second floor of Wanska Street, #2. This was a dark house, where even during the day the sun's rays hardly entered. In that *cheder*, the boys also studied *gemara* [Talmud] and *tosefos* [commentary].

Reb Yosele Weistuch ("Lame Yosele")

One of the colorful personalities in town was the teacher Reb Yosele Weistuch, or as he was known in town by his nickname, "Lame Yosele." He limped on one foot and because of that he always walked with a cane which served him as a support, and then also as a weapon of punishment for his students in his "*cheder*" which was located in the women's section of the synagogue "Koler's *minyan* [quorum]" in the yard of Halberthal's house in the large town square.

[Page 171]

The older generation simply called him Reb Yosele Weistuch. He was a refined Jew, a radiating face, a scholar, and the principal leader of prayers in Koler's *minyan*. This was a beautiful, clean synagogue, in the shape of a long, narrow prayer hall, where generally, the congregants were committed Jews who loved and greatly respected Reb Yosele.

For us youth, Reb Yosele was simply: the "lame Yosele," always with his stick in hand, of which we were terrified, up to a fear of death. He was an easily angered Jew, and at any opportunity he would use his stick and provoke his students, who sat half asleep and lazy during his lessons, and forced them to learn with more enthusiasm. In his "*cheder*," the boys studied actual *chumash*. Studying *gemara* [Talmud] already had to be done with other teachers, and so he was involved with only the very young, upon whom he threw great terror.

In truth, generally, he was not as bad as he appeared. His was an unusual anger, which was clad and covered with a love for his boys. The *Rebbe*, Reb Yosele, never used a whip, as other teachers did, but then his stick played an important "pedagogical" role. As every teacher, he would sit at his table, at the head, always with his bent head, beautiful, covered with dove white hair, and always holding in his hands his "tool," the stick, that rested on the table itself. From his rigid face, decorated with a snow– white round beard, from behind his white, tin glasses that hardly stayed on the edge of his nose, there looked out at you two large, sky blue eyes that were always in motion. These eyes saw everything and noticed everything and nothing could hide from them.

[Page 172]

For even the smallest discipline infraction committed by a *cheder* boy, the stick, with the quickest and most incomprehensible motion, immediately landed on the hand or arm or back of the "criminal," and the victim felt this slap all too well. Reb Yosele did not accompany this slap with any shout or word from his mouth, but the slap was always accompanied with a wink of his eye, and a strange grating of his teeth, some kind of muttering, not understandable, that was heard from his teeth.

During recess, the young boys would run around in the yard and Reb Yosef would mingle among the noisy boys, smiling with pleasure with the boys who were playing, taking pride in them and having great enjoyment. Then the young boys took to pushing each other and included Reb Yosele himself, and if one of them would scream out, to incite the others: "Lame Yosele!" then immediately, like an arrow shot from a bow, the stick flew from Reb Yosele's hand right towards the feet of the boy, accompanied by his well–known curse used for everything: "A *kalik* [handicap] and a *bolik* [sturgeon] in your bones!" Reb Yosele shouted this in a loud voice. Then the little boys would run off into all corners of the yard leaving behind, all alone, the Rebbe's stick, until the angry Rebbe called over one of the boys to bring his stick back into his hands. This game with the Rebbe would evoke an excited mood among the boys, and they would intentionally provoke the Rebbe wildly, to get him angry and drive him out of his mind. Then they waited until the Rebbe would once again throw his stick, but many times the boys would be perplexed when Reb Yosele did not want to, or did not have enough time to play this "pushy" game.

Reb Yosele Weistuch raised several generations of *cheder* boys in Jaroslaw, and I remember that we really were very frightened of him, but we also loved him and always listened to him.

His son now lives in Israel.

Translator's Footnote:

1. Religious schools for young children.

[Page 173]

Supporters of the Military

by Shmuel Schleider

Translated by Pamela Russ

In the years 1916 –1918, during World War One, when the war was still in its fiery times, the flow of older Jewish reservists to the army was still great, and among them there were many religious Jews who were very strict about kosher food. Many of them were poor and did not have the ability to feed themselves and so, they did not want to eat anything from the military kitchen because of these religious reasons.

Their situation was very difficult and critical, almost without any hope.

On the initiative of Rabbi Yitzchok Enker, who came from Nisko, the young men established a kitchen by the name of *Tomchei Hatzava* [supporters of the military]. Members of this committee were: Rabbi Yitzchok Enker, chairman; Shmuel Schleider, secretary; members Dovid Graf, Yosef Sacher, Michoel Zilber, Moishe Kalchheim, Asher Kalchheim, Yitzchok Hass, Naftoli Rozenboim.

The goal of the *Tomchei Hatzava* was to feed each soldier one meal a day in the afternoon, after completing his duties, and two meals on Shabbat and on the Jewish holidays.

It is worth noting, that even with the great shortage of products and large number of soldiers (more than 200), *Tomchei Hatzava* enabled each Jewish soldier to eat his fill, and on Shabbat and on the Jewish holidays, delicious foods were prepared that were served generously.

The expenses were very great, but the profits, primarily comprised of volunteer payments [donations], basically covered all the expenses.

[Page 174]

The name of the *Tomchei Hatzava* reached very far into many cities and towns and the rumors about the Jewish soldiers' kitchen were extensive. There were many donations from many well–meaning friends and also from private people in order to enable a regular existence of the *Tomchei Hatzava*. The Jaroslaw merchants donated all kinds of products, flour, meat, sugar, and other necessary foods. The generosity of the people was exemplary.

The blessed activities of *Tomchei Hatzava* went on until the end of World War One. The Jewish people were proud of the activities of this necessary institution, which enabled hundreds of homeless Jewish soldiers to use a kosher kitchen and not to leave them hungry, and also maybe to even give them life.

[Page 175]

Religious Life

[Page 176] Blank

[Page 186 -Yiddish] [Page 177 - Hebrew]

The Synagogues

by Moshe Kalchheim

Translated by Pamela Russ

"A Jaroslaw holiday!" – This is what the Jews in our city called it. And actually, there was always a distinct holiday atmosphere in the city.

I knew many cities in our area: from the smallest, such as: Pruchnik, Przeworsk, Lubaczów, Radimna (Radymno), and larger ones, such as: Przemysl to the east, and Rajsze (Rzeszów) to the west, but there was no city more beautiful and clean than our Jaroslaw. That is not to say that in our city there were no neglected houses, but the general panorama of the city was pleasant to the eye, both for the visitor and the resident of the city.

Those Jews who comprised about a third of the residents of the city (8,500 Jews out of 27,000 residents), lived primarily in the center of the city; on the streets around the "*Ratusz*" (city council), that stood in the middle of the large marketplace (*duzy rynek*), all the houses around the city council and on the following streets: Sabjeski, Tribunalska, Opolska, Spitka, Grodzko, and others, all belonged to the Jews. All the trade and Jewish business life was concentrated in this area. Here also, were synagogues, *chassidic* courts [belonging to specific rabbinic dynasties], *Batei Midrashim* rooms [study halls], and many *minyanim* [prayer groups], and also the centers for the Zionist youth organizations and Zionist parties.

With time, the Jews spread out onto other more aristocratic streets, such as: Grunwaldska, Kraszewski, Dicjus, and others. In general, it was the wealthier Jews who inhabited those streets, but you could also find some of "those" Jews among the residents of the other [former list of] streets.

As mentioned, the Jaroslaw streets were clean and filled with greenery. The city council made sure that the street cleaners did their jobs properly. Their jobs were mainly gruelling and tiring, done on Fridays, when the weekly fairs took place on the "large" and "small" marketplace, when hundreds of farmers with their horses and wagons would come from the surrounding villages to the fair to sell their land–grown products and handiwork. When they left the city at the end of the market day, they left behind a lot of grime and all kinds of trash on the "large" and "small" marketplace. At that time, the street cleaners went right to work, and in a short time the place became clean as before, as if nothing had taken place there. On Friday evenings, when the Jews went to *shul*[synagogues] to pray, all clean and dressed up in their Shabbat clothing, ready to greet the Shabbat, they blended well into the surrounding city panorama. Until this very day, this holiday atmosphere that reigned at sunset on Shabbat eve over the "large marketplace" and its area is etched in my memory. The holiness of Shabbat embraced the streets, the houses, and the people. You could never imagine that only a few hours earlier, the farmers' peddling rowdy noise was heard, as was that of the merchants, and buyers, mixed with the neighing of the horses and noise of the animals. The air was mixed with the smell of human and animal sweat. It left the impression that even the Christians who lived in that area also participated in our Shabbat joy, because they also threw off their weekday clothing and mixed into the holiday [Shabbat] atmosphere that ruled the city.

The Great Synagogue

[Page 187]

The Large *Shul* [synagogue]

Among the large Houses of Prayer that were in the center of the city, were the large *shul* and the *Beit Midrash* [Study Hall]. Both were almost connected to each other. The large *shul* shone with its majestic glow from the outside, but it was even more beautiful on the inside. The entrance to the large *shul* was

[Page 188]

through two steel gates, made in a highly artistic style. On the Shabbat and Jewish holidays, both gates were widely open, welcoming the approaching congregants. According to the old custom, you had to go down two wide steps in order to enter a wide corridor, and then one more step at the entrance of the *shul* itself. The height inside the *shul* was three levels, and on the third level there were about 20 huge windows with colored panes, through which the sun's rays shone with many colors into the rich prayer room, which created an extraordinary atmosphere within the group of congregants.

Along the full length of the walls large calendars [with schedules] were attached, with information [texts] about the Shabbat prayers written in large, bold letters, so that each congregant would be able to read it from a distance.

The large Holy Ark and the large podium in the center of the prayer room were rich in artworks on a prominent artistic level. Everything here was royal and magical. An exemplary "*yekishe*" [Germanic Jewish; pristine and orderly] organization always reigned in the large *shul*. The prayers were according to the *nusach Ashkenaz* [text and melodies of prayer according to *Ashkenaz*, i.e., Central and Eastern Europe style] and were small in numbers, in the city. In honor of the Shabbat, the beadles came in tall, black, cylindrical hats. The children here were forbidden from performing any pranks as they were prone to doing in the other *shuls*. Everything here was majestic and tranquil.

In the large *shul* Rav Yitzchok Shteinberg the chief rabbi of Jaroslaw, prayed regularly. There was also a permanent cantor there, Reb Meshulem Lamm, a Jew of average size with wide shoulders and a black beard. A children's choir assisted him, and every person with a good cantorial voice wanted to sing in the choir. I remember the soprano solo of the choir – Mechele Fogel (lives in the Soviet Union) and the tenor Avrumik Dagan (lives in Israel). In the large *shul*, official ceremonies were celebrated: both Jewish and governmental. I remember after the death of the ruler of Poland, Marshal Pilsudski, they set up a mourning ceremony in the *shul* which many people attended. The famous cantor Moshe Koussevitzky, who that week was a guest in the large *shul*, recited the *"eil malei rachamim"* [prayer for the dead], and Rav Shteinberg delivered the eulogy for Pilsudski in a pure Polish language in honor of the esteemed guests from the magistrate and from the army, who were present at the event of the mourning ceremony.

[Page 189]

In the corridor, to the left, at the entrance to the prayer room, there was a small *"minyan"* [designated quorum] that was called "the tailor *shul*." On Shabbat morning, that was the first *minyan* for prayer at 6:30 am. I prayed in that *minyan* for a long time while I was a student of the "blue gymnasium," that was named Youzef Pilsudski. I would come to that *minyan* with my backpack and then after prayers, I rushed off straight to the gymnasium in order to arrive there before the lectures began, that meant 8 am.

There was a cantor there with a small, sharp goatee, whose name I do not remember. I only remember that he had a convenience store on Spitka Street, and his son was a student in the so-called "red gymnasium." He had a strange voice, whistled through his nose, and always enjoyed his own praying. At the end of the prayers, he would turn to the small group of congregants and he would say to them, in doubt with a question and in doubt with excitement: "So, what do you say about my praying today? It was wonderful, right?"

When the Germans occupied the city they turned the large *shul* into a warehouse of grain.

The *Beit Midrash* [Study Hall]

To the right of the large *shul*, on the same, broad sidewalk was a beautiful, steel gate, through which there was a path leading to the *Beit Midrash*. They said that this was the gate to the Jewish ghetto in the city in the Middle Ages. The *Beit Midrash* was large and spacious, but without the glow of the large *shul*. Also, the group of congregants was different. Here, everything simply was more "homey." Here, the prayers were conducted according to *"nushach Sephard"* [Nusach Sefard is used nearly universally by Hasidim, as well as by some other Ashkenazi Jews but has not gained significant acceptance by Sephardi Jews] and the congregants were *chassidim* from several rabbinic courts.

In the large *shul*, there were hardly any congregants with beards, and in contrast, in the *Beit Midrash*, the majority of the people were bearded. It is worthwhile to mention that in the *Beit Midrash*, there was a Jew by the name of Yosele who prayed there. He was a strange, unusual person, who distinguished himself from the congregants with his odd expressions and behavior. All kinds of rumors about him circulated in Jaroslaw, and many people saw a hidden visage in him – a "hidden person" [mystical term referring to one of the "39 hidden righteous persons" in each generation].

[Page 190]

At the entrance of the large prayer room in the *Beit Midrash*, the *minyan* of the *"Hapoel Hamizrachi"* [religious labor party for Israel] set themselves up. It seems that this was done with the initiative of the leader of the movement, Shiye Lang (known by everyone as "Comrade Lang"). I enjoyed praying with that *minyan* sometimes, because of the Zionist atmosphere there. During the reading of the Torah, they would go out into the corridor and have lively discussions about the problems specifically of the Zionist movement and about politics in general.

The *Minyan* of the Rebbe, Reb Shiyele

On the side, behind the *Beit Midrash*, stood the house of Reb Shiyele, the youngest son of the Belzer Rebbe [leader of the Belz *chassidic* dynasty]. He also had a regular *minyan* every Shabbat and Jewish holiday, and the Rebbe himself would stand before the congregants and recite the Shabbat prayers with his pleasant voice.

Fate had it that his son, who was also my classmate in the *Talmud Torah*, took a different route in life, may G–d have mercy on us, which, according to us in those days was called a "bad route," may we be spared our own. The young boy actually tried to study secular subjects and did not want to follow the ways of *chassidic* life, like his father. The talk was that the "hand" of his mother, the beautiful *Rebbetzen* [Rabbi's wife] was involved here, that she encouraged her only son to go in the ways contrary to his father and the Belzer *chassidim*.

[Page 191]

The Talmud Torah [religious school]

Not far from there, at the decline of Lubelska Street and in the corner of Spitka Street, there was the Talmud Torah building. This was the central, religious institutional building in our city, and I think there was not one single boy, or youth, who did not go through the Talmud Torah system, beginning with the entry level of the system, that means from learning to read, until the studies in the yeshiva. This was a proper building, with five study rooms and a prayer room. There were about 200 or 250 students who regularly studied in the Talmud Torah.

Around the building there was a courtyard enclosed by a nice wooden fence, and in the middle a tall chimney thrust out, built from red brick; [the chimney] was from the nearby Jewish baths and mikveh [ritual baths] which were close to one another. The yard actually was shared by the Talmud Torah and the baths and served as a playground for the students during the school breaks.

The baths were an important service for the community, and they loyally served not only religious Jews, but also "heretics" and even Christians.

There were two divisions in the baths: the first and the second. The first shone with its cleanliness and was decorated with a modern orderliness. I also want to mention the nice "steam baths" which was well–known to the bathers. They set up contests to see who could withstand the hot steam on the tall wooden steps the longest, when the [person who] heated the ovens would, from time to time, pour cold buckets of water on the huge rocks which warmed themselves on the large pieces of wood during the night.

[Page 192]

Until today, I hear the cries in my ears: "[Put] a bucket full into the stove!" That's what the Jews would cry out, those who sat on the wooden steps and hit their bodies with brooms [switches] made from small branches with leaves, to accelerate the blood flow through their veins. Understandably, the intention was to pour another bucket full of cold water onto the steaming rocks in order to intensify the steam that poured out of the stove and filled the space.

But let us go back to the Talmud Torah:

I studied there until I became a student at the gymnasium [high school]. My last teacher there was Reb Hershele Meller. I liked him very much and valued him greatly. He was a Jew with a beautiful visage, was tall, with a long beard, into which many gray hairs were interwoven, but the blond color was still strong. I was particularly impressed by his large eyes that looked at you with intelligence and astuteness, and with his beautiful and pleasing voice both as he studied and as he spoke.

In addition, Reb Hershele was an outstanding *Baal Tefilah* [leader of prayer]. Reb Hershele had a great influence on me, and when I left my studies in the Talmud Torah, I continued studying with him for a long time in his home on Mickowycz Street, opposite the Sokol cinema.

In the *shul* of the Talmud Torah, there were daily services in the mornings and evenings, and of course on the Shabbats and Jewish holidays. Reb Hershele was gladly taken on by that *minyan* of congregants and the esteemed businessmen of the city.

I would also like to mention a figure that was connected to the Talmud Torah, Reb Mekhele Gelernter. He was a tall, short–sighted Jew, who wore thick glasses, and every student was scared to death of him. He was the administrator of the Talmud Torah, and took care of all the issues of the school and of the *minyan*. His son Karol was my good friend in Akiva [youth group], and he immigrated to Israel in the mid–30s, and lives in Haifa today.

[Page 193]

It is also worthwhile to mention another *Baal Tefilah* who prayed in the *shul*, Reb Moshe Hass. He was a well–to–do Jew, with a handsome, black beard and black sparkling eyes. He had a very pleasant voice, and his style for prayers was of the most enjoyable that I knew. When he had the position of leading the prayers for the congregation, many Jews streamed into the *shul* to hear his wonder child "Yankele," who was the "young nightingale," as he was rightly called in our city. He had a rich soprano. His father would let him sing solos for all the prayers, to the enjoyment of all the congregants.

It is interesting to note that Yankele had difficulty in speech. It was hard for him to speak easily, but when he began to sing the stuttering soon started to disappear and his young voice took on an angelic tone.

Reb Moshe Hass had nine children, among them three sons. All were famous cantors, who today live in America (Yankele), England and Israel.

"The Czortkow Court" [followers of the Rebbe of Czortkow's *chassidic* court]

Uphill on Lubelska Street, near Grunwaldska Street, there was the so–called "Czortkow Court" of the *chassidim* of the Czortkow Rebbe. This was a single level building, built from bricks and wood that belonged to the Tentzer family who owned a bakery where they baked bread and *challah* [braided bread for Shabbat].

Many of the congregants belonged to the *"Mizrachi"* [religious Zionist] movement. The Czortkow court comprised seven or eight *minyanim*. My cousin Yankel Liber–Fushteig also prayed there. He was well known as a fine singer and was praised by everyone.

[Page 194]

The *Kehat* Court

Of all the *shuls* in our city, without a doubt the most famous was the *Kehat* Court. This *shul* was located in the small marketplace, not far from the city council.

The popularity of the *Kehat* court was because of the rabbi, Reb Dovid, who was the main *Baal Tefilah* in that court, until his death. The court presented a large prayer room, where long, heavy tables were set out, and on both sides of each table were long, wide benches. The Holy Ark was not a great artistic piece of work, and did not glow with its beauty and richness as in other *shuls*. Instead of a podium, there was a tall table upon which they read from the Torah. Everything in this court was simple, intimate, but without question, the main treasure of this court was the beautiful and enjoyable voice, that was filled with depth [devotion], of the leader of the prayers, the *rebbe*, Reb Dovid. He had a set style for the prayers, as if he prayed from actual notes.

The congregants already knew all his melodies by heart, every "wrinkle," and his personal sigh. It was a tremendous spiritual pleasure to hear him, and generally, the congregants would join in with his singing and Shabbat songs. Often, when the congregants would "support" him, he would suddenly stop his prayer, and that was a hint to the congregants to allow him to do his own presentation of the prayer, and understandably, the congregants soon stopped their singing.

For me, the *Kehat* court was an integral part of my childhood, and until the outbreak of World War II, I would often go to the court for prayers on the Shabbat and Jewish holidays. That is where, in the court, I celebrated my bar mitzva, was called up to the Torah for Torah reading, and then celebrated with a beautiful *kiddush* [festive celebration] for the crowd of congregants, as was done in those times in our city.

My brother Bunye, who remained a religious Jew, – one who guards all the *mitzvoth* [Torah commandments], and who is known as a fine *Baal Tefilah* and singer, remembers until today, the specific style of Reb Dovid's prayers. Every time I hear him leading the prayers, I am moved yet again, because in front of my eyes the patriarchal image of Reb Dovid appears, along with the tens of congregants, whom I knew well. I feel the holy atmosphere anew, as it reigned in the *Kehat* court, where I prayed during my youth.

[Page 195]

During the Days of Awe, Jews from all over the city would come here to hear the Rebbe, Reb Dovid, and every year, during these days, the court was filled with congregants, so much so, that not all were able to fit inside, and many Jews stood outside with their prayer shawls and prayed there.

The greatest experience was undoubtedly the *hakaffot* [the dancing with the Torah on the holiday of Simchat Torah], which the Rebbe, Reb Dovid would celebrate on Simchat Torah and Shemini Atzeret [last two days of the Sukkot holiday]. With his singing, he would carry along the large crowd of congregants. More than once, I would ask myself, from where does the Rebbe get such rich thoughts and so much energy to be able to stand for hours in the heat, in a tight crowd among hundreds of congregants, who were standing on tables and benches, drunk with the Rebbe's melodies, and who with great love swallowed every word that he sang out. He really gave great pleasure to the crowd with this song and dance.

It was one of his standing traditions to recite the *tefilat neilah* [closing prayer] of Yom Kippur in the large *shul*, and then many congregants would leave the *Kehat* court and go with the Rebbe to the large *shul*.

He had two sons and one daughter: The older son's name was Menachem, and the younger was Simcha. They were not blessed with the talent for prayer that their father had, but Menachem was a Torah scholar and Simcha was handsome [captivating].

The Rebbe, Reb Dovid died, I think, in the year 1937. His death unsettled the Jews of the city and evoked a great sadness from all the congregants whom he would gratify with his beautiful prayers, and who treasured him greatly.

[Page 196]

Of the patrons in the *Kehat* court, I remember the regular Torah reader Shimon Hafner, the blind person Shloimele Libman, Avrohom Glatt, Zishe Schleider, Leybel Heiberg, Leib Rubenfeld, Shimon Horn, Dovid Fridberg, Dovid Hebenstreit, Gotfried, Shtulbach, Zelig Hafner, Axelrad, and others.

*

Of the other *minyanim* that took place in various places in the city, I remember the *Hachnasat Orchim* [Welcoming the Guest], and the Belz *shtiebel* [small, informal *shul*] at the end of Sabjoska Street; the *minyanim* in the yards of Halberthal's house, Shteinbuk's house, at Maritz's *minyan* with the *Mora Hora'ah* [rabbinic leader of the city] Reb Pinkhas Hemerling on Wonska Street, number 2, where my family lived.

I would often attend the *minyan* of the *More Hora'ah* [rabbinic leader of the city] for the Friday night prayers and for the *Shalosh Seudot* [late Saturday evening with light food, before Shabbat ends]. The *More Hora'ah* customarily delivered words of Torah during *Shalosh Seudot* and would often toss in words unrelated to anything: "... such as these things." Among the jokers, we would kid with each other joking about his speech, and toss about his words: "... such as these things." But he was a respectable Jew and a fine Torah scholar. He was elected into the municipal government as the one responsible in the registrar's office providing birth certificates for the Jewish population in the city. His office was in his house, and he conducted it with the help of his daughter, even though he too knew the Polish language well. And one more interesting detail: The entrance to the *minyan* was through his kitchen. And until this day, the aromas of Shabbat follow me, those that were in the kitchen, and that teased us during the Shabbat prayer. These were aromas of cooked foods that were in pots on the wide cooking plate in the kitchen, and mainly, the soup and the fish, whose aroma filled the space of the kitchen and teased the nostrils of the congregants during the prayer times.

[Page 197]

At the beginning of the 30s, the construction of the large and beautiful *shul Chesed Ve'emet* was completed on Wengerska Street, not far from the large *shul*. This was a large, modern building and the prayer room could hold several hundred congregants.

[Page 198]

My Grandfather's Synagogue

by Moshe Meizler

Translated by Selwyn Rose

My grandfather's synagogue was situated on 15 Dietziusa Street and in its way quite unique. It was located in a distinctly Christian area, on a main street, facing the post-office and next door to the police station, regional government offices and close to the Third Battalion Barracks.

On the days of the Jewish Sabbath and other festivals, tens of Jewish residents, from the most pious, with their ear-locks and beards, *Mitnagdim* and *Hassidim*, wearing their fur hats, caftans and waist girdles, would rush to the area. There were among them the older Yiddish-speaking Jews and also the younger ones speaking Polish – Jews from all sections of the population – wealthy and with standing in the community and traders, representatives of the free-professions and artisans and students.

The synagogue occupied the second floor in the apartment of Grandfather Eliezer Diller. Those close to him called him "Luser". He was a tall man, upright with a typical Jewish face. Everything about him spoke of self respect and elegance. Everyone spoke to him with great respect. He was a man who followed the Commandments with great dedication as a follower of the *Hassid*, Rabbi Elimelech Weisblum of Lizhensk (Leżajsk). On the 11th day of *Adar,* the memorial day of the great Rabbi (Z"L), he visited the local cemetery and communed with his memory. Grandfather's regular place in the synagogue was the most prestigious spot – alongside the eastern wall next to the Holy Ark. Next to him stood a small gaunt man who prayed before the Holy Ark on Sabbaths and festivals.

I am reminded of the first Yok Kippur eve in my Grandfather's synagogue. I lived with my parents in Vienna but every year we visited Grandfather in Jaroslaw. Before my eyes, I see the small narrow hall of the synagogue. Its walls were faded and the decorative curtain of the Ark was of a red rose on a white background. I was only a small boy and that night, I couldn't tear my eyes away from the bearded Jewish men there, dressed in white. All of a sudden, I heard the voice of the gaunt, pale Rabbi, who spread his thin arms towards heaven. His voice was vibrant and high like the voice of a young man. His gaze wandered towards the flickering memorial candles. In answer to my questions as to why the candles were lighted, I did not yet know that everyone was condemned to die. Agitated and afraid I hid myself wrapped under the prayer-shawl of my grandfather in order not to see their flickering.

On the night of the prayer of *Sliḥot* (forgiveness), in the middle of the night, the synagogue Sexton would pass from house to house, knocking on the doors and waking the members of the congregation in a loud voice to come to the important prayer. They woke me as well. Half asleep and chilled to the bone I made my way to the synagogue where all the lights were on, like a burning, illuminated island in the darkness. I immediately sensed the holiness of the atmosphere enwrapping the place. Grandfather Luser proudly held my hand and together with him, I stood in his regular place in the Eastern corner. It was as if a Jewish light was ignited in the darkened Christian world surrounding us.

[Page 199]

The women's section was a small separate room close to the synagogue. On Sabbaths and festivals it was filled with women and girls, dressed in their festive clothes. Sometimes my gaze wondered into this room, to the women wearing shawls when suddenly came the sound of crying and lamenting as if of a woman resembling "Rachel weeping over her sons."[1]

On festivals, the small synagogue was full from wall to wall and many remained standing outside in the corridor. The synagogue had a very special friendly style; its members enjoying a warm friendly relationship with each other. I remember that on Sabbath there were always a number of poor people in the synagogue. The members of the congregation would regularly invite one of them home. The synagogue was known to show much generosity and charity and the local poor and those who came from afar, knew that they would find someone among the congregation who would invite them for a Sabbath or festival meal.

I remember the Purim holidays in Grandfather's synagogue. A group of young people would pass through the city streets wearing costumes. Musical instruments played and the atmosphere was uplifting. The peak festivity that is engraved in my memory is the Festival of Simchat Torah in the synagogue and the dances that the men performed with such vigor and dedication with the Scrolls of the *Torah*. The caftans of the men waving in the wind and swirling from their energetic movements and their voices hoarse from singing, young and old joined together in dancing circles. This Jewish "island" in the Christian street seemed that same moment more than ever, to declare that – "*Am Yisrael Ḥai*" – the People of Israel live!"

There were also days and events that cast a dark shadow on the life of the town. Anti-Semitic hooligans and thugs would attack the congregation as they left the synagogue, shouting abuse and curses, pulling at their beards and even using their fists.

These ugly and gloomy incidents dimmed in the unquenchable memory of the glorious radiance of that small room on the second floor in the house at 15 Dietziusa Street when it was illuminated and filled from wall to wall with the Jewish men wrapped in their flying prayer-shawls, voices raised in joy and praise. I can still hear the cantor's deep voice and in front of my eyes spread the red curtain, which emphasized even more the paleness of Grandpa's synagogue....

Tranlator's footnote:

1. See Jeremiah 31:15

[Page 200]

The *"Agudat Israel"* [religious] Organizations

by Boruch Kalchheim

Translated by Pamela Russ

[ ] translator's remarks

The religious elements of the Jewish settlement in Jaroslaw were primarily organized into two organizations: "*Agudat Israel*" (the older *balebatim* [male heads of households]), and the "*Tzeirei Agudat Israel*" (the religious youth). As part of the *Tzeirei Agudat Israel*, there was also a youth group that was called "*Pirchei Agudas Yisrael*" that was comprised mainly of *cheder* aged children [younger elementary school ages].

The *Agudats Israel* in Jaroslaw was mainly taken up with education and cultural activities. For example, they created a girls' school called "*Beit Yaakov*" where there were more than 120 students. This was run with two teachers: Szianke Prinz (today Zonenblik), and Mina Sperling (today Kalcheim), both of whom live in Tel Aviv today.

"Beit Yaakov" school with the two teachers, Prinz and Sperling

[Page 201] [page 202]

The primary education institution of the *Talmud Torah* was mainly run by the business people of the *Agudah,* and in the *Talmud Torah*, there were hundreds of young boys and young men studying.

The *"Agudat Israel"* and the *"Tzeirei Agudat Israel"* conducted extensive cultural activities that came in the form of lectures, meetings, and also in creating their own library.

In general, the *"Agudat Israel"* was organized according to the *kloyzen* [meeting-house for scholars; elitist learning institutions] of the town, and the central stronghold of the organization was the *"Talmud Torah"* *kloyz*, where they studied mainly classes of the *Daf Hayomi* [designated daily portion of the Talmud] under the direction of Moshe'le Danner, and *"Tehilim"* [Psalms] under the direction of the secretary [record keeper] of the *"Tzeirei Agudat Israel,"* Dovid Freifeld. Other than that, the *"Agudat Israel"* organized its own *minyan* [quorum for prayers] where, every Shabbat, there were five or six *minyanim* [quorums for prayers] of boys, and where *shalosh seudot* [third meal for Shabbat] and *melave malka* [meal after Shabbat ends] were conducted regularly.

Other than those above-mentioned activities, the *"Tzeirei Agudats Israel"* established a *Hachshara* center [pioneer movement to prepare for settlement in Israel] in a specially rented location that was in the house of Reb Efraim Izman. In this *Hachshara* location, there were 16 young people from the province. Two friends from this *Hachshara* group made *aliyah* to Israel, and are there now.

A group of "Tzeirei Agudat Israel" with their leaders Dovid Intatur, Boruch Kalcheim, and Hirsh Brandt

The *"Agudat Israel"* had a strong and representational presence in the community. In the latest term of office in the community, there already were five representatives: two in the administration and three in the community council. In the administration, the following held positions: Reb Moshe Haas, representative of the *"Agudah"* (died in London), and Reb Eliezer-Berish Goldman (a son-in-law of Reb Yankel Klepner, one of the prominent *balebatim* [male head of household] in Jaroslaw (killed by the Nazis). In the community council: Reb Avrohom Glatt (died in Tel Aviv), Reb Mordechai Arenbach (died in Givatayim), and Reb Mendel Shleferig (died in New York, and his casket was taken to Israel).

We must state that the *"Agudat Israel"* along with the*"Tzeirei Agudat Israel"* played a vital role in the religious, cultural, and social life of the Jewish community in Jaroslaw.

[Page 205]

Ways of Life,
Experiences, Recollections

[Page 215 - Yiddish] [Page 205 – Hebrew]

Jews and Poles in Jaroslaw
And Their Relationship in the Years 1918-1945

by Mundek Hebenstreit

Translated from the Yiddish by Pamela Russ

[ ] translator's remarks

When describing the relationship between the Jews and the Poles in Jaroslaw during the above-mentioned period, I was directed by the principle that you cannot explain the life of the Jews in our town of Jaroslaw, not even briefly explain the behaviors between the Jews and the Poles, even though the Poles comprised two-thirds of the city's population, and the Jewish only one third.

For the sake of truth, we must underscore that generally, the relationship between the Jews and the Poles in town was not very close. We Jews used to meet in the locations of the Zionist youth organizations, in various sports clubs, sport locales, and synagogues. On the other hand, the Poles would organize their meetings in their national youth organizations, such as "*Sokoł*" [Polish Gymnastic Society], "*Strzelec*" ["The Shooter"; youth paramilitary association], "*Kasina Oficerska*" ["Officers Club"]. There were recognized sports clubs such as "*Jaroslawjanka*" and "*Ogniska*," but aside from that, there was close contact between the two nations in the everyday life.

The "Sokol" cinema

[Page 216]

In addition, this caused all kinds of situations, and mainly that a significant number of Poles were hired by Jews and their various projects in town, in their businesses, and in the service areas.

For many years, many Poles lived among the Jews, knew their language, and even spoke Yiddish quite well. This was quite a familiar phenomenon in the city. Who, for example, did not hear about the Polish bath worker Pal, who spoke Yiddish like a Jew.

The Jewish youth studied together with the Polish students in all schools, and we used to go with them to all kinds of sport competitions in the city stadium of the Polish army.

The Jewish merchants and artisans would visit the city council (magistrate) on all kinds of opportune times, also the offices of the administration departments, or the finance offices, and in that way, they stayed in contact with the Polish officials in the government offices.

There were even contacts in the Polish police, and particularly with the familiar policeman Wianorwycz. But we were lucky that the contact with him was only in a political context, not a criminal context, since there were really no criminals among the Jews. The Polish police carefully guarded that the stores should be locked at the designated time according to the law, and there were also incidents when the Polish police arrested left-wing Jews just before every workers' holiday.

One has to state that the Jews and the Poles, in large numbers, behaved towards each other with a certain contempt. In the eyes of the Polish student, a talented Jew, or Jew with a strong fist, was no more than a "*Żydek*" [derogatory term for "Jew"].

[Page 217]

On the other hand, by us – and mainly by our parents, every Pole was no more than a gentile, and in the cheders [religious schools] he was called Esau, or *sheigetz* [derogatory term, means someone who openly defies Jewish law]. But generally, we have to say, that the behavior of the Polish people towards the Jews was overall proper. In our city, it was not like it was on other cities – a ghetto where it was exclusively the Jews who lived there. The Jews lived not only in the region of *Rynek* [the main square] and in the nearby streets. Many of them settled in the exclusively Polish streets, such as: "May 3," "Dietziusa", "Poniatowski" and "Kościuszko." On Shabbat and on the Jewish holidays you could see Jews dressed in their *talit* [prayer shawls] and *shtreimlech* [fur hats] on their heads, and religious *chassidim* with long beards and sidelocks as they used to walk by the main streets of the city in the direction of the synagogues or the *Beit Midrash* [Study Hall]. On those same streets, on Sundays and on the days of Polish national holidays, Polish soldiers would march to the church or to the Orthodox Church. We have to emphasize, that in Jaroslaw the Jews were not under the terror of anti-Jewish excesses of the Polish population.

In the Years 1930-1939

In the 1930s, and particularly in the years before World War 2, the good relationship between the Poles and the Jews began to deteriorate.

Part of Grunwaldzka Street
(Page 206 - Hebrew)

During this period, anti-Semitism in Poland increased, finding its expression in open hooliganism against the Jews, and pogroms that broke out in various cities in Poland. For example, in the city of Przytyk, the farmers, heated up by a priest, left a church and threw over the stalls of the Jewish merchants in the marketplace, stole their possessions, and even killed some Jews.

In the city of Mińsk Mazowiecki, a Jewish soldier shot a Polish gendarme out of desperation, since the gendarme was bullying him. As a result of this shot, a pogrom broke out and the Jew who shot the gendarme was sentenced to death by the Polish court.

[Page 218]

In the universities of Warsaw, Krakow, Lvov , and Vilna, the Endek students attacked their Jewish friends with clubs, on the edge of which razors were wedged in. With the help of these types of instruments, they conducted their ideological discussions with the Jewish students.

The relationship of the Poles to the Jews worsened after closing the no-attack clause between the Poles and Nazi Germany at the end of January 1934. I remember the indignant appearance of the anti-Semitic priest Czeczak, the famous appearances of Mrs. Pristarowa who was against ritual, kosher slaughter. In the universities in Poland there was a "*numerus clausus*" [one of many methods used to limit the number of students who may study at a university] established, and the Polish government declared an economic war on the Jews that found its expression in the word "*Owszem*" ["yes"] from the head of government at the time, General Sławoj Składkowski, which meant: "Make pogroms on the Jews, get rid of them physically – no, but fight with them economically – absolutely!"

After an anti-Semitic incident in the Polish high school, there were the "left ghetto chairs", the so-called "ghetto chairs," that were set up for Jewish students in the higher education institutes. The Jewish students did not agree to this "ghetto" in the high schools, and in protest of this discrimination, they would remain standing as they listened to the lecture. My brother, who at that time was a student in the Lvov polytechnic, told me that he and his friends were prepared to stand for hours and listen to the lectures, and not sit on the "ghetto chairs." These types of anti-Semitic incidents were also felt in our town, but not in such a sharp manner as it was in other cities in Poland. But very often, you could see "academics" in the streets with "Mieczyk Chrobrego" ("the sword of Chrobrego") [Boleslaw Chrobrego's sword; a symbol used by Polish nationalists, representing the coronation sword of Polish kings] placed on the lapels of their shirts, and "*corporants*" [the corporations, businesses], with flyers that told them to boycott the Jewish stores: "Poles, buy from your own," or "Fish for the holidays, only from a Pole."

Leaflets circulated by Antisemitic pickets in front of Jewish shops
(Page 208 Hebrew)

[Page 219]

The leader of the anti-Semites was the despicable Kazimierz Tumidajski, whose face actually did not fit the representation of the "pure Aryan race." With government blindness, the Poles would cry out "patriotic" praises, such as: "Commander, take us to Zaolzie [land beyond Olza River, part of Czech]," that was said to the marshal of Poland, Edward Rydz-Śmigły, or: "Strong, United, and Ready!" "*Silni, Zwarci, Gotowi*" . These encouragements blinded the Polish nation that did not sense the approaching danger of Hitler's Germany.

We, the Jaroslaw Jews, felt the looming windstorm. We saw the danger that was coming towards the Jewish people, even though none of us, in our worst dreams could imagine the gruesome results of the approaching catastrophe.

In the Years 1939-1945

Only after the Germans expelled the Jews from the city, did the Poles begin to understand the danger that the German occupation brought for them as well. The well-known Volksdeutsche [ethnic German, non-citizen] Schmidt, whose activities on the Jewish street became limited, now looked for new activities for himself. He would search for and find nationalist elements, among whom there were also many Endeks. In many different ways, he pursued them, informed on them to the German government, and in the end, he delivered them to the Gestapo. Among those arrested were the Poles Szimlakowski, Trojanowski, the engineers Rynjak, Dubrzinski, Albinowski, Nazarkewicz, Galinski, and others. Many of the Poles were arrested and they were later deported to Auschwitz. A total of 70 people. Only a few of them survived and the rest perished in the camps. One of them, Galinski, a native of Jaroslaw, was mentioned in the Eichmann trial in Jerusalem by the eye-witness Raya Kagan.

[Page 220]

Galinski was a son of the caretaker of a middle-school, and when he was in Auschwitz, he met the Jewish girl Mala Tzimetboim from Belgium. Both decided that they would flee from the camp. With the help of several Jewish prisoners, Galinski was able to get a uniform of an SS officer, and thanks to this uniform he was able to escape the camp together with Mala Tzimetboim. His goal was to get to Slovakia. On the way, not far from the city of Bielska, his Jewish girl friend became ill and they were forced to hide at a farmer's place, who later handed them over to the Gestapo. Galinski was hanged in Auschwitz and Mala Tzimetboim sliced her own veins and died agonizingly before the Germans could pass their death sentence on her, by a hanging.

It is worth noting that for three weeks, both withstood the worst tortures that the Germans afflicted on them in order to find out who had helped them escape the camp. But despite all the tortures and pain, they [the two martyrs] did not reveal anything.

In the second group that was taken to Auschwitz, there were officials from the magistrate. They were accused of illegally listening to radio broadcasts. The magistrate officials were given over to the Gestapo by city councilmen Podgurni and Hanaiko. In connection to that, I want to stress that we Jews well knew that most of the Polish population were indifferent to the fate of their Jewish neighbors. Some of the Poles, the so-called "*szmaltzowniks*" ["blackmailers"], delivered the Jews to the Germans. But despite the toxic atmosphere, there were still individual Poles from the "*chasidei umot haolam*" ["righteous among the Nations"] who, disregarding the danger that was pressing, still saved Jews from death. But Poles who gave their own brethren to the Germans, is a fact that speaks for itself.

[Page 221]

In the year 1940, another group of Poles was arrested by the above-mentioned Schmidt and his Nazi friends. Among those arrested were the director of the finance office Aslanowicz, the director of the postal company – Kurek, and also the directors of two gymnasiums: Dr. Mertowski, engineer Sobolewski, and the Pole Wajdowycz.

Not long before the end of the war, the 25-year-old student Basha Pozan and the teacher Ziemnicka were arrested and later shot in the Kidloweica forest.

But the main goal of the above-mentioned Nazi Schmidt was to persecute the Jews. Even though there were no Jews left in the actual city of Jaroslaw, he searched for Jews in the nearby towns and in the forests.

In June 1942, Schmidt and the German security police conducted an Aktion, murdering 360 Jews, who had been sent to the Pelkinia camp.

Schmidt was also guilty in this: In the summer of 1942, at the wall of the monastery "Anna Kasarnia," Schmidt killed the father and son of the family Sztelcer.

It is worth noting that Schmidt was also the murderer of 30 residents of Jaroslaw, Jews and Poles, whom he shot at the same wall of the monastery.

At the end of the war, Schmidt fled to West Germany, and now he lives a calm life there, since there were no living witnesses found to report his crimes against the people. This year, after lengthy searches for witnesses in the "Department of Investigation of the Nazi Criminals" of the Israeli police, a significant amount of material was collected that enabled him to be put on trial.

When there is talk about the Nazi Schmidt, it is worthwhile to mention another Pole – a lowlife type by the name of Geroi. This Pole, a former Polish officer, occupied himself, during the Nazi occupation, with delivering Jews and Poles to the Gestapo, those Jews who were hiding in all kinds of hiding places in villages around Jaroslaw. This same Geroi also informed on Zosia Szpac (the daughter of a well-known doctor from Jaroslaw). At that time, she worked in an agricultural colony Demitrowica. He was even accused of having informed on his own brother-in-law – the judge Topolinski – whose own roots were Jewish, and who, after long and harsh tortures, was murdered by the Gestapo.

[Page 222]

At the time of the war, after the Germans expelled the Jews from Jaroslaw, our town's Jews spread out in the eastern regions of southern Poland and found temporary shelter with relatives and friends. Some of the Jaroslaw Jews settled in the cities: Sambor, Drohobycz, Jaworow, and other places. But the majority settled in Lvov.

In the year 1940, when the Soviets ruled the area the NKVD conducted a raid on the "refugees" and many of our Jaroslaw Jews were deported to distant areas of Siberia and there they spent the rest of the war years in very harsh circumstances.

To our great joy, the majority of these deported Jaroslaw Jews survived, whereas of those who remained in the area and fell into the hands of the Germans only very few managed to save themselves.

In the year 1945, I met several Jews in Krakow who survived the Nazi hell. From their reports I found out that many of them were living witnesses to the murders of their relatives by the Germans.

One year later, I met our Jaroslaw Jews who returned from Russia. From their reports as well, I found out about the terrible conditions in which they had lived in freezing Siberia during the war. A terrible fate had greeted our Jaroslaw Jews during the years 1939-1945. The majority of the Jews were murdered by the Nazi thugs. This period of time demands substantial investigation.

[Page 223]

* * *

To end my brief discourse, I want to mention how I separated myself from our dear city and from the Poles, who, before the war, served as spokesmen in the merit of being the guard of the "pure Polish race."

Not long before the end of the war, as I was a cadet in the officer's school of the Polish army, I went on a mission for one day to my city of Jaroslaw in order to take care of some things. After completing all the things that were connected to my mission, I went out to see the city which I had not seen for years.

City Hall Building

My excursion across the city was started at the "small *Rynek*" [square]. Leaning on the railing, I gazed at the beautiful plain that spread out before my eyes. Somewhere in the distance the waters of the San River flowed calmly and slowly.

I remembered that not far from here, as if stuck to the scruff of the mountain, was the location of *Beitar* [Revisionist Zionist Youth movement] and *Hashomer Hatzair* [Socialist Zionist Youth movement], where the life of Jewish youth once throbbed. Understandably, these two places were located at a certain distance from one another as if the two Zionist organizations wanted to distance themselves ideologically from one another as well.

I looked around and I could not believe my own eyes: Not far from here there once was a small synagogue that was known as the "*Kehat Kloiz*" [small *shul*, place for prayer]. In my youth, my father and I would go to this *shul* for prayers on Shabbat and the holidays. This was

[Page 224]

a holy place where the beloved voice of the dear and honored Rav, Reb Dovid was always heard. This shul no longer existed. The shul was destroyed and its walls collapsed into the ground.

I crossed over the abandoned and silent square and went to the corner of Rynek and Spitka streets. The house that once stood on the left was destroyed. From Tribunalska Street, I came to the place called "*Wały*," and from there I went down the steps and remained still in front of the building that once was the "*Yad Charutzim*" [social hall and artisan association]. In this place, there used to be Yiddish theater performances, and also lectures and readings of Zionist activities in town and in the center. Here, our youth had fiery, passionate discussions among themselves, and sometimes these discussions took on a sharp edge. We would come to the *Yad Charutzim* to spend Shabbat evenings, the days of Chanuka, and for Purim celebrations. Now the building is empty, there is no living soul there. Only a sign in the front of the building testified in irony of fate, that the Poles had changed it into their "House of Culture."

Corner of Słowackiego, Kraszewskiego and Grunwaldzka streets

[Page 225]

"Yad Charutzim"
(Page 213 Hebrew)

I returned to Grodska Street. Once, this street was the center of trade for the city. Here you were able to feel the pulse of Jewish life. And now? All the shops were closed, only two of them had been changed over to cooperatives. I turned right to Lubelska Street, to the place where once there was the center for Czortków *hassidim*, but which was now an empty, abandoned place, overgrown with weeds. With pain I asked myself: How could this happen? In the end, the Jews of Jaroslaw comprised not more than a third of the population of the city, and now without them, life in the city died. A strange emptiness covered everything. (At that time there was only one Jew in the city, that was Zilberman, who had the bakery in the square.)

I returned and I feared new disillusionments. Not far from the place where I was standing there once was the Talmud Torah, and close to that was the Jewish bathhouse and the *mikvah* [ritual baths], and who knows what was there now!

As I went through Grunwaldska Street I met two people. When they saw me, they stopped. One of them was Zadarazhni, who once worked for my father in his business. The other person was his friend, an official in the magistrate.

[Page 226]

In order to underline that with both Poles who, before the war were vocal supporters of the Nazi ideology, I held lengthy and sharp discussions about Judaism. And now, meeting them, there was a paradoxical situation: I was in the uniform of the Polish army with a gun on my shoulder, and they, the Poles – representatives of the "ruling race" stood opposite me with downcast heads. They politely asked me about the fate of my family, and asked for pardon for their earlier anti-Semitic talk from before the war regarding the Jews. I thought that it was very sad that the destruction of their ideological youth came years after the time when our Jewish nation lost millions of victims of our brothers and sisters.

There were eight hours left for me until the time when I would leave the city, but I felt it was beyond my strength to remain even one more minute. The city where I was born and raised, the city that is dear and close to me, was now dead as a cemetery. I left to Słowacki Street, and then with the first train I left the city. This was my last parting from the city of my youth, from Jaroslaw.

On the beach of the San River
(Page 214 Hebrew)

[Page 227]

The Town Wherein
I was Nourished by Zionism

by Attorney Moshe Aridor (Weihenmayer)

Translated by Selwyn Rose

There were cities in the Jewish diaspora that the nickname "Metropolis of Israel" clinging to the title by virtue of being centers of Jewish culture, the "cribs" of great *Torah* scholars and renowned educators, ancient synagogues and centers of the economic life of Diaspora Jews. Events occurred within them that were recorded on the pages of history as milestones in the annals of the people. The town Jaroslaw for me was a "Motherly Metropolis" because of its maternal qualities where I was reared and nourished with the doctrines of Zionism. Pure, maternal, natural Zionism, with no spices, like the pure natural genuine milk the mother gives her baby, granting him life and like the mother's milk, that same Zionism was free of infection, sterile but not unfruitful. Warm as if a mother's heart – not frigid and cold with pure reason usefulness and not destructive like coals afire, glowing with the fervor of flag-carrying Marxism and all the other threats. If I am immune in today's Israeli society after the *Yom Kippur War*, when I am faced with questions such as "What are we doing here?", I must thank the cradle that permitted me to suckle Zionism, devoid of those venomous bacteria that threaten to destroy the very tissues of the Jewish State.

* * *

In retrospect, in the world of my childhood and youth, that I lived through in Jaroslaw, things now look a little different than we imagined them at the time. The Zionist youth movements represented the majority and the best of the Jewish youth in the town, from the Hebrew Youth Association *Akiva*, *Betar*, the Young Zionists and the religious youth movements, and including *Hashomer Hatza'ir*. Much of our innocence was in our perception of Zionism in terms of a worldview rather than a movement for the national liberation of the Jewish people, devoid of political independence. A mixture of scouting, mysticism and sometimes abstinence from the pleasures that nature gives to a young boy. A dividing line separated the majority of the organized youth in the Zionist movements in the city, from the so-called assimilated minority, who aspired to resemble their gentile friends, those same "golden youth" who looked with compassion and pity on those who trained themselves to immigrate to the Land of Israel, learning a profession to work there, or to wear the uniforms of *Betar*, or trained to use weapons that will liberate the land of Israel. We used all sorts of derogatory nicknames for them.

[Page 228]

* * *

Much of the innocence sprang from the image we created for ourselves in spite of the reality at that time in Israel. We did not want to know the "truth from the Land of Israel" but thanks to that innocent Zionism, which I nursed from in my youth, I can today stand tall, and not bow my head in front of the "realists" of all kinds, for whom the word "Zionism" is used in quotation marks and who ask: "What is our right to this land?"

* * *

When I try to go back in my memories and recreate the sights of the same city (which, sometimes instead of "Jaroslaw" I say "Tel Aviv" and is often perceived as a Freudian mistake), two images always come to mind. One - of those Sundays of a Polish-Christian holiday, with army battalions marching through the city streets, and cavalry on white, sleek horses, with their flags honoring and glorifying their bearers, followed by rows upon rows of elementary and high school pupils in their uniforms and glittering symbols, accompanied by bands playing marches, all of them on the way to the church; everyone, that is - except the Jews. We do not belong. The flag, the symbols, the melodies – they are not ours.

* * *

On those Sundays, I looked forward to the coming of *Shabbat* and the traditional assembly of the Movement's branch and the large blue and white flag that flew with all its beauty and grandeur before the rows and rows of the Jewish youth, training themselves for the establishment of their State. Then the air would be filled with Hebrew orders: "Attention!" Then and only then did I feel myself of value and equal to them – the Poles: I have a flag, I have a National Anthem, I have a language and I have a country to which I must go. That was the compensation for the pain that I suffered on those Sundays in which I had no part. In the afternoon, on *Shabbatot*, when we marched out of town to enjoy the open countryside, to the nearby hills for activities and debates to strengthen the mind and body of young Zionists, no Polish youth dared to bother us, or to call after us with their insults. Only the grinding of teeth could be heard. It was then that I felt the force of the Jewish strength and its flag. They learned to respect those that respected themselves.[1]

[Page 229]

The town of Jaroslaw was not counted among the largest of towns in Poland but it was unique. It was among the oldest towns in Poland. The name Jaroslaw is associated with the history and struggles of the country whose enemies tried many times to "partition" it. The educators of the new Poland knew how to instill into the Polish youth a sense of National pride and the school fulfilled that task successfully. I, as a young Jew, who identified with the plight of the Polish people against their oppressors studying the Polish history created a sense of jealousy. For every evil act carried out upon the Polish heroes in their wars against the Russians, the Germans and even the Tatars, I asked myself: have we, the Jews, no warriors, heroes and victors? And when we had religious lessons, we were separated from the Polish students and when the Jewish teacher of religion, Distenfeld, taught us about Yehoshua Bin Nun, Moshe, the Maccabees and the Hasmoneans, my heart was filled with satisfaction and my wounded pride was healed.

* * *

The town of Jaroslaw was far removed from the model of Jewish towns and villages of Eastern Europe, identified by their Jewish ghettos. Jaroslaw was distinguished by its cleanliness, its broad streets in keeping with the period's style, and its tolerance of the "Jewish minority", a minority, where the cynics at times provoked the anti-Semites: "The streets are yours but the houses ours." Here the physical exile was not one of the hardest exiles in the world. Therefore, the memories themselves are not saturated with dramatic events. You cannot dredge up from the depths of your memories feelings of excessive hatred, nor excessive feelings of affection. Whenever I recall this city, the huge town hall, with its tower and dome towering up to the heights of the sky and the municipal building with its huge clock come to mind. Then the little boy's fears came back to me, of the little man who patrolled the heights around the tower turning back and forth night and day, on fire-watch of the city, lest he fall from the high tower and smash himself on the stones of the town square. But the huge clock in the tower continued to ring and count its hours placidly, its sounds calming and with that calm the fear of that little man falling from the heights of the tower gradually faded.

* * *

There was a town in Poland called Jaroslaw. It was one among many. For us, it no longer exists. Our memory is the memory of our mothers, our fathers, our brothers and sisters who lived there and are no more. Them, we will remember forever. For us "A Metropolis in Israel" is Jerusalem, Tel-Aviv, Haifa and every town in the land of Israel. In Jaroslaw I was reared and nourished by Zionism – Here, I live it!

Translator's Footnote:

> 1.   See Pessaḥim 49a, (freely paraphrased): "…not flatterers of goyim and those who dance, but those who stand up to them and give them a stern look."

[Page 237 – Yiddish] [Page 230 - Hebrew]

With Jaroslaw Jewry

by Yeshayahu Rabinowitz[1]

Translated from the Yiddish by Pamela Russ

[ ] translator's remarks

My encounters with the Jaroslaw Jews were accompanied by a feeling of strangeness and loneliness. In the city, I felt like an immigrant who came to a strange land. The language of the land, which the majority of the Jews spoke, and particularly the nationalist youth, was foreign to me. Few people understood my Yiddish, and very few spoke Hebrew.

I remember a day when I was invited to the home of the parents of one of my students of the "Yavneh" school. During a conversation, with a cup of coffee, I received a "compliment" from a woman: "You speak Yiddish so beautifully, that I did not understand even one word."

I came to Jaroslaw from a real Yiddish environment, where everyone from the water carrier to the religious, worldly intellectuals, spoke Yiddish, and the sounds of the Hebrew language were heard by the students in the Hebrew schools and from adults as well. There was a great difference between those Jews and the Jews of Jaroslaw. Here, in Jaroslaw, the Jews were dressed in their traditional clothes, wearing *shtreimlech* [round, fur hats] on the Shabbat and on the Jewish holidays, and the worldly, Jewish youth did not, more or less, distinguish themselves from the non-Jewish youth. Here, the Jewish youth spoke Polish, and their knowledge of Judaism was very limited. For me, the lifestyle and habits of the local population were also unusual, with their exaggerated politeness. At meetings, you could hear: [Polish] "My respects"; or [Yiddish] "I bow to you" [repeated in Polish]; and greetings to a woman: [Polish] "I kiss your hands"; and so on.

But despite my difficult integration into Jaroslaw, I remained in the city, and that was thanks to the chairman of the school committee of the Hebrew school, Shimon Spiegel, of blessed memory.

[Page 238]

He brought me closer to him and had a warm relationship with me. The same was for his wife Regina, who, with her great understanding and wisdom, addressed my inner stress. In this absolutely venerable family, whose Torah and Zionism were their beliefs and their motto, the activities and needs of the Hebrew school were their focus. I found a familiar warmth in this Spiegel family – the most important thing for a person who finds himself in a strange environment, and really, their warm connection to me, as to a family member, enabled me to acclimate myself to Jaroslaw.

In the center of Jaroslaw, in the marketplace, there was an old, historical building with huge thick walls. Its ceiling was arched, and in the upper part of the building there were special openings where you could place cannons in case of enemy attack. I had the impression that this old-time building symbolized a tombstone of the Jaroslaw Jewry.

Among the Jaroslaw Jews you could still find young people dressed in specifically traditional clothing. I heard them say that the Rebbe's *shamash* [beadle] "conquered worlds" to bring the youth close to the Rebbe, but when they got older, they left their Rebbe and then the devoted *shamash* cried out in pain that they would not live to get older.

Whereas the parents of boys attending the government school wanted them to extend their religious studies, the girls were totally released from Jewish studies. The religious Hebrew school "Yavneh," brought in a great change to the education, but could not make a significant change to the situation. The students of the "Yavneh" school were only boys. But in those circumstances, the school activists did not want to introduce essential changes into the religious school system, and dealt with it accordingly, and did not establish general studies for both the boys and girls.

[Page 239]

It's a wonder that it did not occur to them to worry about a traditional Jewish education for girls too.

We have to underline that it was actually the *Agudat Yisrael* who was the pioneer in this area, as they opened a "*Beit Yaakov*" [religious] school for girls. They invited a compassionate teacher to the *Beit Yaakov* school who taught the religious girls subjects in Yiddish traditionally and national spirit. In these conditions, the Zionist youth organizations became the main source for some of the girls to strengthen their traditional education as a barrier against assimilation. Later, the party of the general Zionists established the primary school for boys and girls in Jaroslaw, and Polish was the language of study. In that school, other than the studies in the Polish language, they also studied the Hebrew language and *Yahadut* [Judaism]. In this school, there were no classes on Shabbat, the environment was really a Jewish one with a traditional spirit, but if the students in this school excelled in Hebrew or *Judaism*, is very doubtful to me.

* * *

Jaroslaw was a cultured, European town that had a particular charm. Life in the city flowed quietly, without disturbance. The streets were clean and straight, the city garden was large and well tended to. The city had a large electricity station, gas, and an urban canal system with a central water line. But there were still houses in the city, with outhouses in the courtyards, and where water was drawn from artesian wells.

Even though the inter-party frictions among the Zionist parties in Jaroslaw did not bear a sharp feel, as it had in various other cities in Poland, this did not prevent sharp, political, opinionated discussions [from taking place]. I remember the lecture of Meyer Grossman the leader of the "*Judenstadt* [the Jewish state] Party," which took place in the music-school building. During the presentation, leftist Zionist youth interrupted his lecture and threw stones through the window. Some people got hurt when this was going on, by shards of glass from the shattered window panes…

[Page 240]

I will bring another example from my own experience: The split of the revisionist party occurred at the Katowice conference. The central committee of the "*Judenstadt* Party" for western Galicia and Silesia organized in Jaroslaw, with Yehoshua Potasher as chairman. As secretary of the central committee of the "*Judenstadt* Party," I had several presentations in many different cities, and I expressed my views against the decision to leave the Zionist movement. As a punishment for this "sin," the commander of Beitar, Nasik, ordered that the friends of Beitar, to whom I had taught Hebrew, should terminate their studies with me. This order, which caused me to suffer a real material loss, actually had the opposite effect: The students completely stopped making any progress in the Hebrew language. In a discussion with the commander of Beitar, I explained that he dealt very inappropriately with me, and I was very offended. He became very angry, and with sharp words, he argued against my viewpoint, adding that if he would have the chance, he would ship me off to a punishment camp.

* * *

Węgierska street between Grodzka and Mickiewicz plaza

That which was told above, took place in the first half of the 1930s. Life in Poland still flowed smoothly, without any marked upheavals in Jewish life, but inside the country, there were already signs of the approaching storm, in which even the greatest pessimist could not envision the horrific results. This was the time when Hitler came to power in Germany. The tensions between Poland and Germany grew from day to day. As the danger to Poland grew, so the anti-Semitism became stronger. The hatred towards the Jews took a sharp form, and its flow also reached Jaroslaw. Poisonous, anti-Semitic slogans appeared on the walls of houses, as rumors spread that on a certain day it was going to be "merry." The Jewish youth decided that it would defend itself. (I do not know any details about this decision, but the day that was set aside for these troubles passed by peacefully.)

[Page 241]

In the year 1936, when I went as a delegate of *Keren Hayesod* [United Israel Appeal; created in 1920 to provide resources for return to the Land of Israel] to visit various cities in western Galicia and Silesia – I already saw the effects of the poisonous, anti-Semitic propaganda that brought terrible consequences. There were cities and towns where the Jews were simply afraid to go out into the streets in the evenings and leave their homes. As a result of the economic ban on the Jews, the Jewish population in the towns became impoverished. Those Christians who were not anti-Semites, did not have the courage to enter a Jewish shop, knowing that a watchful eye of the leaders of the ban would notice them.

In Poland, the "*Sanatzia*" Party ["Healthy Politics Party"; Polish fascist party] was in the government. Officially, they did not preach anti-Semitism, but they used all the means, kosher and non-kosher, to trip up the opposition party and the parties of the national minorities during the elections to the Polish Sejm [parliament]. During a lecture by the Zionist senator Dr. Schreiber on the eve of the elections to the Polish Sejm, the commandant of the police suddenly appeared in the hall of the "*Yad Charutzim*" ["Craftsmen Union"] * [artisans' hall; see p. 153 of this YB for details of hall], accompanied by an entourage of police, and dispersed the meeting by saying that "the floor of the hall is bad and that it could cave in." It should be noted that the government organizations generally did not disturb the election meetings of the "*Agudat Israel*" [political party representing the Orthodox Jews]. At the election meeting of the "*Agudat Israel*," a *maskil* ["enlightened" Jew] from Przemysl came forward and discussed the meaning of number "1" (the number "1" was the electoral number of the *Sanatzia*). The lecturer later justified his action at a meeting with his acquaintances, explaining that he had no other choice and that he was forced to fulfill the orders of the government party.

[Page 242]

In connection with the situation of those days, I want to relate an episode: In the capital city of Warsaw, a mixed committee of Jews and Christians was created – "Friends of Israel." The "*Judenstadt* Party" invited one of the members of the above-mentioned committee, the duke Pruszinski, who was a journalist himself, who had published a book about his impressions of his own trip to Israel. (After World War Two, Duke Pruszinksi was the official representative of Poland in the United Nations). At that time, we thought that a large number of Christians would be in attendance at his lecture, but we were mistaken. Even his title of "duke" – "editor" – that was written on the posters, attracted only a small group of Christians. Our Jewish brothers filled the hall, those who did not need a pro-Israel election. The following day, after the meeting, I spent a few hours with Potaszer and Pruszinki. During the time of our discussion, we addressed the ways of creating an understanding between the Jews and the Poles – citizens in Poland. Our guest agreed to the necessity of this agreement and promised to occupy himself with this. I asked him, in his opinion, how could a better understanding be established between Jews and Poles. After a brief silence, his answer was: "Sport." I expressed my opinion, that I very much doubted this, that general sport competitions between Jews and Poles would be able to create a better understanding between them. I stressed that the spirit of sport alone was not enough. This "sport spirit" would not be able to prevent fights during the competitions between the Polish sport organizations, and you could imagine that the sport competitions between the two nations would only heat up the national instincts of certain elements, instead of reaching an understanding between the two. Our discussion ended with a *tie*: Neither side was able to offer concrete suggestions for improving the situation. The only solution for the Jews, which is what I thought about during the discussion and could not express openly, was: exodus [to Israel]. Tens of thousands of Jewish youth were aiming for this exodus, but the gates to Israel were locked.

[Page 243]

At night, we invited the speaker to a kibbutz of "*Hechalutz Hamedinati*" ["State Pioneers"], and Gershon Zhelinkowski talked about pioneer life on *Hachshara* ["preparation" for living in Israel], about their preparations for building of the Jewish country, and he stressed that they were waiting impatiently for the time that the gates to Israel would open and they would be able to immigrate to their land. Pruzhinski replied with a short speech and ended with these words: "Maybe you will be able to see the documentary film about the development of the Polish legions at the end of World War One. Some of the legionnaires were wearing sparse uniforms, were barefoot, and were not taken care of with ongoing, military equipment. That's how the soldiers of the Polish army looked at that time. Looking at you today –the pioneers of the *Hachshara* squad, who are preparing to build a Jewish country, I believe, and I am certain, will arise."

Memorial Candle

A row of faces of Jaroslaw Jews pass before my eyes: friends, acquaintances, my students from the "*Yavneh*" school, whom I taught and with whom I was linked with my heart and soul. Also, the grown-up students whom I taught in the evening courses. I feel it is my sacred responsibility to light a memorial candle for all those Jews who died and were tortured, and to put up a memorial tombstone in the Yizkor book. I wish to dedicate my words in the memory of two people:

[Page 244]

Yehoshua Potaszer

Yehoshua Potaszer was a popular Jew and an interesting conversation partner. He possessed an exceptionally magical personality, and he really inspired a person with his words. He was an old Zionist, one of the founders of the Krakow Zionist newspaper, *"Nowy Dziennik"* ["New Journal"]. He would spend his free time in places with intellectuals (the club of the doctors, as it as called at that time). He participated as a delegate at the Zionist Congress, for the Judenstadt Party, and he was also a delegate at the founding assembly of the World Jewish Congress.

As a light to his memory, I would like to present one of his interesting stories that has remained deep in my memory:

As an officer in the Austrian army, he was once walking on Grunwaldska Street, and a Jewish soldier passed by in front of him and did not salute him. Potaszer intentionally walked past him, waiting to see if he would salute him, but without success. Being curious, Potaszer walked by a third time, then approached the soldier and said to him:

"Did you see me pass by?"

"Yes."

"Do you know that I am an officer?"

"Yes."

"Then why did you not acknowledge me?"

"Because you are Jewish."

[Page 245]

I dedicate these words to Potaszer, because I spent much time in his company, in general Zionist work.

Ber

I did not know him personally, because at the time when I started visiting his home, he was no longer there. I was with the Ber family during my last days in Poland, just before my *Aliyah* to Israel.

The Ber family owned a restaurant that was near the train station. The restaurant was open every day, and also on Shabbat. When the Tuczyn Rebbe came to town, Ber was actually a *chassid* [follower] of his he went in and began crying: "Rebbe! I am being forced to desecrate the Shabbat!" .As the Rebbe listened with understanding, he replied: "My child, earning a living is a great thing."

I presented two episodes which cast a light on and characterize the daily life of the Jaroslaw Jews.

There are warm feelings in my soul, of the time when the Jews waited impatiently with great eagerness for the establishment of the Jewish state. Many of the Jaroslaw Jews hoped to come here. It is with great pain and sadness that the Ruler of the People did not have enough strength to protect the survivors – and only very few merited to reach the shores of this land.

[Page 234 - Hebrew][a]

Translated from the Hebrew by Susan Rosin

I cannot add much to describe the Jewish community life in Jaroslaw. I was in Poland unwillingly, staying longer than expected, and I was not paying attention to the local life; In addition to my professional work, I was very involved in the Zionist and party activities.

Taking upon yourselves the honorable task of erecting a monument to the community of Jaroslaw, and to document historical material, to describe the institutions and activists of a Jewish community, I hope that a special emphasis will be placed on "Amcha" (the "common folk/ordinary people). Without this portion of the population, the various institutions and activists would not have been able to exist, the same way that a general cannot conduct a battle without an army behind him. It is very important to immortalize the daily life of the people, the family celebrations, the way they celebrated the holidays, in the study halls and at home; The education and educators of the "Talmud Torah", and so on. During my time in Jarolsaw, I did not hear even one song in Yiddish. I assume that Jewish mothers in the traditional families did sing Yiddish lullabies, and Yiddish folk songs to their children. If I am correct in my assumption, maybe it is still possible to rescue some of these songs, as well as folklore, local sayings and traditional stories popular among the people.

[Page 235]

I can recall two local customs that were new to me and were not practiced where I came from:

A. During the Purim feast, dressed-up groups from the local youth organizations or institutions performed a song or a short play. At the end, they would be rewarded…

B. During Passover eve, singles would send a ship sailing ticket "Steamer to Egypt", stating the location and timing of departure. I heard that these tickets came in various shapes and colors. It will be great if tickets like these could be found, so that they can be added to the folklore section.

I will end with a tale that reflects the local customs of Jaroslaw and the area: A young Yeshiva student was introduced to a girl from a neighboring town. He liked the girl, and promised her that upon his return to Jaroslaw he will write to her. He was in great distress, as he had no clue what to write. Suddenly he had a brilliant idea: he copied the entire "Song of Songs" scroll (שִׁיר הַשִּׁירִים Shir haShirim) Editor's in tiny letters on a postcard and sent it to the girl…

———————

Comments from the editor:

1.   Yeshayahu Rabinovitch died in the year 5731 [1971]. He came from Rasno, and worked for several years as a teacher in Yavneh school on Jaroslaw. He was one of the founders of *Hashomer Hadati* [religious Zionist youth organization].

When the *Judenstadt* Party was established, whose leader was Meyer Grossman, Yeshayahu Rabinovitch was elected as secretary of the Central Committee of the party.

Footnote:

a.   Pages 234 - 235 are part of the Hebrew article (pages 230 - 236), but are missing from the Yiddish (pages 237 – 245).

[Page 246]

Jaroslaw As I Knew It

by Dr. Yitzhak Schwartzbart

Translated from the Yiddish by Pamela Russ

[ ] translator's remarks

I would like to discuss a different part of our small kingdom. I have in mind the "Eastern borders [edges] of our small kingdom. In these borders, there was a second "kingdom," that was started, the kingdom of the "Eastern Galician National Association." There was a really beautiful city there, and that city was called Jaroslaw. This was the central county that was in our proud corner. I loved this city very much. My memory is therefore, particularly connected to it. In the hall of the handworkers' union, very often our Zionist meetings took place. The city was beautiful, clean, Jewish, and it was truly a pleasure to wander through its streets. It didn't have too strong of a temperament. There was not a particularly strong sense of a Zionist unrest, but in spite of that, it was strongly connected to our movement. I personally had another specific reason that I remember this city. In my last wanderings through Poland during the last meeting of the Polish Sejm, at the beginning of September 1939, my road brought me to Jaroslaw, because the road back to Krakow was already torn away. I spent only one day here. It was a real hell. For almost twenty-four straight hours, German bombs fell on the city. From there, the following morning, I left on foot to Przemysl, while the German airplanes covered the sky. These types of experiences very strongly tie the memory to the place.

But let us go back to the beautiful city of Jaroslaw itself. I already noticed that the leaders of the local Zionism movement were not quarrelsome. Therefore the executive felt they (the locals) were able to do the Zionist work. The names of Dr. Spatz, Yehoshua Potasher, remain in my memory. Also, the name of Dr. Rager, a lawyer whom I met in Jerusalem in the year 1953.

The Zionist youth there was wonderful. They were wonderful with their many problems. Well, wherever there are problems, there are also arguments and disputes. It simmered in the pot of youth.

[Page 247]

Occasionally, here on Broadway, in New York, I meet a friend who in my time, was one of the calm directors in Jaroslaw of this local Zionist youth, and today he is a well-known scholar in the area of old Yiddish literature. He is an expert in Yiddish knowledge, and he is also the pride of the city of Jaroslaw. This man is Shalom Spiegel, the well-known professor of the Theological Teachers Seminary in New York.

Excerpted from the book "Between Two World Wars," pages 45-46.

[Page 248]

Zionist Jaroslaw

by Dr. Yitzhak Schwartzbart

Translated by Susan Rosin

Slowly our state organization became almost a country in itself within the Zionist life.

In the eastern borders of this country was the beautiful town of Jaroslaw. It was a district in our organizational activities. My memories of this town are not necessarily just because I lectured there many times and also participated in meetings that took place there. They are mostly related to my dramatic wanderings after the last meeting of the Sejm in Warsaw. During the first days of the Second World War I stayed in the hell of this town for 26 hours while the German bombs were dropped mercilessly.

The Jaroslaw Zionism was moderate, even-tempered, and completely in tune with the rest of the movement. The Zionist leaders of the town were not quarrelsome people. Therefore the executive felt confident they can leave the Zionist work to the local leaders in town. I remember the names of Dr. Spatz, Yehoshua Potasher, and the lawyer Dr. Rager, whom I met in Jerusalem in the year 1953. At the time he was a night guard on mount Herzl.

The Zionist youth there was amazing. They were amazing with their many problems. Wherever there are problems, there are also arguments and disputes. It was a boiling cauldron of youth.

Occasionally, here on Broadway, in New York, I meet a friend who in my time, was one of the Zionist youth leaders in Jaroslaw, and today he is a well-known scholar in the area of old Yiddish literature. He is an expert in his field, and in my opinion he is also the pride of the city of Jaroslaw. This man is Shalom Spiegel.

Such were the roses in the Zionist life bouquet in western Galicia and Silesia. Is it possible - roses without the thorns? There were thorns and quite a few of them.

During the early years after Poland was resurrected [after world war one], the head of the executive was dr. Shmuel Warhaftig. He was the epitome of a Zionist leader. He was heavy set and was measured in both his personal and public life, but was completely devoted to the Zionist ideas. Because of his dedication to the movement, he sacrificed quite a bit in his professional life as a lawyer. When he passed we followed his coffin in silenced mourning with our heads bent through the historic Grodzka street to the Jewish cemetery.

Excerpted from the book of Krakow, page 214.

[Page 249]

Purim in Town

by Moshe Kalchheim

Translated by Pamela Russ

[ ] translator's remarks

As soon as the writing saying "*Mishenichnas Adar marbim besimcha*" ["as soon as the month of Adar comes in, the simcha increases"] appears in the courts and in the *shteibelech* [small, informal synagogues], written in colorful letters and decorated with two, large carp fish, and sometimes also with a bottle and a cup – it became festive in the entire city.

The holiday of Purim is arriving!

Even though my fellow townsmen called it a "Jaroslawer holiday," and truthfully, whoever spent a Purim in our town could not forget it for a long time, nonetheless, the term "Jaroslawer holiday" actually had nothing to do with Purim.

Purim afternoon was the time to exchange *mishloach manot* [gifts of holiday foods], and there was a rushing and lots of action, enough to make one's heart proud. Those who carried the *mishloach manot* were women, young boys, young girls, and beadles of the rabbis, [rabbinic] court judges, and rabbis of *chassidic* courts and *shuls*. And under the covers of the plates that they carried, there sneakily appeared hamantaschen [a triangular pastry symbolizing Haman's hat], all kinds of cookies, and sometimes a bright red orange as well. Shrewd housewives would sometimes intentionally cover the plates with cloths that were too small, so that the neighbors would be able to see what was underneath, and explode with disappointment. And what was "heard" from the plates was:

So, you see how tastefully we are baked, as if we were just taken out of the oven!

On Purim afternoon, the beggars and wanderers also lived it up. Traditionally, the businessmen increased their regular donations – from one *coin* there were two, and from five there were ten. These beggars went from store to store, dressed a little better for the holiday of Purim, and were happy with themselves and with the donations.

[Page 250]

At the time of *mincha* [evening prayer], they closed the shops, and the holiday evening of Purim would start with festivities in the streets.

As if under a magic wand, the city changed its normal appearance. The three principal streets, Sobieskiego, Rynek, and Grodzka, were now filled with all – old, young, and children. They were all waiting impatiently for the time that the tens of local Zionist youth, who were living there, would show their masks.

For a long time, it was already an established that every Purim the Zionist organizations would put together groups of costumed people who would go from house to house, and then at the festive tables of the hosts, they would perform a brief artistic program and collect money for the various Zionist activities.

They went – and suddenly there was a tumult and a cry. Everyone ran over there, where the first group was. People pushed to see them. They were enjoying themselves, and laughing, and mothers and fathers were proud of their young sons and daughters who had suddenly turned into bold cowboys and rich maharajas, decorated with gold and silver, and thieving Arabs dressed in long robes with daggers under their belts.

Oh, what you see here! Wild negroes, yellow Chinese with braids at the bottom [of their heads], Japanese women in floral robes, bold Apaches [Indians] with red scarves around their necks, rich lords in black smocks, Cossacks in flaming red pants, beautifully embroidered shirts, and shiny boots on their feet, and tens of other types from all corners of the world. A real *dor haflaga* [generation of the dispersed].

It was shining and glimmering from crowns and brooches, white, green, and red, which were taken from the grandmother's dresser, scarves and shawls of all colors – an ocean of color.

[Page 251]

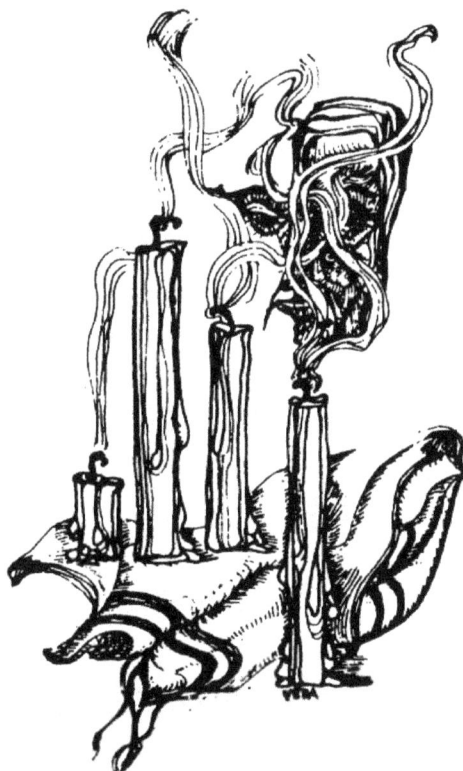

The greatest applause, though, went to Achashverosh and Queen Esther, Mordechai and Haman, or a different group with a very large *pushke* [charity box] for the Land of Israel that they wore on themselves, or the Peel Commission [Palestine Royal Commission headed by Lord Peel, 1936, to investigate Palestine] with cylinders and binoculars, which did not stick to the eye but fell down every minute.

And that is how one group went after the other, accompanied by festive cries and amazement from the gathered crowds.

The most important part, however, took place in the homes of the local businessmen, at the festive tables laid out with good food, with drinks and whiskey, festive breads and baked meats, cakes and all kinds of preserves.

A group of 10-15 men would tear into the house with song and an uproar, dance a flaming *Hora* [Israeli dance], sing a few funny songs, or perform a short or biting sketch of a "*heimish*" type [typically of homelife], and soon drink one or two or three cups [of whisky], and with the same liveliness and rush that they had when they entered, they left so that there would be place for the next group that was already waiting at the door, and who sometimes was already impatiently waiting for the room to be emptied.

There were other festive tables where they would stay for longer periods of time, as, for example, by Reb Steinberg, by Melech Reich, Dovid Kramer, by the Belzer Rebbe (understandably, there the women remained behind the door), and by others, where tens of businessmen from the city would gather, and where a greater amount of money would greet those who were in costumes.

That's how they went from house to house, from room to room, rushed and hurried, so that they could visit everyone, and this went on until the late hours of the night.

All sweaty, and with messed up beards, makeup smeared all over their faces, and with blisters on their feet, the costumed crowd would gather in the streets that were already empty at midnight, and in the glow of the shining moon that lit up Purim night, the crowd would dance in middle of the street until … the police came and chased everyone home.

[Page 252]

Shushan Purim [the following day] was no longer a holiday. More than one person had his bones aching, others developed a bad cold, and the greatest number of the young performers was so hoarse that no one could hear their voices.

And who took this all in?

The mothers.

[Page 253]

Jewish Sport in Jaroslaw

by Mundek Hebenstreit

Translated by Selwyn Rose

I cannot pretend to write about the history of sport in our town because I simply don't have the information. I only wanted to convey a few memories of the sports life of Jaroslaw, things that I carry in my memory thirty years after they occurred, from the day the Jewish population was exiled from the town in 1939. That was the day that the sports life of Jaroslaw's Jews died.

Tears fill my eyes when I recall the memory of those days and of the Jewish youth in the period between the two World Wars (1918-1939). This youth was full of life and youthful energy. They filled the *Ḥadarim* and schools, the youth associations and the sports clubs every day and on Saturday nights, at *Hanukkah* and *Purim*. They spent time in the "*Yad Harutzim*" Hall or "*Szkoła Moziczna*". This Jewish youth was imbued with ideas, beliefs and ideals, which explains the fact that eighty percent of the Jewish youth belonged to Zionist youth movements and the number of different associations was over ten, in a town that was not so large. The activities of the youth were not confined to the field of idealism alone. In keeping with the saying "A healthy mind in a healthy body" the youth of our town developed a vibrant life of sports either within an organized framework or even without it.

Groups of boys and girls would go sledding on the slopes outside of town or play ice-hockey on the frozen Zilinski Lake. The truth is that not every boy or girl had skates or other equipment for winter sports training. Quite frequently, a bent wooden stick served us as a "hockey-stick" or one ski or skate tied to the foot served as two real ones but we didn't let that stop us. The only target was "go faster", "get further". So far as skating was concerned, some of the Jewish girls at the time, were very capable, especially the sister of D. Hentzel and on more than one occasion we followed her in wonderment as she danced across the ice.

On summer days, we spent our time on the banks of the San. Youngsters were accompanied by their parents. They would simply go to bathe while the older children at the same time would swim in the river; the weaker swimmers swam with the current while the stronger ones against it or they swam from bank to bank. The older ones rowed up and down the River San. Another branch of sports activities for which the youngsters would train was weight-lifting. More than once a couple of circuses visited town. It was a real attraction for the youngsters to see the trapeze artists training. Every little Jewish youngster wanted to copy the heroes of the circus and try his strength lifting weights or swinging on the trapeze or simply trying to display his physical strength in striving to at least emulate the strength of Zishe Breitbard whose physical strength was equal to our legendary hero Samson.

[Page 254]

The youngsters taking part in the various sports programs were members of Jewish sports associations. It was only within the organized framework that they could play football, volleyball, table tennis, participate in bicycle races and also boxing, a sport that was considered to be a gentile domain.

I remember the years we played football on the "Mały Rynek" Square and afterwards we would go to the "Wandoły" square to compete in football against the youth teams of "*Akiva*", "*Betar*" and "*Hashomer Hatza'ir*".

During that same period, there were competitions against "*Hapoel*", I think on the ground behind the Great Synagogue or in the "Targowica", an area close to the municipal park. These were real competitions and the names of the players on these teams were known to the public. Among them were: Siegel, Renner, Lipper, Licht, Aftilon, Kaufstein, Bienenstok, Fogler and others.

"*Dror*" also had a football team in those days and its leaders were the Bergerfreund brothers, Krieger, Reich and Sandig. The sportsmen of "*Dror*" were the only ones who played tennis. Among them were: Sandig, Krieger, Reich, Rabinowitz and Meister. Tennis practice took place on the grounds of the "Casino Oficerska" and later on the grounds of the "Stadium".

The young sportsmen, who up until now had played only football, yearned to broaden their sporting activities and in order to do so they had to form a new sports organization. The existing Zionist youth organization dedicated all its time and resources to educating the youth and had no spare time to enter the field of sports.

At the beginning of the 1930s a group of youngsters, among them Kalchheim, Fuks, Glatt, Hemmer, Guttman and the writer of this article, decided to create a Sports Association - "*Maccabi*".

"*Maccabi*" had a club on "Mały Rynek" Street and its activities quickly grew.

[Page 255]

The "'Dror' Team"

From right to left: Horn, Kaufstein, Hebenstreit, Rot, Fuks, Krieger, Reinherz, Sprung, Kaufstein

The main sports of "*Maccabi*" were football and table-tennis. The organization was equipped with an assortment of sports gear, in spite of the fact that there was no revenue, not from support foundations and not from various other "donors". All the necessary equipment was acquired with revenue from the faithful, "*Maccabi*" members' dues. Nevertheless, in time, it became necessary to widen the "*Maccabi*" club because the framework became inadequate.

At the time, a large sports organization, "*Dror*" existed where most of the Jewish sportsmen were active. The "*Dror*" club was located on Grodzka Street, in the Warhaftig building. Its secretary was Manek Fliegel and the football manager was Klang. That was in the early 1930s. Outstanding football players were Alec Lipiner, Nadel and Renner.

[Page 256]

We, members of "*Maccabi*" joined the "*Dror*" club because it allowed us the opportunity to take part in other sports.

And here, I would like to mention a unique attribute of our town Jaroslaw. In other towns the Jewish sports organizations were sponsored by the various political parties or movements. For instance, the *"Gwiazda"* ["Star"], was under the influence of the *"Bund"*, *"Ha-Poel"* included among its ranks the Zionist Socialist Jewish youth while the ranks of *"Maccabi"* and *"Ha-Gibor"* had youth from the "General Zionists".

The "Maccabi Team"

From right to left, first row: Israel Kneitel, Kaufstein, Moshe Kalchheim, Israel Fuks, Izio Krieger
Second row: Moshe Hebenstreit, Chaskiel Fogel, Siko Gutman
Bottom row: Reuven König, Lonek Pokard

[Page 257]

Such a schism did not exist in our town. The youth from all the different political persuasions came to our various sports associations without any reference to their political opinions. In that way the sports associations in our town were a unifying factor of the Jewish public.

After *"Maccabi"* joined, *"Dror"* moved to a large apartment in the building on Dietziusa Street, belonging to Rosenblatt. The Chairman of the organization at that time was Engineer Schneebaum and Mauritz Schneebaum served for many years as manager. For a certain period, Glasberg (now living in Haifa), was the Chairman of *"Dror"* and also its patron.

Within the framework of the club, a few other departments operated: At the head of football department was the writer of these lines, table-tennis was in managed by Hendzel and boxing was managed by Dym. Cycling was managed by Fruchter.

The football team trained at the stadium grounds on Kolejowa Street and the trainer was Sh. Kaufstein. For a short time the trainer of our team was Chudzinski. He was well-known as a player with an established football team "*Ognisko*".

The "*Dror*" team entered into matches against teams of neighboring towns: Radymno (Redem, Radimno), Przeworsk (Pshevarsk, Pshevors'k), Sieniawa (Shinova, Shenova) and others. Among the outstanding players of the team were: Reinhertz, Metzger, Königsberg, Sprung, Weinberg and Gerblich. I recall that at a few games we were joined by the well-known Polish player Antek Tiszarski from the "Ognisko" football team in our town. The intention was to strengthen the team and to have the "*Goy*", dressed in blue and white, competing against his fellow Poles.

A group of cyclists from "Dror"
Korn, Fliegel, Mundstein, Fruchter (manager of the team), Sh. Kaufstein, Metzger, Friedel

[Page 258]

The table-tennis players practiced their ping-pong in one of the club rooms containing a table. Most of the day it was occupied and during the hours Hentzel, Fuchs and Königsberg played they were surrounded by many eager spectators.

Among the well-known boxers were Sh. Dym and Sh. Kolman who more than once demonstrated their capabilities in the ring at the "Casino Oficerska".

The cyclists of "*Dror*" organized bicycle races to local towns and more than once were seen flying along Grunwaldzka Street, Trzeciego Maja, Rynek and Grodzka Streets.

In the volleyball section, the players were mostly the Gymnasium students and pupils of the "Boduwlana" school. They trained in the field on Kraszewskiego Street.

It is impossible to write about sport in our town without noting the hundreds of noisy spectators - the fans. They were supporters of the different teams. With them were sportsmen of the past or simply fans whose support for the various branches was enthusiastic. Among many, I remember two who were really "crazy" about sports. One was Henio Hauben, the "games manager" of Maccabi. He went to all their matches and was the first to enter the ground. Tired, his face covered in sweat, dragging with him suitcases of equipment; complaining about every torn shirt, missing shoe and above all living to the depths of his being his team's victories and unfortunate defeats.

A Group of "Beitar" Sportsmen

Standing from right to left: Sh. Dym, N. Tanzer, Korman
Sitting in the center: Y. Glatt, M. Pasczer

[Page 259]

David, the brother of Shimon Dym, was another dedicated supporter. He was nicknamed "Goose". He walked by foot to every game, however far; to the town of Sieniawa, or Radymno or even Przemyśl. One would see him walking for many kilometers. He personified the image of the "supporter" and the "walker" at one and the same time and there were many like him – "crazy" about the game - in our town of Jaroslaw.

Nevertheless, the sportsmen in our town didn't achieve the levels of ability of the well-known national sportsmen of Poland but everyone in his sport tried to emulate the well-known Jewish sportsmen. The footballers dreamed of achieving the standard of Steuerman or Blatt, the well-known players of Lvov's famous "*Hasmonea*" team. Table-tennis players sought to copy the champion table-tennis players of the time, Ehrlich of "*Hasmonea*" or Gutek from the town of Tarnow. The famous boxer, Rothholtz, from the Warsaw "*Gwiazda*" team, was the "ideal" of the boxers in our town. Rothholtz was the only Jew in the boxing team to represent Poland in the boxing contest against the United States of America, beating his American opponent. Incidentally, it should be noted that the world champion boxer was the Jew Max Baer, who reached the championship after his victory over Primo Carnera.

The greatest Jewish sportsmen in the world were idolized by the sportsmen in our town in the 1930s.

The "HaKoach" ("Strength") team of Vienna, one of the most famous football teams in the world, was the pride of our generation. I clearly remember the team visiting our town Jaroslaw. It was in 1931. "Strength" then played against the best team Jaroslaw had, "*Ognisko*". The game ended with the Viennese team winning 6-1. We were then quite young brats and it was the first time that we bought tickets and entered the ground through the main gate. Most of us were "gate-crashers" and entered the ground through holes in the fencing surrounding the stadium. With obvious pleasure we found ourselves watching the match between the two teams and saw how Ehrlich, Folk or Guttman with their excellent play "subdued" the "champions" of "*Ognisko*". With heads held high and with pride we returned home from the stadium and never stopped talking about the tricky maneuverings of "Strength" on the field. Even religious Jews that we met on the street asked us: "Well – by how many goals did we beat the "*Goyim*" with?" Those were the days!

[Page 260]

It seems appropriate to notice that two targets stood out for the Jewish youth in those days: the physical development of their bodies and the development of their intellectual abilities. During the morning hours, the youngsters studied in the high schools or were working, while during the afternoon hours they dedicated themselves to sporting activities. The evening hours were spent in various social and Zionist organizations, discussions, or reading books.

In perspective, these were the lives of sportsmen in our town. The youth of those days was magnificent.

The Holocaust brought an end to that generation of youth in our town and dispersed some of them throughout the world. The majority of the surviving refugees live in Israel and only on a few occasions like memorial meetings or chance encounters do we bring to mind the people of the town of Jaroslaw, who are engraved on our hearts.

[Page 261]

Recollections of my Town

by David Isman

Translated by Selwyn Rose

It isn't easy to bring up many memories of the town wherein several generations of my forefathers and I were born. In that town, I lived and grew up until the age of 21. It is now 30 years since I left my town, Jaroslaw.

It is difficult for a man to be objective regarding his way of life in the town, where he was educated to reject life in the Diaspora, for it requires dispassionate judgment to bring up memories objectively in a way that is as close to the truth as possible. Today it seems to me those were days of idealism and romance among the youth, and faith among the adult population who came from different sectors of the population: "*Haredim*", free-thinkers, wealthy and needy. Many dedicated much of their time to the Zionist movement and a significant portion of them prepared themselves for immigration to Palestine in order to take a meaningful part in rebuilding the country. They all took part, either physically or financially in the revival project. As a result public life displayed a noticeable ebullience, hundreds of lectures were presented and arguments took place on ideological topics, both Jewish and general and understandably there were many different points of view and opinions on the present and the future. Every group put greater emphasis on the theme that was closest to its heart and justified developing it. In the end, they all came to terms with each other. The meaning given to the "National Home" and how to build it also occupied the time and energies of many circles. It is to everyone's credit that can be said that everything possible was done to instill the love of Zion and Jewish cultural values. It was done not only with words but with deeds as well, like: imbuing the youth with a fondness for physical effort, professionalism, military activity, excursions, summer camps and general studies that broaden the knowledge of the youth. At that time there wasn't much work available or significant employment. As a result, for some hours each day they would help their parents, either in their shop or in their workshop (there were professional artisans among Polish Jewry). They remained living with their parents for quite a few years with a very uncertain future.

In the evenings, the youth would gather in their various movements and spend the time in pleasant companionship, reading or listening to a lecture, studying, folk-dancing and so on. All this gave meaning and content to their young lives. Shabbat eves and festivals were particularly notable. Adults also spent their evenings in cultural pursuits: the "*Haredim*" – in prayer, studying the *Talmud*, conversations in the Study House on matters of the day, holidays were spent actively in the organizations on various public affairs (voluntarily and with no thought of reward).

[Page 262]

The cultural connections and mutual assistance were well developed. As an example, I can note a specific case: the room used by the Federation where we used to meet for a weekly conversation on Shabbat was at the foot of the high hill. It was one snowy night in winter, freezing cold with strong winds and the approach to the building was very difficult with the added danger of slipping on the snow and breaking bones. Nevertheless nearly everyone came including those who lived at some distance. No one wanted to stay away and miss the meeting with neighbors and friends. Poverty existed throughout the Jewish population, but there was also joy and gaiety in life: there were social and family events. Ways were sought to improve the situation in order to make life more interesting and culture-filled. Each one of us retains some sentiment for those days, especially Shabbat and Festivals, Passover evening and the Days of Awe. Their characteristics were the chief feature for the Orthodox "*Haredim*".

Part of the Market Square

All of them gave content and taste to life and the daily struggle for existence that was by no means easy for most of the Jewish population. We must never forget that thanks to the education we received we have arrived where we are today. From the cultural standpoint as well, we draw on that period; in those days, people were involved with matters of culture and courtesy to others.

[Page 263]

As usual, like in every large population group, there were good people and some a little bit "less good". I am reminded of someone who appeared to be a little "grey" to observers. The name of this man was Eliezer "the lemon-seller". He would wander round the streets of the town with a basket of lemons in his hand selling them to housewives, barely making a living. But on Thursdays, he would beg for money. I once asked my father (Z"L), who knew him well, if he didn't make enough to sustain himself from the sale of the lemons and had to beg for money. My father answered me saying that he begged for money in order to purchase supplies for destitute people and others in the hospital where he would visit them and offer some comfort, adding from his own resources often leaving himself without sufficient to sustain himself or purchase a fresh supply of lemons. He did this for many years without anyone knowing so that the mitzvah would be greater – giving to others anonymously.

It is possible to provide a gallery full of such people. Perhaps because people like this, the Jewish people survived in spite of all the suffering.

I am writing these few lines not only for those people who were residents of Jaroslaw for many years and know, more or less, the style of living in the town, but especially for our children. Perhaps one day they will want to know about their forefathers. Then they can open this memorial book, read it and from its pages draw a picture of the life of Jaroslaw's Jewish community – their fathers – the previous generation, and what happened to them under the Nazis.

———

[Page 264]

The "Incident"
at the Opening of the Wiata Targowa Town Market

by PinHas Wintgreen

Translated by Selwyn Rose

I recall the "incident" that occurred at the opening of the new Municipal market "*Wiata Targowa*" at the corner of Grodzka Street and the "Big Rynek" [marketplace]. The Municipal authorities had deliberately fixed the ceremonial opening for a *Sabbath* in order to prevent the participation of the town's Chief Rabbi Yitzhak Halevi Steinberg and other Jewish representatives who comprised a major portion of the shop and stall-owners. The senior officials of both the regional civil and military authorities had been invited, as had the heads of the Roman Catholic priesthood and the Greek Orthodox clergy, and also the Chief Rabbi of the Jewish community – Rabbi Yitzhak Halevi Steinberg. The City Fathers were sure that the Rabbi would not appear because of the sanctity of the day.

That same Sabbath in the Great Synagogue, in which Rabbi Steinberg prayed, tempers raged. The congregation could not be pacified in view of the affront to the community by the town's authorities. After the Rabbi had been "called to the reading of the *Torah*", he addressed the congregation in a trembling voice and briefly explained to those present that he had been invited to be present at the ceremony on that *Shabbat*. Rabbi Steinberg expressed the view that he should take part in the ceremony in spite of the wrath of the inviters. He asked permission of the congregation to agree to his attending the ceremony in order to sanctify the status of Israel and begged the congregation to delay commencing the Additional *Shabbat* prayer until his return.

Dressed in his *Shabbat* finest, he walked the few hundred meters from the synagogue to the site of the ceremony and there, after the opening addresses of the Municipal authorities and assembled clergy, the Rabbi was invited to address the assembly. He ascended the podium and in clear and fluent Polish gave the assembled crowd a brief lesson in the history of Jaroslaw for the last several centuries. The assembled audience stood mouths agape listening to the impressive content of the Rabbi's lecture. Many comments were heard from the audience to the effect that the Municipal representatives and Clergy needed to approach Rabbi Steinberg and learn from him how to conduct a speech.

At the close of the ceremony, the Rabbi returned to the Great Synagogue with a handful of Jews who had taken part in the official opening of the new market, for the additional prayer where the rest of the congregation had patiently waited.

[Page 265]

Music and Entertainment

by Erna Zilberman

Translated by Selwyn Rose

The musical and entertainment life in Jaroslaw was, to a certain degree associated with the Geiger Family. The band of David Geiger, his son and Erna Zilberman-Geiger always took part in every theatrical or cinema event in town.

The band performed concerts for the town's residents, and the revenues accumulated were dedicated to the Jewish orphanage situated on Avenue 3rd May under the patronage of Mr. Strisover, the deputy mayor and one of the outstanding community leaders.

The band was known beyond the borders of the town, thus for instance, it appeared on occasion at the court of Baron Potocki and Baron Wettman and even reached Vienna and India where they played before the King in 1938.

The Geiger family also managed a dancing academy where the students from all walks of life in Jaroslaw, Jews and non-Jews, received lessons. The family also ran a school of music where the residents of Jaroslaw, especially children and teenagers learned the basics of music and played violin, viola, saxophone and accordion. As a result, a variety of musicians became available for the musical life of our town and elsewhere.

[Page 266]Blank [Page 267]

Holocaust and Heroism

[Page 268]blank [Page269]

0.12

ISRAEL ישראל

השואהוהגבורה

HEAR, O ISRAEL...
Deuteronomy 6, 4

יום השואה והגבורה
HEROES AND MARTYRS DAY

ISRAEL ישראל

ישראל 0.60

אלה אזכרה...
תהלים מב, ל
THESE I REMEMBER...
PSALMS 42, 5

[Page 270]

Poem on the Murdered Jewish People

Yitzhak Katzenelson

Translated from Yiddish by Judie Ostroff-Goldstein

How can I sing – so that the world will know?
How can I play with broken hands?
Where are my dead? G-d, I am searching for my dead,
In every hill of ash: - Oh, tell me, where are they?

Shout out from the sand, from under every stone,
From all the dust, shout, from all the flames, from all the smoke –
It is your blood and sap, it is the marrow from your bones,
It is your body and your life! Shout, Scream, loud!

[Page 271]

Shout out from animal entrails in the forest, from fish in the river –
I want a shriek, an outcry, a voice from you,
They ate you. Scream from the lime kiln, scream small and big,
Scream murdered Jewish people, shout out!

Oh, alas, my people appear. Raise your hands
Out of the deep, mile long graves and sealed shut,
Layer upon layer, doused with lime and burned,
Up! Up! Ascend from the obstacle, the deepest layer!

Everybody come, from Treblinka, from Sobibor, from Ostrolenka,
From Belzec come, come from Ponar and from others, from others, from other!
With eyes torn open, raise a cry and without a voice,
Come from the swamps, from deep in the mud, from Poland -

Come, you who are drained, ground down, crushed. Come. Stand up,
In a circle, a large circle around me, one large ring –
Grandfathers, grandmothers, mothers with babies in their wombs –
Come, Jewish babies of powder, of a bit of soap.

I am the man who watched, who saw
How men threw my children, my wives, my young, my old
Into wagons, like stones you were flung in there, like discards,
And they beat you without pity and spoke to you as wantons.

And now? You see wagons, trucks now, you watch,

[Page 272]

You silent witness of such burdens and of such pain and of such distress!
Silent and closed, you watched, Oh, tell me wagons, where
You are traveling to. You the people, the Jewish people, have departed to death?

The first killed were the children, forlorn, little orphans. They are called
The best of the world, the most beautiful that the dark earth possesses!
Oh, from the loneliest little orphans and children's homes should grow our comfort, from the
cheerless, mute, little faces, the gloominess will not be allowed to take us!

They were the first to be taken to their deaths, the first ones on the wagon,
Men threw all of them in the wagons, like a handful of garbage, like rubbish –
And took them away, murdered them, destroyed them, there is no trace
Of them, of my best, no more remains! Akh, alas, woe is me!

The sun will rise once more over small villages in Lithuania and Poland never to meet a
Jew again
A light in the dark, an old man, a man reciting a chapter of Psalms, a man going into the
synagogue -
After all, the peasants will travel in wagons on all the roads, they will travel to the fair after all,
So many gentiles – good gracious! Yet more than before! And the market, the market is dead.

The market is full and is not full!

There is no longer a Jew to beautify the fair for great distances around, they are no longer
lively, there is no longer any spirit
And no longer will a Jewish long, black coat flap over the market with a sack of potatoes, flour
and grain, and a Jewish hand
Will no longer raise a pot, a soft chicken, caress a calf...the peasant a drunk, whips
His horse in grief pulls the full wagon back to the village... gone! Gone, there are no longer any
Jews in the country!

And Jewish children – they will not wake up from sleeping, from dreams, every one of
them bright in the morning –
They will no longer go to school, no longer let their minds wander, no longer play pranks, no
longer play in the sand,

[Page 273]

Oh, you Jewish youngsters, oh, bright eyes! Little angels...where are you from? From here,
in this town? And not from here!
Oh, beautiful young girl, your brightness, your neatness, everything in order, your little face is not
messy.

They are gone already! Oh, on the other side of the ocean, do not ask, do not search in
Kasrylewka, nor in Jehupiec...leave it alone!
Do not search for any one...not the Menachem-Mendels, the Tuwia Milkhikers, the Shlomo
Nagids, the Motke ganefs, oh, do not search!
Like your prophets, Yeshaya, Jermia, Jehezkiel, Hosza and Amos, from the eternal Bible

They will cry out to you from Bialik, speak to you from Scholem Aleichem, from Scholem
Ash, from one of their books.

It is that lost voice from the Torah no longer heard from any yeshivas, from any study house
and pale yeshiva students,
Noble in learning, poring over the Talmud, deep in thought...no, no, not pale, there is such a glow!
Already extinguished...rabbis, heads of yeshivas, Jews studying, geniuses thin, dry, weak and full
of Talmud,
With post Talmudic commentators, small Jews with large heads, with high foreheads, clear eyes,
they are already gone, they will no longer be.

[Page 274]

Our Town is Burning

by Mordecai Gebirtig

Translated by Selwyn Rose

It is burning, brothers, our cherished town, it burns!
Our poor unhappy town is on fire!
Enlivened by evil spirits
And from the wild-fire ruins

Everything is already burning all around.

And you who look upon it while folding your arms!
And you stand and just stare and look.
How our town burns!

It is burning, brothers, our beloved town, it burns!
Our poor unhappy town is on fire!
You already know full well how the tongues of fire swallow all, -
Everything is already burning all around.

And you just stand and look...

It is burning brothers, our dearest town, see how it burns!

The moment may come when the town will remain – G-d forbid,
Together with you, like after a battle, -
Blackened and desolate.

And you stand and just look…

Only your hand, your hand can prevail!
And if the town is dear to you,
Take tools and quench the flames, quench them with your hands

And prove your hands failed you not!

Do not stand, brothers, like that to the end, with folded arms!
Do not stand, brothers, put out the fire, for our town is on fire!

[Page 275]

Our Exile from Jaroslaw to the Siberian Forests

by Moshe Katz

Translated by Selwyn Rose

"How doth the city sit solitary, that was full of people (Jaroslaw) and her Jews are not."[1].

It was that same fateful summer of 1939, a short time after Nazi Germany attacked Poland and the Second World War broke out. One bright morning we found the Jackboots of the Nazi army in our town, captured virtually without a fight and without a shot being fired.

The sorrows of the Jews began the following morning after the Germans mobilized the Jews for work (sometimes simply fabricated and unproductive). The work was intended to abuse and humiliate the Jews more than any other purpose. While working the Jews were beaten mercilessly by the Germans. Anti-Semitic Poles took part in that and goaded and aggravated the Jews.

It was the morning hours of a lovely day when the writer of these few lines, together with his mother, were in their grocery store at 4 Spytka Street when suddenly a German entered the shop accompanied by two Poles. The Nazi spoke a couple of sentences to my mother that could only be understood in one way and that was:

"All the Jews of the town of Jaroslaw and the area must congregate today, no later than three this afternoon in the town's stadium, with a parcel of belongings to take with them. The Jews must lock their apartments and business premises, workshops and arrange all the keys together with the addresses of the properties and the personal details of the owner."

Many of us, in our innocence and naïveté did as the Germans commanded and reported to the stadium. The Germans body-searched everyone carefully taking everything of value they could find, especially money, gold, diamonds, rings and other articles. Many at the same time bullied the Jews with blows and then moved them across the River San.

Many of them (my family among them), understood the intention of the Germans and crossed the river on their own initiative and in so doing saved themselves from robbery, insults and pain. And thus, within one day alone, our town was cleared of all its Jews, leaving behind them quantities of personal property, homes, stores full of goods, workshops and also much public community property – splendid synagogues, Study-Houses, schools, the "*Yad Harutzim*" building, public and other meeting rooms. Most of the buildings in town were owned by Jews and everything remained, everything was confiscated, rapidly and completely and we even had no time to prepare provisions for the journey; The Jews left behind them the organized Jewish lives and traditions that sustained them in Jaroslaw for many generations.

[Page 276]

Within two or three days, we were met by the Red Army that was advancing rapidly towards the San which according to the Molotov-Ribbentrop Agreement was to be the international border between the Soviet Union and Nazi Germany after the fourth carving-up of Poland.

Most of the Jews of our town spent the winter of 1939-40 in Eastern Galicia.

The spring of 1940 did not bode well, although our townspeople somehow managed to survive with acquaintances and relatives and among ordinary Jews and sometimes with Poles from the Righteous Among the Nations. We were only sorry that there were so few of them.

The Soviet Union brought order to the annexed territories and offered the population Soviet citizenship. The Jews of Jaroslaw as one rejected the offer, considering themselves refugees with the hopes that at the end of hostilities they would return to Poland. They asked to remain as refugees and waived the offer of Soviet citizenship. There is no doubt that the rejection wasn't pleasing to the Soviets and Stalin's reaction was came quickly.

It was a dark summer night when the N.K.V.D. came to visit the refugees - the Jews of Jaroslaw. They ordered our refugees (together with tens of thousands of other Jews who fled when the war broke out), to gather their belongings and once again fulfill the biblical injunction "Get thee out of thy country…"[2].

That same night, guards transferred us to railroad wagons with small windows and we journeyed eastwards in the closed wagons. When we passed Lvov, many of the town's Jews brought us bread, something to drink and other supplies. A few Yiddish words were all that was needed for them to bring as much food and supplies for us as they could get their hands on before the train moved on eastwards. After three days, confined within the wagons and travelling in the direction of Kiev we noticed at every station a conspicuous sign with the word "*Kipiatok*"– we didn't know why the town "Kipiatok" had so many stations.

At fixed times during the journey, the wagons were opened once a day and we received bread, soup and tea. It was only during the journey eastwards we learned the that meaning of the word – "Kipiatok" was "boiling water" - "boiling water" that was so essential for the preparation of tea during long journeys lasting several days.

[Page 277]

We continued eastwards.

The train passed through all of European Russia, travelling for a week or two (during which we often stopped for a number of hours). And here we were already in Asiatic Greater Russia. If there had been earlier doubts among the Jews as to where we were going, those doubts now disappeared. The thought of forced labor now gnawed at our minds. We travelled on and on for about 4 weeks until the transport arrived at a town called Barnaul. The biblical injunction of "get thee out of thy country…" continued as far as the area of Topchikhinsky and the village of Topchikha as we penetrated deeper and evermore deeper into endless forests. It was possible to travel for days on end through the Taiga[3]. areas, imprisoned by the forests from which there is no escape or exit.

Our final destination in the Topchikhinsky raion (district) was barrack number 3. It was our "resting place". We were about seventy Jewish families, some from Jaroslaw: the large Kaufmann family, with Yeshiayhu Kaufmann, the Shachne Rubinfeld family, the Blond Family, owners of the paint shop with their son the veterinarian, Dr. Korman[*]. The Zadok Prinz family, the Sonnenblick family- metal-workers from Jaroslaw, Leib (Arieh) Katz and his family, owners of a grocery store at 4 Spytka Street (who immigrated to Jerusalem and lived there for many years and was privileged to see the reunification of the Eternal City). There were additional families from Jaroslaw whose names have unfortunately slipped my memory.

The first winter started before *Rosh Hashanah*, we began to bury our dead in ever increasing numbers due to poor living conditions. We suffered from hunger and the cold weather.

When we arrived, we found a large bare barrack block with no partitions and that is where about seventy families were placed. There was no kitchen and no facilities. We "lived together" communally throughout the first Siberian winter. We were selected to work in various forestry works such us chopping down trees. The payment for the labor was barely enough to maintain us for about one third of our needs. We had two Russian work managers as overseers and also an N.K.V.D. officer. We were told quite clearly that we would never leave that place – "No one is ever released from Siberia"; and "if we build for ourselves living quarters it will be for our own benefit for we have hands, there is an abundance of timber and no restriction about building a place to live."

[Page 278]

The distress, the hunger, the lack of sanitary conditions and the hard labor had a devastating effect on our community. The religious traditions constituted a crime - public prayer - a crime. During that first winter, we began to count our dead. Among the first were Mr. and Mrs. Kaufmann, who died of starvation and the hard conditions they were unable to withstand. Shachne Rubinfeld lost his son from starvation and lack of medication and hospitalization. A significantly equipped clinic was tens of kilometers away (the nearest mail facility was 32 kilometers distant). During the twenty months period we were there, tens of people died, among them the entire group of elders and the youngest children. Only the strongest in body and spirit managed to hold on and were granted "Amnesty" through the Sikorski-Stalin agreement, leaving Siberia for central Asia at the end of the two-year period spent in that "Garden of Eden".

In the hot central Asiatic zones in the difficult tropical climate of Tashkent, Dzhambul, Alma-Ata and so on (Kazakhstan), we met up with other Jews, many of them from Jaroslaw. The shortage of food and the minimal conditions for mere existence as a result of the war, against the Nazi beast, the illnesses – malaria, dysentery and so on – all these made us very frail.

It was only at the end of the war that a small number of our townspeople returned to Poland but not to Jaroslaw. The anti-Semitic beast had decided unequivocally that the Jewish property and Holy places in our town will remain free of Jews. And thus, it was.

I visited Jaroslaw in 1946. I strolled around many different parts of the town. I was shocked. I didn't recognize my town at all. It was Jaroslaw without Jews – I felt as if the heart had been torn out of me. But worst of all – there were no acquaintances, no friends, no family, no *ḥassidim*, no *Mitnagdim*, no Zionists, no Socialists. Everything was strange everything was foreign. Even the Jewish cemetery with its impressive tombstones was as if it didn't exist.

[Page 279]

***The Northern Part of the Central Square;* On the left Grodzka street**

I spent about two weeks in Jaroslaw in the summer of 1946 with my mother, Batya-Basha Katz (Z"L). I covered the town from side to side and from top to bottom, from the church as far as the River San, in the direction of the railroad station, to Dietziusa Street area near the home of Lazar Diller and the municipal hospital in the direction of the *Wandoły*. Everything was there and in place – but the soul – non-existent. We have suffered enough pain. We left the deserted Jaroslaw without Jews, never to return there.

Again and yet again, our souls directed us onwards – to the Land of Israel.

Footnotes:

* The family of Baruḥ Kalchheim (the brother of Moshe Kalchheim - the mainstay of the "*Akiva*" Zionist youth movement in Jaroslaw before the war

1. Taken directly from the opening verse of the Lamentations of Jeremiah.
2. Taken from Genesis XII; 1.
3. Taigas are subarctic scrub areas found throughout the northern latitudes from Canada to Siberia

[Page 280]

In Memoriam

by Alexander Silberman

Translated by Selwyn Rose

When the first days of September came and with them the threats of the bloodthirsty leaders of the criminal people, together with the Polish leaders' proud declarations concerning the "undefeatable weapons of war" that Poland possessed; In an atmosphere between hope and despair, it was possible to hear the weak voices of Jewish optimism of "...the demon is not so terrible".

And thus, on the first of September, 1939 the Second World War broke out with massive bombing attacks by the Germans on defenseless towns and cities and the fate of Europe's Jews and with them the Jews of our town Jaroslaw, where its Jewish community had thrived for centuries was sealed. The contribution of that community to the cultural life of Poland is well known.

On the 8th of September, the Nazis entered the town and conquered it and we, the Jews, were degraded to nothing more than hunted animals by blood-thirsty criminals. Confiscations, robbery, collective punishments and cruelties became daily occurrences.

On 28th of September, we were forced, under weapons' threat, to leave all our homes open and vulnerable for several hours and afterwards we were deported across the River San. That same day, Jaroslaw Jewry ceased to exist and the Jewish citizens of our town became homeless wretches, wandering from place to place, in Siberia in the east, or became prisoners in extermination camps that the Nazis built in the "New Europe".

Torments and suffering were the lot of some of the Jews of our town and we together with our brethren chopped down trees from the forests of Siberia, mined coal in the Urals, rotted in concentration camps, ghettos or fought with partisans against the common enemy.

And now we are the survivors of the Jaroslaw's Jewry. We have no idea where the bones of our mothers and fathers are strewn, where the children are buried or where our relatives were murdered, whether in Bełżec (Belzhetz) or Treblinka or Auschwitz, Mauthausen or Bergen-Belsen. And now we are the remaining Jewish survivors of Jaroslaw, living in our homeland understanding and knowing full-well the enormous obligation we have to perpetuate the memory of the magnificent Jewish community and how important it is to honor and respect those who are no longer with us; to hand down to our children and future generations a diligent description of Jaroslaw's Jewish community before its total destruction.

———

[Page 281]

In the Struggle against the Nazis

by Mundek Hebenstreit

Translated by Selwyn Rose

Tragedy was the fate of Poland's Jewry during the Nazi occupation. Before the war the Jewish population numbered three and a half million Jews. At war's end only few thousands remained.

It was particularly hard for Jaroslaw's Jews and their chances of surviving were slight. After being expelled from the town by the Nazis, they were dispersed to several different places completely strange to them and at decisive moments, when the ghettoes were liquidated, they had no acquaintances among the Poles who may or may not have been in a position to prepare hiding places for them and those who did were few and far between. Because of that, the Jews of Jaroslaw perished in their multitudes without the slightest possibility of defending themselves as did some Jews in other places.

Mordecai Hebenstreit

Not all of them, for all that, were tortured to death in the camps or at the times of the *Aktzia*s by the blood-thirsty Nazi beasts. There were tens of young Jewish Jaroslaw-born young men, who fought in the ranks of the Polish army or in the Red Army, some of whom fell in battle against the Nazis.

Since I have no names for these fighters, or information as to how they fell, I will describe one of them and by doing so commemorate for eternity all the fallen of Jaroslaw who died with weapons in their hands in battle against the Nazis.

Mordecai Hebenstreit was known in our city as a humble and quiet guy who was interested in studies. He was first educated in a *Ḥeder* and later in a *Talmud Torah*. Like most children his age, he attended an elementary school and in the latter years there he began to find much interest in social ideologies and his perceptions, apparently, tended more and more towards the left. He himself never displayed his views publicly.

[Page 282]

His father, a religious Jew, favoring tradition, never sent his son to the gymnasium because there it was obligatory to attend on Shabbat. Mordecai was forced to study his high-school curriculum privately and at the end of his studies successfully passed his matriculation examinations that took place externally, in Lvov. After that, he registered to study at the Lvov Polytechnic.

Mordecai was fully immersed in his studies and only occasionally could be seen on the streets of the town and that was in spite of the fact that his circle of acquaintances was quite wide and he was liked and welcomed by everyone. He was always ready to help, active and modest – and was also very handsome according to the opinion of the girls in his age group.

With the outbreak of the war in 1939, on the 6th day of battles between the Germans and the Poles, Mordecai and I, together with a group of Jaroslaw youth, made our way over the eastern border of Poland. Our leaving was with the blessings of our parents because it seemed more than likely that with the occupation of the town by the Germans they would start torturing and murdering Jewish youth of military age.

It seems that our father was not aware of Mordecai's views because at the time of our departure he gave his son, among other items for his journey, his phylacteries and prayer-book neither of which had been used for a while, saying: "Take them with you and G-d will protect you and have mercy on you".

We went on our way. After wandering around for a week, we met some units of the Red Army that had crossed the eastern border and invaded Poland. In light of the new situation, we decided to return to our town of Jaroslaw. But at the village just before town, we were stopped in our tracks by what we saw before us.

The Jews of our town, from whom we had parted just two weeks ago appeared terrified while meandering around the rented carts of the local peasants, unloading their belongings and carrying them to the attics of the meager houses of the villagers. Some acquaintances explained to us what was happening.

The Germans had ordered all the Jews of Jaroslaw sent across the River San. All their property, the labor of years and perhaps of generations was confiscated. The people told us that after the town had been occupied, the Germans took thirty Jews, among them our father, as hostages and imprisoned them in the cellar of the Municipality where they were cruelly tortured.

The reunion with our family was painful. My father's appearance whose hair had turned white, and his beard chopped, stunned us; we saw the shock on Mordecai's face and we knew that at that moment his hatred of the Germans grew enormously. The Nazis were the enemies of humanity but especially were they the enemies of the Jewish people.

[Page 283]

In 1940, Mordecai completed his studies with excellent grades and entered into competition for a post as an aspiring mathematician under Professor Bartel (ex-Prime Minister of Poland). Mordecai won the competition and remained at this position until the outbreak of the war between Germany and the Soviet Union.

On the third day of that terrible bloody war, the authorities in town organized the evacuation of college employees to Russia. By doing so, the administration intended to save the *intelligentsia*, who were among the first – together with the Jews taken out and executed, in all places occupied by the Germans.

Mordecai and his wife, Hela Krug, left Lvov and turned eastward intending to get as far away as possible from the battle areas. But on the way, when they got as far as Kiev he suddenly changed his mind. He left his wife and enlisted in the Red Army in order to fight against the Nazi conqueror. In a short while, he attained the rank of an officer and was sent to the front.

At the same time, the strong German army succeeded in encircling the Red Army in Ukraine. All this was within the framework of the well-known "Operation Barbarossa".

The encircled Russians disposed of their arms and uniforms and sought a way eastwards knowing what awaited them if they fell into the hands of the Germans.

Yitzhak Damast of Jaroslaw, and other eye-witnesses serving in the same unit stated that his comrades in arms suggested that Mordecai join them in trying to find a way out of the siege because their situation was hopeless.

Mordecai refused. He voluntarily decided to remain and fulfill his obligation to fight the Nazis. Mordecai stood by his decision and told his comrades that he will not desert the field of battle and will fight the enemy with all his strength.

And thus, it was. A few days later he fell in battle. That same modest man from Jaroslaw died the death of a hero.

[Page 284]

From the Ghetto to the Forest
(The last hours of my stay in the Vilna ghetto)

by Moshe Kalchheim

Translated by Selwyn Rose and Susan Rosin

Looking for Prowodnik[1]

I lived with my friends Jacky Pillersdorf and Steffi Shanzer (today Spiegel, living in Shavei Tzion) in Straszuna number 2 street. On one of the last days of July in 1943, a messenger arrived and told me that Abba Kovner[2] wanted to see me at the headquarters of the FPO[3]. When I arrived, I found a blond woman named Dunka Shapira and from her and Abba Kovner I heard the following story:

A few days ago, a messenger from a partisan unit in the nearby Narocz forest under the command of Fiodor Markow[4] arrived in the Vilna ghetto. The messenger, whose name I believe was Haim, was to get a group of FPO fighters and guide them to the forest. While in the ghetto, Haim began to organize a group of the boys and girls to join the partisans, charging them large sums of money.

Dunka and Kovner said that last night thirty boys and girls left the ghetto in small groups, most of them paying large sums of money, on the way to the assembly point outside of town, as appointed by the guide. When they arrived at the meeting point, it became clear to them that instead of waiting for all to arrive, the guide took thirteen of the group with him and went on. Seventeen people remained, among them some girls, in a wooded area, with some scattered houses. They had no idea where to go.

All night long and well into the morning, they lay low unmoving in the forest anxious to avoid being noticed by the nearby residents fearing they would be reported to the police. In the end, they decided that Dunka Shapira, one of the girls who had distinctly Aryan features, should return to the ghetto headquarters of the FPO and report on the situation. When she arrived in the vicinity of the ghetto entrance, she waited until a group of laborers were retuning and with them, she was able to sneak into the ghetto.

Dunka pleaded that the 17 remaining people be moved from their vulnerable situation in the direction of Narocz forest. I was familiar with part of the way to the Narocz forest.

[Page 285]

I told Kovner that I would be willing to go on condition that my two friends, Steffi Shanzer and Jacky Pillersdorf could come with me and with an additional man who knew the way from Bezdonys to Narocz. An hour later, they called me again and told me they had found a Jewish man, a timber-merchant, who knew the area very well and would lead the group on the second part of the route.

I returned to my friends and found there Hillel Seidel[5] who, unlike us, had lived in the ghetto since it was established and belonged to the group of fighters led by Yeḥiel Sheinbaum[6]. I told them about the conversation with Kovner and my refusal to accept his suggestion to go without them.

While we were still talking about it, the messenger from Abba Kovner came again, calling me back to headquarters. When I got there, Kovner told me that I could take Jacky and he committed to send Steffi with the next group in a few days. I told him I couldn't accept his claim that Steffi's inclusion would endanger the whole operation and added that without her I wouldn't go. But I told him that I would give him my final answer after I had discussed it with my friends.

Leaving Kovner, I found Steffi, Jacky and Hillel waiting for me on the street. They urged me to accept the proposal. Their argument was that not one of us was armed and we had no money to purchase arms. Abba Kovner's promise (to get them out) was worth more than arms. Therefore the plan should be accepted.

I returned to Kovner and told him that I agreed to go with Jacky on the condition that Steffi would be sent to Narocz forest with the next group.

Inside the headquarters, they introduced me to the timber merchant whose task it was to guide us on the trip. I saw in front of me an elderly Jew and with him was his young daughter who was about 13-14 years old. Some unexplained feeling caused my heart to flutter. I asked the Jew: "Are you really sure you know the way beyond Bezdonys?" He replied by stretching out his hand and saying: "You see my hand? I know the area as well as I know that hand; I have lived here nearly all my life." Although I relaxed a little, I remained skeptical. Unfortunately, I was proven right. Throughout the entire journey, the man was a nuisance. The difficult journey was especially hard on his poor and sickly daughter. It was agreed that we would meet at 7:30 at headquarters; the merchant with his daughter, Dunka Shapira, Jacky and I and from there we will set out, through a secret passage, to the Aryan side.

The separation from Steffi was particularly difficult. For two whole years, we lived together literally 24 hours a day in each other's company as friends and companions under very difficult conditions in the work camps of

Bezdonys and Biala-Waka and the ghetto. Together we suffered from different illnesses, persecution and harassment and the need to wander from place to place and together we were happy when we began to profit from trade with the peasants and when life became a little bit easier. And now – after 700 long days and nights together like this, we had to part. I consoled myself with the thought that Hillel Seidel, who had proven his faithfulness to us in the past, will certainly care for Steffi when I leave her on her own.

[Page 286]

At 7:30 in the evening, we all gathered at headquarters. In place of Kovner there was a member of the Headquarters staff, representing the Communist Party, Chiena Borowski. She informed us that she was going to get us out of the ghetto by a secret passage to Niemiecka Street, on the other side of the ghetto. We began to walk but when she saw Jacky Pillersdorf, she stopped and said that it was decided not to include him in my group but to attach him to the group leaving in two days. At first, I began to protest and said I wouldn't leave without him and it is impossible that within an hour headquarters would break a promise that was given to me by Kovner. She began screaming at me accusing me of sabotaging the safety of the group and the success of the entire operation. She said I should trust the Headquarters of the FPO, and that I cannot endanger the entire operation at the last moment. To this day, I have no idea why Jacky and I eventually gave up. We hugged each other before I went into the building. I waved to him with a sad smile on my face and he did likewise.

After me, there were many groups of FPO fighters who left for the Narocz forest and also to Puszcza Rudnicka. Steffi Shanzer, Jacky Pillersdorf and Hillel Seidel were not among them. All three of them were taken to Estonia in a big Aktion during of the liquidation of the ghetto. Hillel and Steffi survived and are in Israel. Jacky perished in the Klooga camp in Estonia.

The Trek to the Narocz Forest

Translated by Selwyn Rose,
Edited by Susan Rosin

In the evening twilight, after we had found our way via the attic of the house bordering Niemiecka Street, we were on the Aryan side of Vilna: Dunka Shapira and I walked arm-in-arm like two lovers, while behind us were the timber-merchant and his daughter. We continued towards the hiding place of the group. After a while, we found them without difficulties, safe and sound but extremely tense and nervous. It is difficult to describe their great joy, even though they had to keep it down but they surrounded us, happily kissing and hugging us. I asked Borka, one of the group to give me his pistol and he did so without any problems. I began to lead the group and after about an hour we were far from Vilna and the city lights had faded in the distance. We sat down in the forest and for the first time in 24 hours felt we could breathe more easily. We distributed what little food we had among the girls who dined on it gratefully and recovered somewhat, and then we continued on our way.

[Page 287]

We knew we had to cross the railroad of the main line between Vilna and Minsk which was most certainly heavily guarded by the Germans. I searched for the easiest way to cross, far away from any station and indeed after many hours of searching, found it. I instructed everyone to remove from their pockets any object that might make a noise to ensure that the guards posted along the tracks would hear nothing as we ran across.

The one person who failed to obey the warning was, as it happens, the second in command – the timber merchant. The moment he started running across the tracks with his daughter a loud noise was heard that froze all of us with fear and dread. It was the rattling sound of tin army mess kit that had been hanging on his belt, had fallen off and rolled on the rails and ballast and in our ears sounded like a thunder. I immediately instructed those who remained with me across the rails to run forward but as soon as we started running gunfire opened from several sources – although fortunately we were far enough away and out of range.

We ran like madmen in the direction of the forest at the side of the track and on into the forest itself until the sound of firing stopped and we found ourselves deep in a swamp that reached almost to our hips. We dared not progress further for fear that it got even deeper – yet neither could we return to where we came from fearing we may not find our way out of the forest. I knew that we were safest in the swamp, hidden by all the tall weeds. Once I was sure that all twenty people were together, we decided to remain where we were until dawn.

When dawn came, we suddenly discovered that the swamp covered only a small area on the edge of a lake on the banks of which stood a single house and anchored close by were two boats. There was a small raised area that was drier. We climbed up there and kept ourselves warm by hugging each other. We were wet, tired and hungry and the morning was bitterly cold. The little girl began to cry and barely stopped all day long. Fortunately, the house on the other side of the lake was far enough away and the sound of her crying didn't carry that far. I found some candies in my pocket and they helped to calm her a bit. Around noon, one of the girls remembered that she had a small vial containing a few drops of valerian. She gave the child a large dose and she fell asleep.

[Page 288]

The undergrowth hid us all quite well and we could not be seen from the house opposite but we could see what was going on around the house and the area. At about 9 o'clock in the morning one of the residents approached one of the boats got in and began rowing in our direction. We were gripped with fear and it was clear that if he got close he could not avoid seeing us, and then – we knew for sure – that would be the end of us.

Fortunately, the young man rowed to the center of the lake and then turned the boat towards the dry area where he moored it, collected some dry wood from the shore and loaded it into the boat. He worked there for a while before returning home with his cargo.

Throughout the whole day, we sat huddled without moving, making sure to keep low so we wouldn't be seen. In the meantime, the sun came out, warmed us up and dried our clothes. At the same time, thirst began to be a problem and one of the men crawled towards the water and filled a small container and passed it round among the group. Drinking was not simple at all, because in order not to swallow the dirt in the murky water, we spread a handkerchief over the container and through it we slowly drank the filtered water. The hours dragged on endlessly until twilight. We decided to skirt the lake on the dry side, but to do so we had to cross a certain area of swamp that separated the island on which we sat, from the dry area we noticed during the day and assumed it continued to the house in front of us.

When darkness fell, we left the island and through the swamp arrived at the dry area. The swamp was not deep but we still got wet above knee level. When we arrived at the dry area I left the group at some distance from the house. With three of the armed men we approached the house, knocked on the door shouting to those inside to open. Our intention was to obtain food and water.

After a few minutes, the door opened. Together with another man, I burst into the room, leaving the remaining two guards outside. The people inside were very frightened and immediately agreed to our demands bringing bread, white cheese, a portion of butter wrapped in cotton and the woman even took some hot potatoes out of the stove and laid them on the table. At that moment I had an idea. I turned to the owner and told him he has to take us to Vilna because we didn't know the way, threatening the family that if they informed the police, their father would never return home; but if they remained silent and kept the secret, he would return towards morning and all will be well. In the meantime, the remainder of the group outside found two large jugs of cream and sour milk. They told the rest of the group to come closer and within minutes all the food was gone. We shared the bread, the butter and the cheese and also the potatoes.

[Page 289]

All that took less than 15 minutes and we were on our way again. When we were about a kilometer from the house I told the farmer not to take us to Vilna but actually to lead us in the opposite direction, adding that no harm would come to him but if he deceived us he would be killed.

To our great surprise, he told us he had seen us that same morning but didn't know whether we were partisans or Jews who had fled the nearby town and he had followed our movements all day long and that now he could see we were partisans. He went on to say he hated the Nazis and will willingly help us escape them and get us to our destination. Nevertheless, I decided he should stay with us all day until nightfall and only then we would release him to go home.

We walked rapidly while I, and one of the men walked with the farmer and the rest of the group trailed along behind. We were in a good mood after a day and night of fear, hunger, and thirst. Hearts were quiet, stomachs full and the hike light and easy.

We walked nearly the whole night without a break. From time to time the farmer stopped for a couple of minutes to make sure that all was in order and so before dawn, we arrived at the forest and settled ourselves on a hill from which we could "control" the surroundings without being surprised by sudden "visitors"; all that with thanks to our farmer who now introduced himself to us as Stefan and a true and serious hater of the Germans. He was even prepared to continue onwards with us for another night but was afraid that if he failed to return home that night there could be a disaster. Eventually, during the afternoon hours we decided to let him go and after talking to him some more I knew exactly where we were and how we were to proceed.

At about 4 in the afternoon, it was time for him to leave us. He said goodbye to us with hugs and heartfelt greetings.

As darkness fell, we began walking. On this night, also, we carried on without stopping and towards morning, we arrived at a village known to me. Before entering the village, I left the group behind sheltering in a forest and went in alone. I arrived at the house of a farmer I knew from "business dealings" I had with him when I was in Bezdonys. He was surprised to see me and thought I was long since dead because he had heard that all the workers of the forced labor camps had been murdered by the Gestapo. I told him that I was with a group of friends that were waiting for me outside the village, making our way to join partisans operating in the Narocz forest. I asked him if he could spare some food for my friends and me. He cut off a few kilograms of smoked meat added two loaves of black bread and a chunk of white cheese. He put it all in a sack, placed it in my hands and afterwards accompanied me to the outskirts of the village parting from me with the blessing: "May G-d preserve you."

[Page 290]

I returned to the group and when they saw the "treasure" I had brought with me, their joy was unbounded. We shared the food among us and decided we would "dine" either in the middle of the night or in the morning, because it was important to get away as far as possible from the village to avoid any trouble.

That night also passed without incident. In that area I was "at home" and towards morning I found an excellent hiding place where we could spend the day. We sat and ate although thirst was a problem especially after eating the salted meat. We had no option other than to suffer since we could not go out in search for water in the forest.

This time we decided to split into three groups, each had a mix of men and women so that we could sleep in shifts: two groups would sleep while the third would be on guard. Thus, the night passed uneventfully.

When darkness fell, we went on our way. Before we started, I spoke with the timber merchant and told him that starting the next day he will have to lead the group because I no longer knew the area. I estimated that we had another two nights of walking ahead of us to reach the Narocz forest. It then became clear to me that I had no one to rely on. He began to cry and told me that he couldn't remember the area at all and had no idea where we were. He begged my forgiveness in tears for deceiving Headquarters and us but that it had been ten years since he was last in the area and he hadn't the slightest idea how to continue telling me that at night he was completely lost. One of the men attacked him and began beating him and I had to separate them. I managed to calm everyone down by telling them that from tomorrow we would revert to our old tactics of the second night, when we got into the swamp.

I chose the two men again who had the appearance of seasoned partisans and we agreed that we would enter a house at the appropriate time. Encouraged by that decision we went on our way.

[Page 291]

That night everything went wrong. First of all, we were "accompanied" by pouring rain all night long that made walking difficult even within the forest. The mud stuck to our boots and our feet sank into the soft ground. In the middle of the night, a ferocious thunder storm began. It was difficult to continue because we couldn't see what lay ahead of us. In spite of the storm we continued walking. I knew that somewhere in the vicinity was a police station of sorts, always manned by German soldiers. There was no way we could allow ourselves to fall into their hands or we would be lost. Soon we heard through the thunder the barking of dogs but it was difficult to discover how far away they were. We stopped and I sent two men forward to scout out the area. A few minutes later, they returned and told us we were right next to a large village. We decided to take a large curve around the village. It was not an easy task but we had no other option because entering an unknown village was unthinkably dangerous. German units might be there, like the "Todt"[7] or even the Gestapo.

In the meantime the rain had lessened somewhat and we managed to proceed a little quicker. We arrived at the edge of the forest and saw before us open fields and over to the right edge were the last of the village houses. We had to run across the fields – a distance of more than a kilometer. Unfortunately, the fields had just been plowed and we found ourselves in deep mud. Not only was it impossible to run, it was even difficult just to walk because our boots simply got covered with kilograms of mud. We sent the girls on in front and we followed behind so that we could always be there to pull them out of the mud. Eventually we got to the edge of the forest on the other side of the fields, exhausted and at the last reserves of our strength. In the meantime, the rain had strengthened again. Luckily, no one in the village had discovered us and even the dogs had stopped barking.

We sat down in the forest and tried to remove the kilograms of mud that had stuck to us. After about an hour, we started to walk again. We were very tired and wet and just before dawn we found an ideal place: a barn full of hay. We knew we were close to a swamp because usually in these areas, the farmers built their barns next to marshlands and it was a sign that we were not close to a settlement. We went into the barn and buried ourselves in the hay to help ourselves get dry. I told everyone not to fall asleep because wet straw produced intoxicating gases that deaden the senses. (I learned that from the farmers I knew). I set an efficient guard up until daylight. In the morning dry but hungry, we settled down in the attic of the barn that had a small window through which we could see the outside area and everything that happened in the surroundings.

[Page 292]

During the day, we saw some people picking crops and understood that we might be close to a small settlement or village or maybe just a few homes in the area. I favored the last assumption because there were only few adults in the fields.

We waited until it was completely dark and only then did we leave the barn and began walking in the direction that the people had come from during the day. After about half an hour, we came across an isolated house. I left the rest of the group some distance from the house and together with those same two men from before, we approached the dilapidated house. We knocked on the door and the window at the same time telling the occupants to open the door. The door opened immediately. "We are partisans" I shouted and I entered a large shabby room where I saw five or six people spread out on the floor lying on mattresses.

In spite of the fact that we were all hungry, not having eaten a thing for two days, I couldn't bring myself to demand anything from them but I ordered the oldest one to get dressed and come with us. I said loudly that he was going to take us to the village close by where we stayed the previous night.

The man slowly got dressed and the women began to cry. I told them not to be afraid because the man would return that same night after he had shown us most of the way. As on the first occasion, I warned them that if they told the police or the Germans the man would die and their house would be burnt. My words didn't help and the women continued to cry. We left the house and told the man to lead us. As before, after we had gone about a kilometer, we ordered him to reverse course and take us in the opposite direction. When I asked him if there were Germans in the area he answered that the same morning, the Germans had burned an entire village after they had confiscated a herd of cows, the horses and all the food they could find. The farmers dispersed throughout the swamp area before the Germans had arrived taking with them all that they could manage to carry from their homes. After a walk of about two hours, we were suddenly attacked with gun-fire from the hills parallel to the road. The man who was with us suddenly began to run and in a moment disappeared. We didn't know who had opened fire on us or where the shots came. We started to run across the fields and in a moment became separated from each other. The gunfire stopped just as suddenly as it had started. We began to quietly to call the names of the group and slowly we all became reunited again. We returned to the main road where we found the farmer lying with a gun-shot to his leg. He was the only one who got hurt. One of the girls bandaged his leg. He told us that most certainly the shots were by partisans because they came from the high ground where there were no houses.

[Page 293]

We asked him if he could walk and he begged us not to leave him because his life would be in danger, from both the Germans but also the partisans who often came to "collect taxes" from the farmers. He also promised he would bring us to a village where he had an acquaintance, who was a contact-man for the partisans in the area.

In spite of hunger and fatigue that we felt, we were happy to hear this information. Two of our people assisted the farmer all the way because of his injury. Another night passed before we arrived in the village and he took us to the contact-man's house on the far side of the village. He knocked on the door calling the name of his friend. When he appeared in the doorway half asleep, our man simply crumpled and collapsed on the threshold and fainted. It was clear to us that he had lost a lot of blood during the walk and using the last of his strength had managed to hold on until he arrived at his friend's house.

The whole house filled with people. The people living there, awakened from their sleep, gave us food and drink, which we did not have for the last 36 hours.

In the meantime our injured guide recovered somewhat and one of the women cleaned and dressed the wound. Towards morning, the contact-man took us out to the swamp, a distance of about 6 kilometers from the village and told us to stay there until evening when he would return to get us. He told us that there was nothing to fear but that the Germans were likely to appear and disturb the neighborhood as had indeed happened the previous day and therefore it was dangerous to walk to the woods in daylight, about 20 kilometers from where we were. That really was a day of rest. At about 4 or 5 in the afternoon, he arrived and told us he had heard that the previous night a group of partisans had attacked a German guard post about 10 kilometers from the village and during the fight two Germans had been wounded.

He brought us food; we ate and then he took us on our way.

Finally with the Partisan

Translated by Susan Rosin

After six nights of wandering we finally arrived at the partisans' encampment. We walked fast, and before dawn we entered into a forest. The guide told us that from this point on we were already in the Partisans' territory and we should continue on our own to reach the base. A short while later we heard voices: "Stop. Do not move" – two partisans with rifles stood before us on two sides of the road. I told them the secret password I received from Abba Kovner. The guards led us immediately into the base and to Wolodka, the commander of the Otriad (a partisan detachment). After I gave him the note from Abba Kovner, we found ourselves in the midst of Vilna people. When they heard about the arrival of the FPO group, they jumped out of their underground clay homes encircled us with hugs and kisses, asked us endless questions, yelling and dancing.

[Page 294]

My old and dear friend Walter Zisser appeared into this pandemonium. He left the ghetto a few weeks before me with a group of FPO members.

[Page 295]

Among them were members of our kibbutz that were arrested by the soviets, but released by the Germans when the ghetto was established. The FPO command decided to send them to the Narocz forest when the first groups started to leave the ghetto.

Not far from Vilna, the group encountered German soldiers who killed two of the members and captured the rest. Walter was the only one who managed to escape. He swam across the Wilia River[8] and after many hardships managed to get to the partisans' base.

For a long while we remained in an embrace, without speaking. Then, we each talked about our escape to the forests. We both had one prayer: May Steffi, Jacky and Hillel and his family join us soon, so we can be together again.

So ended the first period of the holocaust for us, the labor camps and the ghetto and the second period started. This was the time with the Soviet partisans and it was filled with adventure, drama and tragedy. It was a period of armed struggle against the Nazis, but also a serious struggle in the partisan camp itself. It was a struggle against Antisemitism, discrimination against Jews and Jews' hatred by the Soviet partisans.

Translator's Footnotes:

1.   A guide
2.   Abba Kovner (Hebrew: קובנר אבא?; March 14, 1918 – September 25, 1987) was an Israeli poet, writer and partisan leader. In the His attempt to organize a Vilna ghetto uprising failed, but he fled into the forest, became a Soviet partisan, and survived the war. After the war, Kovner led a secretive organization that aimed to take revenge for the Holocaust by killing six million Germans, but he was arrested by the British before he could carry out his plan. He made aliyah in 1947. Considered one of the greatest poets of modern Israel, he received the Israel Prize in 1970.
3.   Fareynikte Partizaner Organizatsye ("United Partisan Organization"; referred to as FPO by its Yiddish initials) was a Jewish resistance organization based in the Vilna Ghetto that organized armed resistance against the Nazis during World War two. The clandestine organization was established by Communist and Zionist partisans. Their leaders were the writer Abba Kovner, Josef Glazman and Yitzhak Wittenberg.
4.   Soviet partisans were active in the Narocz forest from the beginning of 1942. The leader of the first organized partisan group in the area was Fiodor Markow.
5.   Hillel Seidel (Hebrew: הלל זיידל?, 9 October 1920 – 14 February 1999). A member of the Akiva youth movement, he was involved with the anti-Nazi underground movement in the Vilna Ghetto, and headed the underground in the Klooga concentration camp. After World War II he headed the Akiva movement in Poland until 1947, and was a commander of the Berihah movement until the end of 1947. In 1948 he made aliyah to Israel, where he became head of the Immigrant Absorption department of the World Confederation of General Zionists, a post he held until 1952. He also became secretary general of the HaOved HaTzioni movement and a member of the Progressive Party's directorate.
6.   Yechiel (Ilya) Sheinbaum (1914-1943) led the Second Fighting Organization in the Vilna Ghetto.
7.   "Todt" – named for its founder, was a non-military Nazi organization eventually responsible for organized forced slave labor
8.   The river Neris, (Viliya (Belarusian) or (Polish: Wilia)) rises in northern Belarus. It flows westward, passing through Vilnius (Lithuania's capital) and in the south-center of that country it flows into the Nemunas (Neman), at Kaunas, as its main tributary. Its length is 510 km (320 mi).

[Page 296] Blank [Page 297]

<u>Personalities and Characters</u>

[Page 298] Blank [page 299]

Translated by Sara Mages

Rise up, O well, from the source of our childhood you were honored, rise up from the depths of longing, come back and reveal all our robbed melodies - the virtues of mercy and kindness; the Jewish grief. Its restrained and melancholy joy, with the anxiety of the Diaspora which rises and sets. Come back and instill in us the emotion of our ancestors' wise heart, the righteous and hard workers. For our souls have not ceased to aspire all their precious virtues. We wanted to go back and feel all the kindness and all the gifted minds - the flavor of your elders with the rage of your youth, and the dream of your innocent children. Rise up, O well, and reveal, thanks to you our thirst was quenched, we call on you with all our might.

[Page 300]

HaRav R' Yitzchak HaLevi Steinberg z"l
(Lines to his character)

by Moshe HaLevi Steinberg, Rabbi of Kiryat Yam

Translated by Sara Mages

With a trembling hand I approach to draw in general lines the wonderful and rare character of my master, my honored father and rabbi z"l, to describe his distinguished personality, for my father z"l was great not only in Torah and wisdom, but also in his exalted virtues, his charming manners and deeds.

HaRav R' Yitzchak HaLevi Steinberg
Chief Rabbi of the community of Jaroslaw until the
outbreak of the war

My father z"l was born on 21 Tevet 5647 [17 January, 1887] in the city of Tarnow in Galicia, to his father HaRav HaGaon R' Shmaya z"l president of the court of the community of Przemyslany [Peremyshlyany] , and to his mother Sara daughter of the Hasidic rabbi, R' Moshe Wechsler. Even as a child he became famous as a "prodigy" in his quick perception, his memory and common sense, especially in his unceasing perseverance in the study of the Torah. At his Bar Mitzvah meal he preached in Halakhah[1] and Aggadah[2] as a distinct scholar, and even knew how to orally recite the entire Tractate Shabbat[3].

When he was seventeen he was ordained for teaching by the genius of that generation, "The Maharsham" of Brezhan[4]. During this period he had in his possession a handwritten essay on Tractate Makkot[5], and because of his modesty he did not publish it even though all the great Torah scholars, who saw the manuscript, praised it exceedingly. After he got married at the age of nineteen he settled down in Brody and studied with his genius grandfather, R' Avraham Pinchas z"l, the Rabbi of Sniatyn [Snyatyn] and later in Brody, and became famous in the rabbinical world as a great Torah scholar. When he was a twenty two year old married yeshiva student, he was ordained to teaching by the Gaon, Rabbi Meir Arik z"l.

[Page 301]

With the outbreak of the First World War he moved together with his father, grandfather and the whole family to the city of Vienna, and when the battles were over was accepted as rabbi in the city of Halych near Stanisławów [Ivano-Frankivsk], and in 5682 [1922] was appointed Rabbi of the large and important Jewish city of Jaroslaw and served there in splendor until its destruction. As the Rabbi of Jaroslaw he took a place in the front row of the great rabbis of Galicia. He acted a lot as a chairman of *Kupat Gemilut Hasadim* [Interest-Free Loan Fund] and for the Jewish soldiers who served in Jaroslaw.

In 5687 [1926], he was offered to take on himself the rabbinical chair of the city of Radom. After expressing his consent he changed his mind because he learned about the conflicts and quarrels within the community there. When the position of Rabbi of Lvov (Lemberg) became available, my father z"l was a serious candidate and almost all parties and factors agreed to that, but, in the meantime, the Second World War broke out and everything came to naught.

With the outbreak of the Second World War he was exiled with the Diaspora to the forests of Siberia, and went through many adventures and troubles, especially the illness and death of his son, Binyamin Zev z"l, whose soul was bound with his soul.

Even in those difficult times, cut off from the entire outside world, he found peace of mind in studying the Torah orally. While hiking in wild forests he thought about the Torah. He even put his innovations in writing, which became a high-quality and wise essay. And everything without a book, with extraordinary accuracy he quoted every page and column in the Bavli Talmud and Yerushalmi Talmud. However, for fear of the men of the NKVD, he burnt all of his manuscripts. Until the Holocaust he had many important manuscripts in Halakhah and Aggadah, and especially an entire book on the laws of mezuzah by the name, *Shaare Zedek*, and everything was lost from the world during the Holocaust.

After the Holocaust he was a rabbi and president of the court in Brussels, the capital city of Belgium. In the few years he served there as a rabbi he reorganized the spiritual and religious life, founded a Jewish school, took care of the *mikveh*, the synagogue and more. Thanks to his dedicated work in all fields, the community life in Brussels began to develop in the desired direction.

In 5711 [1951], he was invited by the Chief Rabbi, Maran[6] HaRav R' Y. Herzog, the Minister of Religions HaRav Maimon z"l, and the Chief Rabbi of Tel-Aviv Maran Rabbi Isser Yehudah Unterman z"l, to take on the role of President of Tel-Aviv-Yafo Regional Rabbinical Court. All the pleas of the members of the community in Brussels were to no avail, for his strong desire was to live in the Holy Land. After retiring he served as Rabbi of Yeshuron Synagogue in Tel-Aviv. There, he taught Torah to the masses, preached morality and guided the worshipers to Torah and reverence. In addition to his extensive knowledge of various fields of wisdom and science, he knew foreign languages, and in particular excelled in the Polish language. He often sanctified the name of Israel in public in his speeches in this language. As a gracious speaker he was even suggested by the Union of Jewish Political Parties in Poland to be nominated as a delegate to the Polish Sejm.

[Page 302]

In the morning of 27 Marheshvan 5727 [10 November 1966], he returned his pure soul to his Creator.

A father, grandfather, a dedicated husband and a first-class religious figure, a public activist, a classic figure of a Jewish rabbi and judge with charitable qualities, precious and unforgettable soul.

May his memory be blessed for the life of the world to come, and he will be a good advocate for us and for all the Jewish people.

Translator's Footnotes:

1. Halakhah - the collective body of Jewish religious laws derived from the written and Oral Torah.
2. Aggadah - a legend, parable, or anecdote used to illustrate a point of the Law in the Talmud.
3. Tractate Shabbat deals with the laws and practices regarding observing the Jewish Sabbath.
4. "The Maharsham of Brezhan [Berezhany] - Rabbi Shalom Mordechai HaCohen Schwadron.
5. Tractate Makot ["lashes"] deals primarily with laws of the Jewish courts and the punishments which they may administer.
6. Maran - an honorific title for exceptionally respected rabbis who are considered influential teachers and leaders.

HaRav My Father,
Dr. Yitzhak Rabinowitz

by Arye Rabinowitz

Translated by Sara Mages

My father, Dr. Yitzhak Rabinowitz, was born in 1881, and during his high school and academic studies he was already active in the Zionist movement.

His activity during this period was reflected in the organization of Zionist classes among the students in the cities of Tarnow, Krakow and Jaroslaw. In 1909, my father was registered in the Golden Book of Keren Kayemet LeYisrael [JNF] by the Association of Zionist Academics. For decades he headed the Zionist movement in Jaroslaw, was a member of the district and national leadership of the movement, and the driving force of all the Zionist activity in our city. He headed all the important Zionist enterprises such as Keren Kayemet LeYisrael, Keren Hayesod [UIA] etc. He participated in several Zionist Congresses, and the last he attended was the Zionist Congress in Prague. He initiated the establishment of a Jewish elementary and high school in Jaroslaw, and headed this important enterprise until the day of his death. He was the chairman of the local Zionist Committee in Jaroslaw.

In addition to the above Zionist activity, he represented the Jewish population in Jaroslaw in many public institutions, was a member of the City Council, etc.

[Page 303]

Lines to the character
of the author Eisik Schealtiel Graeber

Translated by Sara Mages

Eisik Schealtiel Graeber, who was a veteran of the National Movement in Galicia, was born in Jaroslaw in 1856. He started to write popular articles in [the newspapers] *Ivri Anochi*[1], *Yehudi, ha-Boker Or*, and *Ha-Tsfira*[2]. In 1879, he published in Przemyśl, together with Avigdor Mermelstein, a Hebrew bi-weekly, "The one who loves his people and his homeland," in the spirit of assimilation and rapprochement with the Polish people. Only 13 issues were published. In 1887, he published a collection of Jewish literature and science *Otzar Hasifrut*[3], from which volume one was published in Przemyśl, and volumes two-six in Krakow (1888-1902). Eisik Schealtiel Graeber also published the book *Yesodei ha-Torah*[4] by Samuel David Luzzatto[5] (Lvov 1881), and his letters in nine volumes (Krakow 1882-1894), *Peninei Shadal*[6] (1880).

Eisik Schealtiel Graeber was among the leaders of the *maskilim*[7] circle in Przemyśl. Under his influence, the *maskilim* of Przemyśl tended to national recognition and were drawn to the doctrines of Samuel David Luzzatto. At the initiative of E.S. Graeber and Heinrich Messner, the youth association, "Seekers of Torah and knowledge for the purpose of disseminating the Hebrew language and literature among Jewish youth," was founded in Przemyśl in the 1870s.

The history of the Zionist Movement in Galicia
Volume one, pages. 65-66

Translator's Footnotes:

1. *Ivri Anochi* - I'm a Jew; *Yehudi - Jew; ha-Boker Or* - The Morning light.
2. *Ha-Tsfira* - The Epoch - was a Hebrew-language newspaper published in Poland.
3. *Otzar Hasifrut* - The Treasure of Literature.
4. *Yesodei ha-Torah* - The Foundations of the Torah.
5. Samuel David Luzzatto, also known as Shadal, was an Italian scholar, poet, philosopher and Biblical commentator.
6. *Peninei Shedal* (The Pearls of Samuel David Luzzatto) is a collection of 89 of Luzzatto's letters.
7. *Maskil* (pl. *maskilim*) - followers of the *Haskalah* (Jewish Enlightenment) Movement.

Steinbock

by Moshe Kalchheim, Jerusalem

Translated by Sara Mages

Steinbock was a well known figure in our city. He arrived in Jaroslaw before the First World War immediately after he married his fiancée. At that time he was still an orthodox Jew and accordingly he wore a long black coat and a *shtreimel*[1] on the Shabbat, and prayed in the Hassidic Synagogue. Over time he changed his cloths, and a rumor circulated among the city's Hassidim that Steinbock was "caught up in" Zionism. It goes without saying, that this change in his worldview was not liked among the Hassidim. In 1920, Steinbock's relative, Yisrael Taub from Dębica, was already a completely committed Zionist and immigrated to Eretz-Yisrael as a *halutz* [pioneer]. He worked as a laborer in Rishon LeZion Winery, but under the pressure of his parents he was forced to return to Poland. The influence of this relative on Steinbock was probably decisive.

[Page 304]

At the beginning of 1926, I immigrated to Israel as a *halutz*. My mother, whom I left in Jaroslaw, was a woman caring for children and, from the day I left Jaroslaw, Steinbock was a father and a patron to my mother. Steinbock was a man of charitable virtues, listened and helped the needy with all the hardships of the day. That period was the period of "Grabski[2]," when many Jews were deprived of their positions by the imposition of high taxes. At that time, Steinbock helped many Jews and in return for the help he rendered them he asked for nothing. At most, he asked for a modest contribution to Keren Kaymet LeYisrael[3]. He himself excelled in his contributions to Keren Kaymet LeYisrael, and in his work, in the redemption of the land from the Arabs, he saw the redemption of Israel.

Wolf Steinbock

Steinbock did not ask for publicity and stayed away from honorary positions. He was a humble and hard-working man. He had a sharp eye and was smart and intelligent. He did not talk much. Steinbock had two loves: one for the Eretz Yisrael and the other for the Jews, and both were bound and attached to his soul.

Steinbock personally helped in the migration of our townspeople to Eretz Yisrael, and he himself was not able to immigrate to Eretz Yisrael. The man was too busy helping others, the unfortunate in his environment, to think about himself. He passed away in Jaroslaw before the war.

Translator's Footnotes:

1. *Shtreimel* is a fur hat that Hasidic Jewish men wear on the Shabbat, Jewish holidays, and other festivities.
2. Władysław Dominik Grabski was a Polish National Democratic politician, economist and historian.
3. Keren Kaymet LeYisrael - the Jewish National Fund.

R' Shimon Spiegel

by Moshe Kalchheim, Jerusalem

Translated by Sara Mages

(Was born in Zhovkva on Rosh Chodesh Shevat 5632 [1872] - passed away in Haifa on Rosh Hashanah 5698 [1937])

R' Shimon Spiegel was a native of Zhovkva, the city of HaGaon Maharatz Chajes[1], and the sage and philosopher, Nachman Krochmal, writer of the book *Moreh Nebukhe ha-Zeman*[2].

R' Shimon Spiegel studied in Beit HaMidrash, and at the age of eighteen began his path in public life. Among his first words in print was the article about the society, *Ohavei Torah* [Lovers of Torah], in the newspaper *Ruach HaZman* [The Spirit of Time], edited by Reuben Asher Braudes and published in Lvov in 5650 [1890].

He saw in the study of the Torah the moral foundation for the existence of the people. He complained, that the young Jewish men were leaving the source of the Torah, will follow nonsense and get hurt. He fought the Haskalah[3] which, according to his words, corrupt the vineyard of the Jewish people and sees the light in the gentiles (Hazal[4] said about the translation of the seventy[5]: "Darkness fell on the world for three days. R' Yochanan ben Zakkai saved the people from the two lions by the establishment of Yavneh and its sages, and we will follow his light").

[Page 305]

At the same time, R' Shimon published a poem for the "Holiday of Shavuot" in the *Yiddishe Tzeitung* [Yiddish Newspaper] of the publisher H. Rohatyn from Lemberg [Lvov]. And here is an excerpt from this poem:

"Raise your voice Yeshurun[6], the law of fire was given to you, your face will shine like the dawn, Torah from the heavens is your portion, it will support you with a strong arm, with an outstretched arm and love we accepted it, it is very dignified, sevenfold refined. From a garland on the forehead it will receive respect and prestige.

After he got married to his fiancée, he moved to Tarnow where he stayed for about a year, and in 5665 [1905] settled in Jaroslaw. He had three sons: the eldest - Shalom Spiegel, who serves today as a professor in the Seminary named after Schechter in New-York, and lectures on medieval poetry. He published scientific books and articles. He graduated from high school in Jaroslaw (he was exempt from writing and visiting on Saturdays and holidays). He studied philosophy in Vienna and at the Schwartz's Rabbinical Seminary and gained a reputation as a scholar of medieval *piyyutim* [liturgical poems]. Shimon Spiegel's second son is Shmuel, a famous Hollywood film producer who won Oscars for the movie "The Caine Mutiny" and others. The third son passed away at a young age, when he was a high school student.

Spiegel's home was known as a religious Zionist home and the sons learned Hebrew from a young age. R' Shimon Spiegel was the first member of "Mizrahi",[7] and members of "Tzeirei HaMizrahi" gathered around him. R' Shimon was a learned man, was among the worshipers of the Ashkenazi Beit Midrash and gave lessons in the Midrash to homeowners. His heart was in the east and all his days he aspired to immigrate to Israel. He took care of the education of the younger generation. Every Zionist emissary, and preacher, stayed at his home. HaRav Mimon z"l visited him several times, and with his help managed to do good work for "Mizrahi" in Jaroslaw.

In 5684 [1924], R' Shimon Spiegel purchased a lot in Hadar HaCarmel [Haifa], and in 5685 built a house for his professor son, Shalom Spiegel, where he lived until 5690 [1930].

In 5696 [1936], R' Shimon Spiegel and his wife immigrated to Israel and lived in Haifa. In this manner R' Shimon was able to fulfill his life dream. In 5697 [1936], he fell ill and his health deteriorated. R' Shimon Spiegel was a devout Jew and was careful with a light commandment as with a grave one. I visited him almost every day. We were connected to the "Mizrahi" idea and he saw in it the future of the nation.

[Page 306]

On the day of his death, on Rosh Hashanah, his son, may he live a long and good life, sat and studied the Gemara. The son said to me: "His time has come to pass away and leave his wife and sons."

R' Shimon Spiegel was buried on the second day of Rosh Hashanah in the Old Haifa Cemetery.

Translator's Footnotes:

1. HaGaon Maharatz - the genius Rabbi, Zvi Hirsch Chajes, one of the foremost Galician Talmudic scholars.
2. *Moreh Nebukhe ha-Zeman* - "Guide for the Perplexed of Our Time."
3. Haskalah - The Jewish Enlightenment - was an ideological and social movement that developed in Eastern Europe in the early nineteenth century.
4. Ḥazal - Hebrew acronym for "Ḥakhameinu Zikhronam Liv'rakha" ("Our Sages, may their memory be blessed"), refers to all Jewish sages of the Mishna, Tosefta and Talmud eras.
5. The Septuagint is the oldest Greek translation of the Old Testament, so called because it was believed to be the work of seventy (or rather of seventy-two) Jewish translators.
6. Yeshurun is a poetic name for the Jewish people.
7. "Mizrahi"- a religious Zionist organization founded in 1902 in Vilnius. "Tzeirei HaMizrahi" was an organization of young "Mizrahi" members founded in Poland in 1918.

[Page 306]

Chelimer the Teacher

by Moshe Kalchheim

Translated by Sara Mages

The teacher Chelimer was our neighbor and three of his five children were my good friends and belonged, together with me, to the "Akiva" movement. I often visited their home and, although we lived in two separate houses, the walls of our houses were shared and, that too, brought us closer acoustically.

"The teacher Chelimer" - so we called him - was short, chubby, with a nice and interesting face. His facial features were very similar to that of Y.L. Peretz, as we knew him from the pictures, the same face, the same forelock, and the same mustache in which many gray hairs were scattered.

He most likely arrived in our city after the First World War, and served as the first Hebrew teacher of the Zionist youth. In his school, which was housed in a nice hall in the building of *Yad Ḥarutzim*, they studied "Hebrew in Hebrew,"[1] and those, who went down the stairs opposite Hala Targowa ["Market Hall"], could easily peek through the large window into the classroom, which bothered the teacher and students quite a bit. Anyone, who seriously wanted to study, and knew proper Hebrew, had to study with Chelimer the teacher.

He was an educated man and an "opponent" [of Hassidut], while most of the Jews in our city were "Hassidim." Maybe that's why Chelimer was on the fringe of society.

Chelimer was an excellent teacher, but it was not easy to earn a living from teaching alone. And Chelimer, in principle, refrained from engaging in occupations other than the teaching of the Hebrew language. Therefore, he, and his family, often knew great distress. Nevertheless - all his sons were educated in high school, but they had to work to pay their tuition.

[Page 307]

Over time, Chelimer became indignant and critical of the Zionist institutions for not properly supporting the Hebrew school. He was mainly critical of the lack of education of the Zionist leaders, and of the intellectual shallowness that prevailed in the Zionist movement. He distanced himself from any political party, or public activity, and devoted his time to teaching the Hebrew language to teenagers and adults. He was isolated and was not involved with people. He had no friends. On my visits to his home, I have always seen him immersed in reading and writing. It seems to me that he did not feel the need for social life.

Although the children spoke Polish to each other, everyone at home spoke only Hebrew, and they all also had Biblical Hebrew names: Arye (Arik), Shulamit, Yochevd, and Gideon.

The whole family perished in the Holocaust.

Yochevd, the youngest sister and a good friend of mine from the "Akiva" movement, a talented and intelligent girl, tragically passed away at the prime of her life when she was only twenty years old. Her death hit us hard to the depths of our hearts, and her sudden departure caused us all a severe and unforgettable shock.

Translator's Footnotes:

    1. "Hebrew in Hebrew" was a method of teaching Hebrew. Its principles were: natural learning close to the way a mother tongue is learned.

R' David Rapp,
ritual slaughterer from Jaroslaw

by Moshe Kalchheim

Translated by Sara Mages

R' David Rapp was born in the year 5630 [1869] in the town of Shchyrets near Lvov, to his father the righteous Hassid, R' Ori zt"l, who was a student of the great and honorable man, the glory of the generation, Rabbi Yosef Shaul Nathansohn, the Rabbi of the metropolis of Lvov. R' David was the student of the famous genius, R' Aba'le Shainblum, the Rabbi of Shchyrets, and he, R' Aba'le, was the son of R' Wawtz'e Shainblum, student of the Seraph of Strelisk[1] [Strelisker]. From his youth he was found to be genius and sharp, and studied day and night until he started to study with the aforementioned, R' Aba'le, at the age of twenty three. After he devoured knowledge in the Six Orders of the Mishnah and Poskim[2], *Rishonim*[3] and *Acharonim*[4], he settled as a ritual slaughterer in Jaroslaw after his marriage to the daughter of the local ritual slaughterer, R' Moshe Frenkel.

From his youth, while he was studying in Beit HaMidrash, dozens and hundreds of students came early in the morning to his doorstep to enjoy his sermons, sayings and innovations. He taught Torah in public, and educated an exemplary generation of devoted scholars who adhered with devotion to the commandments of the Creator. Dozens, of young men from the town and the surrounding area, flocked to hear the young genius, to prepare for the yoke of *mitzvoth* or their marriage ties. They "snatched" his sermons, and attributed his sayings for themselves as achievements they have obtained illegally, and used them in sermons as was customary in those days for the grooms on their wedding day.

[Page 308]

R' David Rapp was not involved in matters of this world, walked in his way of life as if his head was in the heavens, immersed in his thoughts and innovations in the Torah, until one interesting fact may describe his character and the personality of the man. When in the First World War the Russians approached the town, and the whole community was forced to leave the place where they had lived for a long time, and wander afar, his family suddenly felt that R' David had disappeared. After careful searches they retraced their steps a few miles back, and found him sitting on a hill with his eyes closed and engrossed in thoughts, and when they awoke him from his visions and called in his direction, " here, the Russian cannons are roaring and thundering towards us and are already approaching you, and what do you have here that you are sitting still," he woke up a little, blinked his eyes, and replied with a slight smile on his lips: "with God's help an acute problem in Rambam[5] became clear to me, and thanks to his teachings he opened my eyes in this matter."

Even during the war in the Czech Diaspora, he taught Torah in public, and prayed with its greatest, who shared the fate of war refugees. After he returned to his town, Jaroslaw, where he served as a ritual slaughterer until the outbreak of the terrible Holocaust, the number of his admirers and followers grew, and his thoughts spread a great light into the distance.

He was privileged to see a righteous generation follow in his footsteps, his two sons: R' Moshe who passed away at the outbreak of the war in Katowice, and may he live a long and good life, R' Shimon the ritual slaughterer, who now lives in the United States. When the gallows fell on the Jewish people during on the terrible Holocaust, he was also killed by the Nazi murderers, and his last known place was in Lemberg [Lvov].

May his soul be bound in the bond of life.

Translator's Footnotes:

1. R' Uri ben Pinhas of Strelisk, was called the Seraph [the burning angel] for his style of prayer, full of fire, extraordinary fervor and enthusiasm.
2. *Posek* (pl. *poskim*) is the term in Jewish law for a "decisor" - a legal scholar who determines the position of Halakha – the Jewish religious laws.
3. *Rishonim* (lit. "First ones") were the leading rabbis and poskim who lived approximately during the 11th to 15th centuries.
4. *Acharonim* (lit. "Last ones") are the leading rabbis and poskim living from roughly the 16th century to the present.
5. Rabbi Moshe ben Maimon, also referred to by the Hebrew acronym, Rambam, was a medieval Sephardic Jewish philosopher.

[Page 309]

Reb Sender Amster
(The Soul Catcher)

by Moshe Kalchheim

Translated from Yiddish by Pamela Russ

[ ] translator's remarks

The Jewish town lies in devastation, and under the ruins are buried not only our nearest and dearest, but also the former Jewish life of the town and its varied, richly colorful and personalities of businessmen, community activists, unemployed, *chassidim*, *mitnagdim* [opposition to *chassidim*], and all other categories in the Jewish social life.

This town will never be revived from the dead. May these personalities of the fallen Jewish town be a memory and an honor for those who will never rise again.

* * *

Reb Sender Amster was a familiar figure in our town. He was a Belzer *chassid* [follower of the Belzer Rebbe]. This already said a lot, because a Belzer *chassid* was a fiery, fanatic "extremist," who was disconnected from the surrounding world, and had only one ideal: "his Rebbe."

But Reb Sender was different from all the others. Even as a fanatic, he was more freed from this world than the other *chassidim*, so people had great respect and high regard for him, and … also fear [of him].

First, he was different in his outer appearance from the other *chassidim*, as he was always clean and finely dressed. Both on Shabbat and during the weekdays, he wore an impeccably clean overcoat, black, soft slippers and white stockings, which peeked out from under his frock.

When in the street, he attracted all the eyes of those who passed him by, both non-Jews and Jews who were strangers and saw him for the first time. The first glance was to his holy face, which was always bedecked with a clean, well-combed long beard, which was at one time black but became whiter and whiter. His face was framed by two rounded, curled, long *peyos* [sidelocks], which, as he walked quickly (Reb Sender never strolled slowly) raised themselves and shook rhythmically to the pace of his steps.

[Page 310]

And his eyes!

Two black eyes, deeply sunken into his face, as they looked at you half fanatically, half despotically, and for which you had both awe and respect.

He was called "Reb Sender" even when he was single, because he got married, in his forties. He had no worries about earning a livelihood, not before nor after his marriage. Before his wedding, he was a "father's child," who sat for months and years at the Belzer Rebbe's court, bathed in *chassidic dveykut*[deeply closeness to God], ate leftovers [from the Rebbe] and [dribbles] of soup, and then after his wedding … nothing changed. He left livelihood concerns for his wife, and he continued to run his life as before.

Every morning, Reb Sender would rush to the ritual bath, dip into the waters, come home, grab a drink, and go off to the Belzer *shteibel*. He stayed there until noon. He looked into a *sefer* [religious textbook] just for a bit (he was not a great scholar), studied Talmud, waited through several *minyanim* [prayer groups] to finish, during which time he helped the children with their prayers, translating letter after letter of the prayers for them, which gave him great pleasure. Before he himself began his own prayers, he had already recited several *kaddishes* [mourner's prayer recited by others] and *brachot* [recited by all during prayers], and two or three times the prayer of *asher yatzar* [recited after using the washroom]. Keeping the body pure was very important to him, and so during prayers he would leave the room several times in order that no impurity should remain on his body.

Understandably, he actually prayed with the last *minyan* [quorum of men for prayers], and many times on his own. During this time, the school children would already come into the *shteibel* (which served as the *cheder* [school for young children]), and then Reb Sender would tell them of the miracles of the Rebbe, and … create new souls for Belz, meaning that he would produce fresh, young *chassidim* for the Belzer Rebbe.

There were all kinds of *chassidim* in the town: Titchinner (from the town of Tyczyn), Blazhever (from the town of B³a¿owa), Chortkover (from the town of Czortków), Boyaner (from the town of Boyan), Kamarner, and others. But to grab young souls, the Belzers had a master

[Page 311]

When he caught a young soul, he bothered and pestered him until he got what he wanted:

One fine day, a young boy disappeared from home. Reb Sender had "kidnapped" him and taken him to Belz.

The parents created scandals, made uproars in the Belzer *shteibel* and in Reb Sender's home, and finally, with no other choice, they removed themselves from their business, and went to Belz [the town] itself, and dragged home the boy by his ears.

And Reb Sender?

The cries, uproars, and scandals of the parents bothered him like last year's snow, and at his next opportunity, he would snatch up another soul, and take him to the Belzer courtyard.

Understandably, all these young boys who were under his influence were not permitted to go to "school."

That means – Reb Sender would preach to them - you'll have to sit there with your heads uncovered [against Jewish law], God forbid, and even more so, you'll sit in front of "*Yoizel*" [Jesus] who is hanging on the wall? Remember, do not let them convert you!

Sometimes, though, it would happen that his words had no effect, and a Yankele or Moshele would go to school. Then Reb Sender would create all kinds of blackmail methods so that the boy would not be able to go the evil *Tarbut* school [Hebrew secular school]. This actually happened to me, when my mother and mainly my oldest sister decided that I had to go to school. I was already a school-aged boy at that time, and it was natural that I would become a student in school. But the problem was that Reb Sender had one of his agents in our home, and that was my oldest brother, he himself an avid Belzer *chassid*. Reb Sender incited him to take away my shoes and books and hide them so that I would not have nothing to wear to class.

[Page 312]

In the end, my mother and sisters relented. After two or three days of arguments in the home, I was given back my shoes, but I had to resign from any "worldly" education.

Only two years later, when my brother left the house, I went to study in class, after I had prepared privately for the exam for third grade.

Reb Sender already had no control over me.

In the final years before the war, his influence on the young children was limited. He also became more reserved and introverted, but his beautiful face, above everything else, still impressed everyone who met him in the street or in the Belzer *shteibel*.

Also, it is worthwhile to mention that the Belzer *shteibel* was in the large courtyard of the *Hachnasat Orchim* [accommodations for guest] synagogue, which was on Sobieski Street, not far from the church. The *shteibel* was at the very edge of the large courtyard, and was actually no larger than a small room, where several minyanim [groups of 10 men] of Belzer *chassidim*, prayed.

I very likely came there under the influence of my older brother Mendel.

[Page 313]

From among the Belzer *chassidim* – those who prayed in the Belzer *shteibel*, I remember these businessmen: Szlatiner, Jakter (his son lives in Israel today).

The Life and Public Service
of Dr. Moshe (Maurycy) Rager

by Ziva Korn (Rager)

Translated by Sara Mages

Dr. Maurycy Rager

Dr. Moshe (Maurycy) Rager was born in Jaroslaw, Poland in 1887. His origin is from a warm Zionist home. His father was one of the most prominent public activists in *Yad Harutzim*.

His mother came from the family of Dr. Gershon Zipper, chairman of the Zionist Executive in Lvov and one of the founders of Rehavia Gymnasium in Jerusalem. The son, Moshe, absorbed in his home his love for Zionism, Israel and to fellow-man. He studied law at the University of Lvov, and as a student he was involved in public life and belonged to the Zionist Students' Association "Bar Kokhba." After completing his law studies he returned to his city, Jaroslaw, and worked as a lawyer. He was famous as one of the accepted lawyers in his city. Along with his day-to-day pursuits he has acted extensively in all areas of public life. He had a warm Jewish heart and was a loyal Zionist. He was among the founders of the Jewish elementary school in Jaroslaw, and extended his patronage over it and over the Zionist youth movements in the city. He was an avid Zionist, and for many years was chairman of Keren Kayemet LeYisrael [JNF]. As one of the most prominent representatives of Jaroslaw's Jewry, he hosted various Zionist emissaries who came to Jaroslaw, such as Dr. Tohen and others. As a personal friend of Dr. Schwarzbard, he collaborated with him in the Zionist life, and also took an active part in the training of halutzim [pioneers] for immigration to Israel.

[Page 314]

He stayed in the Soviet Union during the Second World War. When he returned from the Soviet Union to Poland, he continued the Zionist activity among the survivors. In 1950 he immigrated to Israel. He was recognized by the management of the Jewish Agency as a veteran Zionist activist and received a pension from the Department of Zionist Activists.

He passed away in 1967.

Aharon Gerblich

by Yakov Gerblich

Translated by Sara Mages

Aharon Shmuel Gerblich was born in 1894 in Sieniawa to a religious Zionist family. He studied in the yeshiva of the Rabbi of Sieniawa, and there he became familiar with the Zionist movement.

When he was a child he learned the Hebrew language and knew it well, he acquired his high school education as an autodidact by correspondence with an institute in Vienna.

After his release from the Austro-Hungarian army at the end of the First World War, he settled in Jaroslaw together with his entire family.

In 1920, two of his sisters and his brother immigrated to Israel. His desire to immigrate was also strong, but his plans changed after his marriage. In Jaroslaw he began to engage in trade, and was also active in the Zionist movement as a member of the committee of Keren Kayemet LeYisrael [JNF], and other Zionist and educational institutions in the city.

[Page 315]

In the 1930s his parents immigrated to Israel in order to join their four children in the country.

Aharon Gerblich

We, his children, also received a Zionist education and were members in the Zionist youth movement.

With the outbreak of the Second World War, we were deported and exiled to Siberia together with the rest of the city's residents. There, he was imprisoned for a period of two years by the Soviet Union authorities and was accused of Zionism.

In 1946, he returned to Poland, to the city of Lubawka in Lower Silesia, and on his own initiative established a Hebrew school there and was the director of the TOZ[1] orphanage.

He also served as chairman of the Jewish Committee and a representative in the city council.

From there, he moved to a refugee camp in Germany and organized there a Hebrew school in which he also taught Hebrew and the Bible.

In 1948, with the establishment of the state, he immigrated to Israel. His son z"l served in the British Army and in the Haganah[2].

When he arrived in Israel he moved to Haifa, and immediately began to work in the Haifa municipality, where he became an address for anyone who needed help. He was among the founders of the Committee of Former Residents of Jaroslaw, and devoted most of his time and energy to this work.

———————

Translator's Footnotes:

1. TOZ - Towarzystwo Ochrony Zdrowia Ludnoci Żydowskiej - Society for Safeguarding the Health of the Jewish Population - was established in Warsaw in 1921.

2. Haganah (lit. The Defense) was the main Zionist paramilitary organization of the Jewish population in Mandatory Palestine between 1920 and its disestablishment in 1948, when it became the core of the Israel Defense Forces.

Shayeh Lang

by Moshe Kalchheim

Translated by Sara Mages

Everyone called him "Member Lang." He was among the founders and activists of "Hapoel HaMizrachi"[1] movement in our city. He devoted his life to the Zionist movement and therefore neglected his family and its livelihood. Even when he stood in his little shop, and when he served his customers, all his thoughts were on public affairs. "Member Lang" was a distinct type of public activist, who knew no compromises in matters of Zionism and the Jewish community. It was impossible to always avoid posing the question "What will the Member Lang say?"

In my time he was already an older man, of average height, a little clumsy, lame on one leg with red hair that fell on his forehead, but his sidelocks and beard were carefully made. And just as it was easy for him to get angry, so it was convenient for him to make excuses. His hand was in everything: in the party, the community, in Kern Kayemet LeYisrael [JNF], in the religious education and social aid. He was among the founders of the Zionist religious school "Yavne," and constantly took care of its existence and development.

[Page 316]

The Zionist and communal landscape of Jaroslaw cannot be described without the "Member Lang." He made a significant contribution to our vibrant Zionist Jewish life, because he believed in the idea and devoted the best years of his life to it without considering that he must also take care of his family's livelihood. His "public service" was the most important part of his life, without it there was no point to his life. It gave him great satisfaction and he believed that this was his main mission. Therefore, he was a man of strife and contention, and did not shy away from struggles.

On the Intermediate Days of Sukkot 5700 (1939), he was exiled together with his family from Jaroslaw to Russia, and there he passed away. The members of the Lang family now live in Israel.

Translator's Footnote:

1. "Hapoel HaMizrachi" (lit. Mizrachi Workers) was a religious pioneering and labor movement in Eretz Yisrael. It was founded in 1922 under the Zionist slogan "Torah va'Avodah" (Torah and Labor).

Berko Winter

by Moshe Kalchheim

Translated by Sara Mages

Berko Winter was three years older than me. In the youth movement, this difference in years is very significant. He was the leader of "Akiva" movement in Jaroslaw and my educator for a number of years.

Berko was a strange young man. He bore the burden of his family: a mother and two sisters older than him. It was an assimilated family and far from Judaism, until the son entered the "Akiva" movement. Very quickly they understood his special character. He was serious and had a desire to delve deeper into things, exceptional friendship and, most importantly, unlimited devotion to the idea.

At the end of the 1920s, when he was a student in the "Blue Gymnasium," he joined the "Zionist Youth" movement. During the split in 1932, with the establishment of the "Akiva" movement, which separated from the "Zionist Youth" due to difference of opinions over Judaism and tradition, he naturally found his place in "Akiva."

The atmosphere at home was difficult and gloomy. His two sisters had long since reached the age of marriage and still lived with their mother. Also the livelihood was not plentiful. And Berko, in addition to his studies at the gymnasium and the activities at "Akiva," had to run around giving lessons to students in order to make a living and support his mother.

In spite of it he did not complain. He accepted everything with love and humility. But he was always thoughtful, always living with the feeling that he had not done enough for his family, the movement and the members.

[Page 317]

He was strange to his friends because he did not resemble the other members. Only once in a long while he laughed with a full mouth and wholeheartedly. He was usually deep in thought, and when he lectured to the members of the battalion, or the group, he would stop his flow of words and be silent for a long time.

On a clear day, Berko Winter became a religious man. He prayed every day, lay *tefillin* and even joined an evening Mishnayot study group in "Kehat Kloyiz" located at the small marketplace.

At that time, he neglected the movement and immersed himself in the search for a lifestyle that bordered on mystery.

With the Nazi occupation we parted ways. He remained in the Lvov area and I made my way to Vilna. Before the mass deportations of Jewish refugees began in the areas of the Soviet occupation, I received some news from him from Lvov. He did not want

to leave his mother and sisters for fear that without him their fate would be bitterer. The last information that reached us in Vilna was the Berko died of starvation, in a small town near Lvov.

Janek Kostman in "HeHalutz"

by Shoshana Kostman

Translated by Sara Mages

This article, about "HeHalutz" Sunday, September 19, 2021[1] movement in our city, is dedicated to my husband, Janek Kostman z"l, who in his life eagerly awaited the publication of the Yizkor Book for our city, Jaroslaw. He himself foresaw the idea of the publication of the Yizkor Book, and also put in writing very interesting things about the movement. However, for some reason, his articles were lost and everything I bring up here comes from the words I heard from him orally. But, I want to point out that I accompanied him all the way in the movement, and was a full partner in the youth experiences in "HeHalutz" movement in our city which conducted a first-class educational and cultural activity.

Since 1922, "HeHalutz" and "Hashomer Hatzair" movements concentrated at the Sobol home. I was very young in those years, and I cannot describe the development of the "HeHalutz" branch in Jaroslaw at that time. I only know from Janek that at that time he was already preparing for productive work values, and began to study carpentry despite the opposition of his parents. As one of the "HeHalutz" counselors, he instructed the young members to realize the pioneering idea: to *aliyah*[2], work, and settlement in Eretz Yisrael. And just as there is no Zionism without *aliyah,* so there is no *aliyah* without *Hakhshara*[3] for *aliyah*. And the meaning of *Hakhshara*: transition to work and acquiring work habits. And work - means, first of all agriculture and all hard physical work.

[Page 318]

Janek Kostman

Among the counselors of "HeHalutz," who were among the first to immigrate to Israel, were: V. Aslowicz, Winnik, Zisha Freifeld, S. Shahar, Stehafel, Steinbock, Laufer, Max Spindel, Rosenfeld, Shoshana Kranz, S. Konigsberg z"l and others.

Janek, my husband, immigrated to Israel in 1930. He settled in Ness Ziona and started to work in agriculture, planting citrus groves and also specialized in citrus packaging. Over time, he became the manager of "Hakal" citrus groves in the south of the country. In the riots of 1936-1939 he was active in the "Haganah"[4] and instructed the members in weapons training. He was bound with all his heart to the building of the country.

With the Declaration of Independence he enlisted in the Israel Defense Forces and participated in battles in the Negev as an officer. At the end of the battles he volunteered to the Civil Defense and received the rank of Major.

When he returned from a tour of the "Hakal" citrus groves, he was attacked by a deserter from the army who fired a number shots and killed several people. Janek was seriously injured. After the injury he never regained his health and, despite his poor health, continued his work with dedication until he was involved in a car accident from which he suffered for many years. His illness did not prevent him from working as a board member of the Organization of Former Residents of Jaroslaw in Israel.

Translator's Footnotes:

1. "HeHalutz" (lit."The Pioneer") was a Jewish youth movement that trained young people for agricultural settlement in Eretz Yisrael.
2. *Aliyah* (lit. "ascent") - immigration to Eretz Yisrael.
3. *Hakhshara* (lit. "Preparation") the process of preparing a person for settlement in Eretz Yisrael based on the Zionist-Socialist ideological basis.
4. Haganah (lit. The Defense) was the main Zionist paramilitary organization of the Jewish population in Mandatory Palestine between 1920 and its disestablishment in 1948, when it became the core of the Israel Defense Force.

[Page 319]

Ziggy Dubshitz

by Moshe Kalchheim

Translated by Sara Mages

Ziggy Dubshitz was a well-known figure in our city due to him being bald. When he was young his hair fell out and he remained completely bald. His baldness "shone" from a distance. His gait was also quite strange. His steps were large and then his body moved like a sail in the wind, back and forth.

In the Zionist circles, young and old, it was known that all his thoughts were given to Keren Kayemet LeYisrael [JNF]. He was the "delegate" of the fund and was fanatically devoted to it without exception. He spurred the youth to action and preached morality to those who had not fulfilled their duty by donating, or collecting for donations from others. And indeed, our city has taken one of the first places in Western Galicia in its contribution for the benefit of Keren Kayemet LeYisrael, although there were cities in which the Jewish population was larger than ours.

Dubshitz was a member of Agudat HaNo'ar HaIvri "Akiva[1]," and was later active in "Bnei Zion" club. He graduated from Commercial High School and became an accountant. He was a member of a well-known Zionist family in our city, which was among the wealthiest in the community (owner of a large fabric store on Sobieskie Street and a large house on the same street). He never knew financial hardship, and despite his young age was involved in every philanthropic activity in the city.

We all appreciated Ziggy Dubshitz for his honesty and innocence, and treated with forgiveness his outbursts that were the result of devotion to the cause and unwillingness to compromise on fundamental matters.

During the war he stayed in the Soviet Union. There, he married a native of Jaroslaw from the Wachtelberg family. He immigrated with his family to Israel, and after the establishment of the state was for many years chief accountant at the "Mekorot"[2] company. He passed away in his place of residence - Givatayim.

Translator's Footnotes:

1. Agudat HaNoar HaIvri "Akiva" - the "Akiva" Union of Jewish Youth - pioneering and scouting Zionist youth movement with special attachment to the traditional values of Judaism.
2. "Mekorot" (lit. "Sources") - the national water company of Israel.

[Page 320]

Yakov Moshe Gilead-Glatt

by Yoel Gilead (Glatt)

Translated by Sara Mages

Yakov Moshe Gilead-Glatt was born in 1913 and passed away at the age of 54.

His father, R' Avraham Glatt, was a wealthy man and his lifestyle was traditional, therefore it was only natural that he was educated in the spirit of Torah and mitzvoth and his main education was Judaic studies. He was not sent to a general school to sit together with the *shkotzim*[1] and without a head covering. But, together with Judaic studies he also studied general subjects with private tutors to prepare for the annual exams. Later, he attended an evening trade school which was almost "Yiddish" in its composition. However, the framework of his life was narrow for him and he threw off his traditional Jewish clothing and became interested in Zionism. Janek, young and energetic, with wide horizons, read a lot and was interested in everything. He felt that he must seek for himself a way of personal life, and also how to identify with the Jewish people. He saw the renaissance of the people in their homeland as the fulfillment of the generations' aspiration for redemption and independence. He joined Betar and was very active in it. He was always on the go, in his lectures and those of others, at conferences, youth camps, summer camps, etc.

Unlike our father z"l, who was a respected member of the Jaroslaw community, a member of various committees and funds, Janek rebelled against the establishment that was represented, among others, by our father, and was an enthusiastic to the Zionist idea. He decided to fulfill his dream, to immigrate to Eretz Yisrael.

The parents' pleas that his place is "at home," in the family business, in financial security and a secure future, did not help. On the contrary - he wanted to convince the parents that, they too, should immigrate to Eretz Yisrael, and that the future of the Jews in Poland and in Europe is no longer safe. He felt the impending Nazi Holocaust.

Despite all his public activity he was a very loyal son. The inevitable contradiction between love for the family, and his strong desire to immigrate to Eretz Yisrael, was resolved in a very painful decision. But, the only possible goal for him: to emigrate. He was sorry for the suffering he was causing his parents, but went his own way.

Janek left for *hakhshara*[2] in Volodymyr-Volynskyi, to difficult living conditions, completely different from his comfortable life at his father's home. At the end of the *hakhshara*, because of his affiliation with the opposition political camp, he waited a long time until he got the coveted certificate[3]. But, finally, Jancze (Janek's name at home) immigrated! When he arrived in Eretz Yisrael he joined a group of workers, and it was not long before he participated in the strike of Betar workers against the unorganized and cheap Arab labor and against their employer, the citrus grower. The police broke the strike and Janek was jailed.

[Page 321]

After serving his detention period in prison, he went through the second severe crisis of his life. He did not challenge the way of his movement and left it. Then, he moved to Haifa.

About two years since his immigration, Hannah, the young woman he met in the *hakhshara* in Poland, joined him and he married her.

Until the outbreak of the Second World War the family lived in far away Jaroslaw, and Janek in Israel hoping to unite. The family was exiled to Russia and the plans for the reunion of the family were postponed to the uncertain future. Janek was happy in Israel, but concern for the fate of his family greatly troubled him. After he finally renewed contact with them, he made every effort, despite his own pressing circumstances, to help.

Slowly, but steadily, Janek progressed in his work. From Haifa he moved to Tel-Mond and from there to Jaffa. Days of happiness came to him when the surviving family members arrived in Israel.

Janek's devotion to his parents, after their arrival in Israel, knew no bounds. He devoted all his free time to them.

With all the happiness of being an Israeli, and that his entire family was in Israel, he did not forget his city - Jaroslaw, that no trace remains in it for the vast Jewish population, the institutions, synagogues, places of culture, etc. He felt great closeness to the people of Jaroslaw, who found refuge in Israel, and to those who scattered in all the countries of the world.

Over the years, until the day of his death, Janek was very active in the Jaroslaw "landsmanshaft." He was always willing to help his townsman, both in the validity of his role and also not in this framework.

The death of our father was very difficult for him and, even more so, the death of our mother a few years later. Until her death, Janek used to devote all his free time, and not so free, to her. He visited our mother three to four times a day. He gave of himself as a son more than can be imagined.

He passed away about a year after the death of our mother in 1967 in Holon.

Translator's Footnotes:

1. *Shegetz* (pl. *shkotzim*) - a non-Jewish boy or youth.
2. *Hakhshara* (lit. "Preparation") the process of preparing a person for settlement in Eretz Yisrael based on the Zionist-Socialist ideological basis.

3. Certificate - the name given to the immigration visa to Eretz Yisrael during the British Mandate. It was divided according to quotas set by the British in negotiations between them and the Zionist administration, based on the regulations of the First White Paper.

[Page 322]

Imek Roschwald

by Haya Ziegel

Translated by Sara Mages

I am afraid, that because of the fog that surrounds my memories many events from the life of Imek Roschwald will also be vague and, therefore, the devaluation of the description of his Zionist activity would be an injustice to this extraordinary man. In any case, it will be easier for me than any another person, since I knew him closely and I can tell about his dedication to public work.

Imek Roschwald

Roschwald was a young man in our city who aroused general attention. He was an influential speaker who knew how to excite his listeners. Therefore, Imek has always been ready for debates and discussions on various topics. He knew how to stick to his opinion with great force and never lacked reasons to contradict the words of his opponent. During his short life he was highly esteemed among the Jewish youth in Jaroslaw. Maybe because of his deep and sincere belief, that indeed, the idea of an independent Jewish state will soon come true. The fact is that Roschwald was an avid Zionist. He acted and preached to everything that had to do with the Zionist idea. He has done his best to gain fans for the Zionist and "Hashomer Hatzair" movements, and spared no effort to recruit his friends from the gymnasium to our movement. His personality, and his intelligence, enabled him to more easily convince the intellectual youth, even the narrow-minded and snobbish by nature that they can only live a cultural and spiritual life within the movement. Imek was aware of all the most important social problems. He collaborated in the cultural field with "Poalei Zion," which treated "Hashomer Hatzair" sympathetically. Under his influence, the non-partisan youth became interested in the problems of the Zionist labor movement. Roschwald initiated the establishment of a library in "Poalei Zion" club, social games and sports. He took advantage of the ideological proximity to the lectures on Saturday nights, which were given by Dr. Blumenfeld z"l, Dr. Meister, Moshe Ziegel and Imek Roschwald. His ambitious aspirations were not limited to public work in his city alone. I remember well the arguments in his parents' home, who hoped that their son would continue his studies at the university, but he argued that no university would satisfy him as much as public activity. In 1938, Roschwald left for Lvov, to the main leadership of "Hashomer Hatzair," and there he dealt with the affairs of this movement. He acquired a respectable place there, but in his letters to me he did not complain that he was not included in the list of candidates for immigration. When he was hundreds of miles from his city his memories brought him back, with nostalgia, to the dilapidated hut in the yard of the Geiger family.

[Page 323]

Imek, the beloved and unfortunate, was murdered, for no sin, by the hands of cruel murderers, and did not get to see the fulfillment of his dream of settling in the Land of Israel. Many years have passed since his life was cut short, but I cannot forget him.

Dulek Altshuler and his Summer Camps
(A bundle of memories)

by Ziva Korn (Rager)

Translated by Sara Mages

Dulek Altshuler was a beloved and revered figure among the children of Jaroslaw. He was a great and dedicated teacher and a personality full of emotional warmth. He was the beloved and respected teacher and the children loved him dearly and adored him. He devoted himself to raising and educating the children of the city by organizing summer camps, which were an unforgettable experience for every Jewish child in our city.

How picturesque it looks now, from the perspective of time, the departure of the children of Jaroslaw's Jews from the crowded city into nature and the beautiful environment. We travelled to the "Halusz" and "Wangrka" forests in horse-drawn wagons of the farmers in the villages, singing and rejoicing with the group of counsellors headed by the organizer who took care of everything - Dulek Altshuler.

I remember the accommodation in the peasants' houses, the rustic natural food and the cold and fresh milk. It is impossible to forget the trips in the area, the children's games, the folk dances, the long walks and the sing-along. I remember the wonderful conversations of Dulek Altshuler, the reading aloud from the books of Janusz Korczak[1], in order to enrich the child's soul.

Dulek took care to provide a foundation for Zionist education and love of the homeland. A lot of emotion accompanied all these impressive conversations. Dulek knew how to utilize the talents of the children in the camp, and at the end organized an impressive artistic program with the participation of the the students' parents. It was our romantic period that I would never forget.

[Page 324]

Dulek Altshuler was a symbol of a great educator and the dream of every child from Jaroslaw was go back to his summer camp. To this day his memory has not disappeared from the hearts of the children of Jaroslaw, and every time I remember his summer camps, I remember Dulek's wonderful image.

––––––––––

Translator's Footnote:

1. Janusz Korczak, the pen name of Henryk Goldszmit, was a Polish Jewish educator, children's author and pedagogue known as *Pan Doktor* ("Mr. Doctor").

[Page 325]

Jaroslaw Townspeople
Societies in Israel

The Committee of Former Residents of Jaroslaw in Tel Aviv and the Environs

Translated by Sara Mages

Until 1959 there was an Irgun Yotzey Jaroslaw[1] only in Haifa due to the fact that most of the immigrants, who came to Israel, and among them former residents of Jaroslaw, settled in Haifa and the surrounding kibbutzim. The wave of settlers among the former residents of Jaroslaw streamed to Haifa and the surrounding area, also in the first years of the existence of the State of Israel on the assumption that they could be absorbed into it with the help of Jaroslaw's people, who, in the meanwhile, managed to gain a respectable status in the institutions of the city of Haifa.

In the 1950s, with the waves of the great immigration from Poland, most of the people from Jaroslaw, who arrived in Israel, settled in Tel-Aviv and the center of the country. Then, the need was felt to establish a separate organization in Tel Aviv as well, to give our people the opportunity for organized meetings, and especially to organize annual commemorations in addition to those held in Haifa. Only a few came to them from the center of the country.

Among the founders of Irgun Yotzey Jaroslaw in Tel Aviv were: Mr. Shayeh Lang and Mr. Yakov Glatt (Gilead) who was elected chairman of the organization in Tel Aviv.

On the eve of the commemoration for the martyrs of Jaroslaw in Tel-Aviv, 1963
From right to left: Yakov (Jacob) Glatt, Rabbi Izak (Yitzchak) Steinberg, Jakter, Moshe Kalechheim, Moshe Heberstreit

200 Jaroslaw Book: A Memorial to Our Town

[Page 326]

A group of Irgun Yotzey Jaroslaw at a meeting in Tel Aviv, 1977

A group of Irgun Yotzey Jaroslaw at a meeting in Tel Aviv, 1977

[Page 327]

The presidium of Irgun Yotzey Jaroslaw at the commemoration in Tel Aviv, 1977

A meeting of Irgun Yotzey Jaroslaw at the commemoration in Tel Aviv, 1977

[Page 328]

Together with them worked for the organization: Yakov (Janek) Kostman, his wife Raiska Kostman (from the Mahler family) and also Yosef Zilberman, Fani Rabinowitz, T. Kiselstein, M. Hebenstreit and Salka Heftler (Shtriks.)

Over four hundred former residents of the city participated in the first commemoration held in the winter of 1959 in Beit Sokolow, Tel Aviv.

In the following years, Moshe Kalechheim (with his immigration to Israel), Motel Faster, Jenia Leshm, Simcha Graff and Jenia Kempinski (Dreyfus), joined the organization's committee.

In 1965, after the passing of Yakov Glatt (Gilead), Moshe Kalechheim took over the management of the committee to this day.

As a first step in the activity of the Tel Aviv committee, it is worth mentioning the commemoration of the Jaroslaw community by establishing a marble plaque in the Chamber of the Holocaust on Mount Zion in Jerusalem.

The committee organized a yearly commemoration and a meeting of members, with the participation of hundreds of former residents of Jaroslaw from of Tel Aviv and the environs. HaRavYitzchak Steinberg - the unforgettable Chief Rabbi of the community of Jaroslaw, and after his passing, his son - HaRav Moshe Steinberg, Moshe Kalechheim from Jerusalem (uncle of our committee member Moshe Kalechheim), and others spoke in them. The prayers at the memorial service were conducted by Mr. Binyamin Unger - Chief Cantor of The Great Synagogue of Tel Aviv, and the cantor Yeshayahu Hess from Jaroslaw. The member of the committee, Moshe Kalechheim, always brought up, with great talent, memories of Jewish community and Zionist life, as well as lines to the characters of various activists and interesting types of our city.

In 1975, the editorial committee for the publication of Jaroslaw Yizkor Book was elected with the members: Moshe Heberstreit, Moshe Kalechheim, Dov (Berek) Fruchtman, Simcha Graff and Raiska Kostman.

The editorial board began to work in two directions: gathering the material, writing articles and raising the funds needed to finance the expenses. After much effort, the members of the editorial board were able to raise the first large sums, which made it possible to publish the Jaroslaw Book. Simultaneously, with the raising of the financial means, the members invested no less effort in gathering the material by contacting the townspeople and encouraging them to write everything they know about the Jewish life in our city.

After two years of intensive activity by all members of the editorial board, and with the help of the book editor, Mr. Yitzhak Alperowitz, the Jaroslaw Book is presented to you.

Translator's Footnote:

1. Irgun Yotzey Jaroslaw - the organization of former residents of Jaroslaw.

[Page 329]

Irgun Yotzey Jaroslaw in Haifa

Translated by Sara Mages

Irgun Yotzey Jaroslaw was founded in 1949 in Haifa, the only representative of former residents of Jaroslaw in the entire country. The founding conference was held in "Maccabi Hall" on Herzl Street. Over seven hundred former residents of Jaroslaw, from all over the country, came by personal invitations sent to them at the initiative of Aharon Greblich z"l. At the same conference the organization's first committee was elected with the members: Aharon Greblich z"l - as chairman, and the members Kluberg, Gretzinfeld, Yehusua Graf of blessed memory, and may they live long the members Palant, Königsberg, Zilberman, Mrs. Schwarz and Moshe Katz.

The goals of the organization were among others:

A. Conducting annual commemorations in memory of the martyrs of Jaroslaw and the environs.
B. Publication of a Yizkor Book.
C. Providing financial assistance to Jaroslaw's immigrants in granting loans in cash and also in bank guarantees for obtaining the loans. Financial assistance to the needy, the elderly and any other assistance to alleviate the difficulties of their absorption, such as: finding a job for them, housing assistance, etc.

A commemoration for the martyrs of Jaroslaw in Haifa
From right to left: A. Zilberman, Z. Katz, HaRav Moshe Steinberg, the cantor Yosef Narcisenfeld, Moshe Hebenstreit

[Page 330]

It is worth noting that the vast majority of loan recipients from our city have met their obligations and repaid their debts.

Until recent years, the commemorations were held yearly with the participation of HaRav Dr. Moshe Steinberg, the chief rabbi of Kiryat Yam (son of HaRav Yitzchak HaLevi z"l, the last rabbi of the community of

Jaroslaw and, after his immigration to Israel, the Head of Netanya Rabbinical Court, who excited the participates of the commemorations in his speeches full of content and rich memories of Jaroslaw).

Over time, with the settlement of the immigrants all over the country, the former residents of Jaroslaw living Tel Aviv and the environs, decided to establish another committee in Tel Aviv, to facilitate the participation of the people living in Tel Aviv and its surroundings in the annual commemorations of the community of Jaroslaw and other activities.

[Page 331]

Commemoration evening for the martyrs of Jaroslaw in Haifa, 1966

Commemoration evening for the martyrs of Jaroslaw

[Page 332] Blank[Page 333]

<u>Pages of Remembrance</u>

[Pages 334-371]

Those We Remember

Transliterated by Ann Harris

אֵלֶה
אֶזְכְּרָה

יאָר־צײַט

Family name(s)	First Name(s)	Maiden Name	Sex	Marital Status	Father's name	Mother's name	Name of spouse	Year of birth	Date and place of death
WILF	Bilah		F		Abba Oskar	Ettel Ella			
RABINOWICZ	Yitzchok (Dr.)		M						
RABINOWICZ	Shaul (Dr.)		M						
RABINOWICZ	Zev Tzvi		M						
KALCHHEIM	Leah Leitsche		F	Widow			Yisrael Avigdor		
HABENSTREIT	David		M	Married			Ester		
HABENSTREIT	Ester	WEISCHSELBAUM	F	Married			David		
HABENSTREIT	Chana Henka		F		David	Ester			
HABENSTREIT	Mira Minka		F		David	Ester			
HABENSTREIT	Mordechai Motek		M		David	Ester			
GRAF	Yoel		M	Married			Gita		
GRAF	Gita		F	Married			Yoel		
GRAF	Shmuel		M		Yoel	Gita			
SCHECKEN?	Shifra (Dr.)	GRAF	F	Married	Yoel	Gita			
SCHECKEN?			M	Married			Shifra		
GRAF	Yakov		M						
GRAF	Mordechai		M						
FRUCHTMANN	Yakov		M	Married			Chaya		
FRUCHTMANN	Chaya		F	Married			Yakov		
FRUCHTMANN	Isaac		M		Yakov	Chaya			
FRUCHTMANN	Chaim		M		Yakov	Chaya			
FRUCHTMANN	Tzvi Herschko		M	Married	Yakov	Chaya			
FRUCHTMANN			F	Married			Tzvi Herschko		
LIPPER	Henya	TELZER	F					1851	1940
MAHLER	Shlomo		M					1881	1941
MAHLER	Natan		M					1912	1942
RIEGER	Chaim		M					1896	1942
RIEGER	Devora		F					1895	1942
RIEGER	Regina		F					1922	1942

Addit'l family	Eulogizer 1	Eulogizer 1 first name	Relationship to deceased	Eulogizer 2 last name	Eulogizer 2 first name	Remarks	Page
	WILF	Harry ?	brother	WILF	Yosef		336
	RABINOWICZ	Francheska		RABINOWICZ	Arye Leon		337
	RABINOWICZ	Francheska		RABINOWICZ	Arye Leon		337
	RABINOWICZ	Francheska		RABINOWICZ	Arye Leon		337
	KALCHHEIM FUCHS	Rachel	daughter	KALCHHEIM MANES	Devora	Uncertain if killed. Eulogisers from Haifa	338
	HABENSTREIT	Moshe Mondek	son				339
	HABENSTREIT	Moshe Mondek	son				339
	HABENSTREIT	Moshe Mondek	brother				339
	HABENSTREIT	Moshe Mondek	brother				339
	HABENSTREIT	Moshe Mondek	brother			Soldier died in battle	339
	GRAF	Simcha Asher	son	KNELLER GRAF	Rivka		340
	GRAF	Simcha Asher	son	KNELLER GRAF	Rivka		340
	GRAF	Simcha Asher	brother	KNELLER GRAF	Rivka		340
2 children	GRAF	Simcha Asher	brother	KNELLER GRAF	Rivka		340
2 children	GRAF	Simcha Asher	brother-in-law	KNELLER GRAF	Rivka		340
	GRAF	Simcha Asher	nephew	KNELLER GRAF	Rivka		340
	GRAF	Simcha Asher	nephew	KNELLER GRAF	Rivka		340
	GEDENSKI?? FRUCHTMANN	Eida	daughter	FRUCHTMANN	Dov Barak		341
	GEDENSKI?? FRUCHTMANN	Eida	daughter	FRUCHTMANN	Dov Barak		341
	GEDENSKI?? FRUCHTMANN	Eida	sister	FRUCHTMANN	Dov Barak		341
	GEDENSKI?? FRUCHTMANN	Eida	sister	FRUCHTMANN	Dov Barak		341
3 children	GEDENSKI?? FRUCHTMANN	Eida	sister	FRUCHTMANN	Dov Barak		341
3 children	GEDENSKI?? FRUCHTMANN	Eida	sister-in-law	FRUCHTMANN	Dov Barak		341
	KROPF??	Selka		KOSTMANN	Reiska		342
	KROPF??	Selka		KOSTMANN	Reiska		342
	KROPF??	Selka		KOSTMANN	Reiska		342
	KROPF??	Selka		KOSTMANN	Reiska		342
	KROPF??	Selka		KOSTMANN	Reiska		342
	KROPF??	Selka		KOSTMANN	Reiska		342

Family name(s)	First Name(s)	Maiden Name	Sex	Marital Status	Father's name	Mother's name	Name of spouse	Year of birth	Date and place of death
RIEGER	Penina Pepka		F					1924	1942
KOSTMANN	David		M						
KOSTMANN	Devora	GEIGER	F						
KOSTMANN	Karola		F						
KOSTMANN	Sela		F						
STEINBOCK	Wolf		M	Married			Chan		
STEINBOCK	Chana		F	Married			Wolf		
STEINBOCK	Henri		M		Wolf	Chana			
LIEBER	Avraham Yakov		M	Married			Adela		Siberia
LIEBER	Adela	FISCHTEIG	F	Married			Avraham Yakov		Siberia
MUND	Richard		M		Shimon	Tzila			
EICHENWALD	Zev		M	Married			Leah		
EICHENWALD	Leah		F	Married			Zev		
EICHENWALD	Monek		M		Zev	Leah			
SILBERMAN	Manya	EICHENWALD	F	Married	Zev	Leah	Henoch		
SILBERMAN	Henoch		M	Married			Mina		
SILBERMAN	Viktor		M		Henoch	Manya			
RENNER	Moshe		M	Married			Mina		
RENNER	Mina		F	Married			Moshe		
RENNER	Orna		F		Moshe	Manya			
RENNER	Tema		F		Moshe	Manya			
KEIL	Yakov		M	Widower			Sara Sheindel		
ORBACH	Golda	KEIL	F		Yakov	Sara Sheindel			
KEIL	Roni		F		Yakov	Sara Sheindel			
GLATT	Bracha	KEIL	F		Yakov	Sara Sheindel			
SCHRECK	Wilhelm		M	Married			Pepi		
SCHRECK	Pepi		F	Married			Wilhelm		
SCHRECK	Norbert		M		Wilhelm	Pepi			
SCHRECK	Adolf		M		Wilhelm	Pepi			
SCHRECK	Fonda??		F		Wilhelm	Pepi			
SCHRECK	Halina		F		Wilhelm	Pepi			
SCHLEIDER	Avraham Alexander Zoshe		M	Married			Hantsche		

Addit'l family	Eulogizer 1	Eulogizer 1 first name	Relationship to deceased	Eulogizer 2 last name	Eulogizer 2 first name	Remarks	Page
	KROPF??	Selka		KOSTMANN	Reiska		342
	KROPF??	Selka		KOSTMANN	Reiska		342
	KROPF??	Selka		KOSTMANN	Reiska		342
	KROPF??	Selka		KOSTMANN	Reiska		342
	KROPF??	Selka		KOSTMANN	Reiska		342
	KIRSCHENBAUM STEINBOCK	Wanda		STEINBOCK	Falk		343
	KIRSCHENBAUM STEINBOCK	Wanda		STEINBOCK	Falk		343
	KIRSCHENBAUM STEINBOCK	Wanda		STEINBOCK	Falk		343
	BRAND LIEBER	Miryam Masche				Uncertain if killed	344
	BRAND LIEBER	Miryam Masche				Uncertain if killed	344
	EMMER MUND	Miryam		RAND	Avraham		346
	EMMER MUND	Miryam		RAND	Avraham		346
	EMMER MUND	Miryam		RAND	Avraham		346
	EMMER MUND	Miryam		RAND	Avraham		346
	EMMER MUND	Miryam		RAND	Avraham		346
	EMMER MUND	Miryam		RAND	Avraham		346
	EMMER MUND	Miryam		RAND	Avraham		346
	EMMER MUND	Miryam		RAND	Avraham		346
	EMMER MUND	Miryam		RAND	Avraham		346
	EMMER MUND	Miryam		RAND	Avraham		346
	EMMER MUND	Miryam		RAND	Avraham		346
	FLASCHEN KEIL	Hinda	daughter				347
	FLASCHEN KEIL	Hinda	sister				347
	FLASCHEN KEIL	Hinda	sister				347
	FLASCHEN KEIL	Hinda	sister				347
	EISEN SCHRECK?	Nina	daughter				348
	EISEN SCHRECK?	Nina	daughter				348
	EISEN SCHRECK?	Nina	sister				348
	EISEN SCHRECK?	Nina	sister				348
	EISEN SCHRECK?	Nina	sister				348
	EISEN SCHRECK?	Nina	sister				348
	SCHLEIDER	Natan Pinchas	son	SCHLEIDER	Shmuel		349

Family name(s)	First Name(s)	Maiden Name	Sex	Marital Status	Father's name	Mother's name	Name of spouse	Year of birth	Date and place of death
SCHLEIDER	Hantsche		F	Married			Avraham Alexander		
SCHLEIDER	Shraga Feiwel		M		Avraham Alexander	Hantshe			
SCHLEIDER	Rela Lieba	KLACHHEIM	F	Married					
SCHLEIDER	Chaim Shraga		M						
SEIDERBAUM	Isaac Yitzchok		M					1897	1944
MUND	Shimon		M					1867	1943
MUND	Tzila	TINDEL	F					1869	1944
DANNENHERSCH	Ann?	MUND	F					1905	1944
BIENENSTOCK	Gitel		F						1942
RADER	Shimon		M						
RADER	Mina Malka Mindel		F		Shimon				
RADER	Alek Alexander		M		Shimon				
LEITNER	Isidore Yitzchok		M						
LEITNER	Berta Breina		F						
LEITNER	Manya		F						
STIEGLITZ	Roza Reizel Gitel		F						
KOENIGSBERG	Efraim		M	Married	Avraham		Yoel		Astrakhan', 03/08/1942
GERBLICH	Aharon Shmuel		M	Married			Puah		
GERBLICH	Puah		F	Married			Aharon ?		
GERBLICH AHARONI	Avraham Romek		M		Aharon Shmuel	Puah			
WASSERKRUG	David		M						
WASSERKRUG	Regina		F						
WASSERKRUG	Aizi		M						
WASSERKRUG	Yerachmiel		M	Married			Rachel Leah		
WASSERKRUG	Rachel Leah		F	Married			Yerachmiel		
WASSERKRUG	Shmuel		M	Married			Ettel		

Addit'l family	Eulogizer 1	Eulogizer 1 first name	Relationship to deceased	Eulogizer 2 last name	Eulogizer 2 first name	Remarks	Page
	SCHLEIDER	Natan Pinchas	son	SCHLEIDER	Shmuel		349
	SCHLEIDER	Natan Pinchas	brother	SCHLEIDER	Shmuel		349
	SCHLEIDER	Natan Pinchas		SCHLEIDER	Menachem Mendel		349
	SCHLEIDER	Natan Pinchas	nephew	SCHLEIDER	Menachem Mendel		349
	SZYDLOWBISKI? SEIDERMANN	Loni?		? SEIDERBAUM	Gina		350
	SZYDLOWBISKI? SEIDERMANN	Loni?		? SEIDERBAUM	Gina		350
	SZYDLOWBISKI? SEIDERMANN	Loni?		? SEIDERBAUM	Gina		350
	SZYDLOWBISKI? SEIDERMANN	Loni?		? SEIDERBAUM	Gina		350
	JANOWSKI BINENSTOCK	Pola	daughter	BIENENSTOCK	Yozka	Uncertain if killed	350
	RADER	Tzvi Henik	son				351
	RADER	Tzvi Henik	brother				351
	RADER	Tzvi Henik	brother				351
	LEITNER	Mondek Micha'el		LEITNER	Wilk Zev		351
	LEITNER	Mondek Micha'el		LEITNER	Wilk Zev		351
	LEITNER	Mondek Micha'el		LEITNER	Wilk Zev		351
	LEITNER				Rader?		352
	KOENIGSBERG	Avraham		KOENIGSBERG	Tzvi	Uncertain if killed	352
	GERBLICH	Yannick	son	GERBLICH	Linka		353
	GERBLICH	Yannick	son	GERBLICH	Linka		353
	GERBLICH	Yannick	brother	GERBLICH	Linka	Uncertain if killed	353
	KALCHHEIM	Gideon		SENDER KALCHHEIM	Gina		353
	KALCHHEIM	Gideon		SENDER KALCHHEIM	Gina		353
	KALCHHEIM	Gideon		SENDER KALCHHEIM	Gina		353
	KALCHHEIM	Gideon		SENDER KALCHHEIM	Gina		353
	KALCHHEIM	Gideon		SENDER KALCHHEIM	Gina		353
	KALCHHEIM	Gideon		SENDER KALCHHEIM	Gina		353

Family name(s)	First Name(s)	Maiden Name	Sex	Marital Status	Father's name	Mother's name	Name of spouse	Year of birth	Date and place of death
WASSERKRUG	Ettel		F	Married			Shmuel		
WASSERKRUG	Losha		F		Shmuel	Ettel			
RAAB	Rachel		F						1940
RAAB	Fonda??		F					1902	
RAAB	Tzila		F					1908	
RAAB	Sheinka		F					1910	
KALCHHEIM	Yitzchok		M	Married			Rivka		
KALCHHEIM	Rivka		F	Married			Yitzchok		
KALCHHEIM	Yakov		M		Yitzchok	Rivka			
AMADA	Soni	SEIDERBAUM	F						
WASSERKRUG	Lozer		M						
LOEFFEL	Yehuda Leib		M	Married			Tola		
LOEFFEL	Tola		F	Married			Yehuda Leib		
LOEFFEL	Yakov		M		Yehuda Leib	Tola			
LOEFFEL	Binyamin		M		Yehuda Leib	Tola			
LOEFFEL	Bronya		F		Yehuda Leib	Tola			
GERSTEN	Hersch		M	Married			Feiga		
GERSTEN	Feiga		F	Married			Hersch		
GERSTEN	Monek		M		Hersch	Feiga			
GERSTEN	Zelig		M		Hersch	Feiga			
BRILLANT	Viktor		M	Married			ora Leah		
BRILLANT	Lora Leah		F	Married			Viktor		
BRILLANT	Karol Ludvig		M		Viktor	Lora Leah			
LISKER	Binyamin		M						
LISKER HASS	David		M						
LISKER HASS	Fruma		F						
BAUMGARTEN	Klara		F	Married			Shlomo		
BAUMGARTEN	Shlomo		M	Married			Klara		
BAUMGARTEN	Leon		M	Married	Shlomo	Klara	Berta		
BAUMGARTEN	Berta		F	Married			Leon		
BAUMGARTEN	Paulina Penina		F		Leon	Berta			

Addit'l family	Eulogizer 1	Eulogizer 1 first name	Relationship to deceased	Eulogizer 2 last name	Eulogizer 2 first name	Remarks	Page
	KALCHHEIM	Gideon		SENDER KALCHHEIM	Gina		353
	KALCHHEIM	Gideon		SENDER KALCHHEIM	Gina		353
	RAAB	Adek??				Uncertain if killed	354
	RAAB	Adek??					354
	RAAB	Adek??					354
	RAAB	Adek??					354
	SENDER KALCHHEIM	Genya		KALCHHEIM	Gideon		355
	SENDER KALCHHEIM	Genya		KALCHHEIM	Gideon		355
	SENDER KALCHHEIM	Genya		KALCHHEIM	Gideon		355
	SENDER KALCHHEIM	Genya		KALCHHEIM	Gideon		355
	SENDER KALCHHEIM	Genya		KALCHHEIM	Gideon		355
	LOEFFEL	Shoshana	daughter				355
	LOEFFEL	Shoshana	daughter				355
	LOEFFEL	Shoshana	sister				355
	LOEFFEL	Shoshana	sister				355
	LOEFFEL	Shoshana	sister				355
	LOEFFEL	Shoshana	niece				355
	LOEFFEL	Shoshana	niece				355
	LOEFFEL	Shoshana	niece				355
	LOEFFEL	Shoshana	niece				355
	BRILLANT	Max Mordechai	son	BRILLANT	Yochanan Ian?	Chemist	356
	BRILLANT	Max Mordechai	son	BRILLANT	Yochanan Ian?		356
	BRILLANT	Max Mordechai	brother	BRILLANT	Yochanan Ian?		356
	SCHIFFMANN	Tzila					356
	SCHIFFMANN	Tzila					356
	SCHIFFMANN	Tzila					356
	BAUMGARTEN	Efraim	son				357
	BAUMGARTEN	Efraim	son				357
	BAUMGARTEN	Efraim	brother				357
	BAUMGARTEN	Efraim	brother-in-law				357
	BAUMGARTEN	Efraim	uncle				357

Family name(s)	First Name(s)	Maiden Name	Sex	Marital Status	Father's name	Mother's name	Name of spouse	Year of birth	Date and place of death
HOFENBRATEL	Hinda		F						
HOFENBRATEL	David		M						
HOFENBRATEL	Hela		F						
HOFENBRATEL	Bracha		F						
HOFENBRATEL	Arye		M						
GELBER	Tzvi Hersch		M						
KATZ	Shmuel		M						Radom, 1943
KATZ	Chava		F						Radom, 1943
KELMER ZHAFANIG??	Arye		M						
DREIFUSS	Moshe		M	Married			Flora		
DREIFUSS	Flora	UNGER	F	Married			Moshe		
SALOMON	Chaya Ester		F	Married			Adolf		
SALOMON	Adolf		M	Married			Chaya Ester		
SALOMON	Regina		F		Adolf	Chaya Ester			
FEIER	Maltsche		F						
FEIER	Wilk		M						
FEIER	Sara Leah		F						
OBER	Mozes		F	Married			Rozia		
RING	Shamai		M	Married			Mina		
RING	Mina	MUND	F	Married			Shamai		
RING	Yechezkel		M		Shamai	Mina			
RING	Yitzchok		M		Shamai	Mina			
HANDEL	Reba	RING	F		Shamai	Mina			
MINNER	Gusta		F	Married			Shmuel		
MINNER	Yisrael		M						
MINNER	Yakov		M						
MINNER	Rachel		F						
MINNER	Elka		F						
DUERSTENFELD RAPS	Leah		F						
DUERSTENFELD RAPS	Yakov		M						

Addit'l family	Eulogizer 1	Eulogizer 1 first name	Relationship to deceased	Eulogizer 2 last name	Eulogizer 2 first name	Remarks	Page
	DUNAJ HOFENBRATEL	Eliezer					357
	DUNAJ HOFENBRATEL	Eliezer					357
	DUNAJ HOFENBRATEL	Eliezer					357
	DUNAJ HOFENBRATEL	Eliezer					357
	DUNAJ HOFENBRATEL	Eliezer					357
	DUNAJ HOFENBRATEL	Eliezer					357
	LEIDNER	David					358
	LEIDNER	David					358
	LEIDNER	David					358
	KEMPINSKI	Tzina	daughter				359
	KEMPINSKI	Tzina	daughter				359
	WEBER	Rozia	daughter				359
	WEBER	Rozia	daughter				359
	WEBER	Rozia	sister				359
	WEBER	Rozia	sister				359
	WEBER	Rozia	aunt				359
	WEBER	Rozia	granddaughter				359
	WEBER	Rozia	wife				359
	FRIEDMAN RING	Ester	daughter				359
	FRIEDMAN RING	Ester	daughter				359
	FRIEDMAN RING	Ester	sister				359
	FRIEDMAN RING	Ester	sister				359
	FRIEDMAN RING	Ester	sister				359
	MINNER	Shmuel	husband				360
	MINNER	Shmuel	brother				360
	MINNER	Shmuel	brother				360
	MINNER	Shmuel	brother				360
	MINNER	Shmuel	brother				360
	SCHRECK EISEN	Nina					360
	SCHRECK EISEN	Nina					360

Family name(s)	First Name(s)	Maiden Name	Sex	Marital Status	Father's name	Mother's name	Name of spouse	Year of birth	Date and place of death
DUERSTENFELD RAPS	Sara		F						
DUERSTENFELD RAPS	Heshka		F						
STEINBRUCH	Fridka		F						
DAMPF	Sidka?		F						
FRIEDBERG	Malka		F						
ROTTENBERG	Rieska?		F						
HORN	Rozka?		F						
STROSSBERG	Itsiv		M						
ROTTENBERG	Falk		M						
HAEMMERLING									
ERDHEIM									
STRAUSS	Dzonya??		F						Lviv, 1941
HEIT	Chaim Yakov		M					1863	1943
HEIT	Elka		F						
HEIT	Chaya		F						
KATZ	Leah	CHAIM	F						1943
LEIDNER	Hinda		F					1908	1942
WAHRHAFTIG	Eida		F						
BORGENICHT	Sara	WAHRHAFTIG	F			Eida			
BORGENICHT	Leontina		F			Sara			
KRIEGER	Natan		M	Married	Markus	Fani	Bronislawa		
KRIEGER	Markus		M	Married			Fani		
KRIEGER	Fani		F	Married			Markus		
SPINDEL	Yenta		F	Married			Shmuel		
SPINDEL	Shmuel		M	Married			Yenta		
SILBERMANN	Fonda??	SPINDEL	F	Married	Shmuel	Yenta	Mayin? Max		
SILBERMANN	Mayin? Max		M	Married			Fonda??		

Addit'l family	Eulogizer 1	Eulogizer 1 first name	Relationship to deceased	Eulogizer 2 last name	Eulogizer 2 first name	Remarks	Page
	SCHRECK EISEN	Nina					360
	SCHRECK EISEN	Nina					360
	KOSTMANN MAHLER	Reiska Shoshana					360
	KOSTMANN MAHLER	Reiska Shoshana					360
	KOSTMANN MAHLER	Reiska Shoshana					360
	KOSTMANN MAHLER	Reiska Shoshana					360
	KOSTMANN MAHLER	Reiska Shoshana					360
	KOSTMANN MAHLER	Reiska Shoshana					360
	KOSTMANN MAHLER	Reiska Shoshana					360
family	KOSTMANN MAHLER	Reiska Shoshana					360
family	KOSTMANN MAHLER	Reiska Shoshana					360
	LEIDNER	David					361
	CHAIM	Shaya		LEIDNER	Chaya		361
	CHAIM	Shaya		LEIDNER	Chaya		361
	CHAIM	Shaya		LEIDNER	Chaya		361
	CHAIM	Shaya		LEIDNER	Chaya		361
	CHAIM	Shaya		LEIDNER	Chaya		361
	KRIEGER	Bronislawa	daughter	MARIN?	Ariela		361
	KRIEGER	Bronislawa	sister	MARIN?	Ariela		361
	KRIEGER	Bronislawa	aunt	MARIN?	Ariela		361
brothers & sisters	KRIEGER	Bronislawa	wife	MARIN?	Ariela		361
	KRIEGER	Bronislawa	daughter-in-law	MARIN?	Ariela		361
	KRIEGER	Bronislawa	daughter-in-law	MARIN?	Ariela		361
	SPINDEL FELDMAN	Malka	daughter	SPINDEL HOSENBERG	Max		362
	SPINDEL FELDMAN	Malka	daughter	SPINDEL HOSENBERG	Max		362
	SPINDEL FELDMAN	Malka	sister	SPINDEL HOSENBERG	Max		362
	SPINDEL FELDMAN	Malka	sister-in-law	SPINDEL HOSENBERG	Max		362

Family name(s)	First Name(s)	Maiden Name	Sex	Marital Status	Father's name	Mother's name	Name of spouse	Year of birth	Date and place of death
NARZISENFELD	Aharon Yakov		M	Married	Asher Shmuel		Reizel		15140
NARZISENFELD	Reizel	UNGER	F	Married	Moshe David		Aharon Yakov		15556
NARZISENFELD	Chana		F		Aharon Yakov	Reizel			
MONTAG	Malka		F	Married			Nachman		
MONTAG	Nachman		M	Married			Malka		
MONTAG	Wolf		M	Married			Elka		
MONTAG	Elka		F	Married			Wolf		
FRIEDER	Rachel		F	Married			Arye		
FRIEDER	Arye		M	Married			Rachel		
FRIEDER	Yeshayahu		M		Arye	Rachel			
GELERNTER	Shmuel		M	Married			Fani		
GELERNTER	Fani		F	Married			Shmuel		
GEIGER	David		M						
GEIGER	Tova Beila		F						
GEIGER	Max		M						
GEIGER	Azi?		M						
GEIGER	Sabina		F						
GEIGER	Benno		M						
GEIGER	Yosef		M						
GEIGER	Gusta	MINNER	F						
GEIGER	Wili		M						
SILBERMANN	Karol		M						
SILBERMANN	Halina		F		Karol				
RUBENFELD	Adolf		M						
RUBENFELD	Sabina		F						
WEISZINGER	Sara		F						
WEISZINGER	Mendel		M						
WEISZINGER	Yoshka		M						
WEISZINGER	Berta		F						
WEISZINGER	Isaac		M						

Addit'l family	Eulogizer 1	Eulogizer 1 first name	Relationship to deceased	Eulogizer 2 last name	Eulogizer 2 first name	Remarks	Page
	NARZISENFELD	Chaim Dov	son	NARZISENFELD	Yisrael		362
	NARZISENFELD	Chaim Dov	son	NARZISENFELD	Yisrael		362
	NARZISENFELD	Chaim Dov	brother	NARZISENFELD	Yisrael		362
	REICH MONTAG	Manya	daughter				363
	REICH MONTAG	Manya	daughter				363
	REICH MONTAG	Manya	niece				363
	REICH MONTAG	Manya	niece				363
	FRIEDER	Binyamin Eliezer	son	SUSSBERG	Ada	Uncertain if killed	363
	FRIEDER	Binyamin Eliezer	son	SUSSBERG	Ada	Uncertain if killed	363
	FRIEDER	Binyamin Eliezer	brother	SUSSBERG	Ada		363
	GELERNTER	Akiva Karol	son				363
	GELERNTER	Akiva Karol	son				363
	SILBERMANN	Orna					364
	SILBERMANN	Orna					364
	SILBERMANN	Orna					364
	SILBERMANN	Orna					364
	SILBERMANN	Orna					364
	SILBERMANN	Orna					364
	SILBERMANN	Orna					364
	SILBERMANN	Orna					364
	SILBERMANN	Orna					364
	SILBERMANN	Orna					364
	SILBERMANN	Orna					364
	SILBERMANN	Orna					364
	SILBERMANN	Orna		SILBERMANN WEISZINGER	Roza		364
	SILBERMANN	Yoska		SILBERMANN WEISZINGER	Roza		364
	SILBERMANN	Yoska		SILBERMANN WEISZINGER	Roza		364
	SILBERMANN	Yoska		SILBERMANN WEISZINGER	Roza		364
	SILBERMANN	Yoska		SILBERMANN WEISZINGER	Roza		364
	SILBERMANN	Yoska		SILBERMANN WEISZINGER	Roza		364

Family name(s)	First Name(s)	Maiden Name	Sex	Marital Status	Father's name	Mother's name	Name of spouse	Year of birth	Date and place of death
WEISZINGER	Loni?		F						
WEISZINGER	Rozia		F						
SILBERMANN	Sophia		F						
SILBERMANN	Halina		F						
SILBERMANN	Simka		M						
GERBLICH	Rivka		F	Married			Chaim		
GERBLICH	Chaim		M	Married			Rivka		
GERBLICH	Aharon		M		Chaim	Rivka			
GERBLICH	Sara		F		Chaim	Rivka			
GERBLICH	Yosef		M		Chaim	Rivka			
LIPPER	Mina		F	Married			Elimelech??		
LIPPER	Elimelech		M	Married			Mina		
LIPPER	Yekutiel		M	Married	Elimelech	Manya	Nina		
LIPPER	Nina	KATZ	F	Married			Yekutiel		
LIPPER			F		Yekutiel	Nina			
SIEGEL	Naftali		M	Married			Rivka	1893	1942
SIEGEL	Rivka		F	Married			Naftali	1893	1942
SIEGEL	Chaya		F					1920	1942
SIEGEL	Yitzchok		M						
FISCHTEIG	Moshe		M	Married			Mala		
FISCHTEIG	Mala		F	Married			Mioshe		
FISCHTEIG	Yehuda		M		Moshe	Mala			
PASTOR	Chana	FISCHTEIG	F	Married	Moshe	Mala	Yakov		
PASTOR	Yakov		M	Married	Yakov	Chana	Chana		
PASTOR	Ben Zion		M		Yakov	Chana			
PASTOR	Mordechai		M		Yakov	Chana			
PASTOR	Shimon		M						
SOFER	Bracha	BUTTERMANN	F						
SOFER	Osias		M	Married		Bracha			
SOFER			F	Married			Osiasa		

Addit'l family	Eulogizer 1	Eulogizer 1 first name	Relationship to deceased	Eulogizer 2 last name	Eulogizer 2 first name	Remarks	Page
	SILBERMANN	Yoska		SILBERMANN WEISZINGER	Roza		364
	SILBERMANN	Yoska		SILBERMANN WEISZINGER	Roza		364
	SILBERMANN	Yoska		SILBERMANN WEISZINGER	Roza		364
	SILBERMANN	Yoska		SILBERMANN WEISZINGER	Roza		364
	SILBERMANN	Yoska		SILBERMANN WEISZINGER	Roza		364
	GERBLICH	Yitzchok Zev	son	GERBLICH	Naomi		364
	GERBLICH	Yitzchok Zev	son	GERBLICH	Naomi		364
	GERBLICH	Yitzchok Zev	brother	GERBLICH	Naomi		364
	GERBLICH	Yitzchok Zev	brother	GERBLICH	Naomi		364
	GERBLICH	Yitzchok Zev	brother	GERBLICH	Naomi		364
	DONNER	Rachel	daughter	GROSSWEBEL??	Fonda??		365
	DONNER	Rachel	daughter	GROSSWEBEL??	Fonda??		365
	DONNER	Rachel	sister	GROSSWEBEL??	Fonda??		365
	DONNER	Rachel	sister-in-law	GROSSWEBEL??	Fonda??		365
	DONNER	Rachel	aunt	GROSSWEBEL??	Fonda??		365
	SIEGEL	Tzvi		SIEGEL	Mendel		365
	SIEGEL	Tzvi		SIEGEL	Mendel		365
	SIEGEL	Tzvi		SIEGEL	Mendel		365
	SIEGEL	Tzvi		SIEGEL	Mendel		365
	MAUERBACH?? PASTOR	Sara	granddaughter	NATTER? PASTOR	Eida		365
	MAUERBACH?? PASTOR	Sara	granddaughter	NATTER? PASTOR	Eida		365
	MAUERBACH?? PASTOR	Sara	niece	NATTER? PASTOR	Eida		365
	MAUERBACH?? PASTOR	Sara	daughter	NATTER? PASTOR	Eida		365
	MAUERBACH?? PASTOR	Sara	daughter	NATTER? PASTOR	Eida		365
	MAUERBACH?? PASTOR	Sara	sister	NATTER? PASTOR	Eida		365
	MAUERBACH?? PASTOR	Sara	sister	NATTER? PASTOR	Eida		365
	MAUERBACH?? PASTOR	Sara	sister	NATTER? PASTOR	Eida		365
	SOFER	David	son				366
	SOFER	David	brother				366
	SOFER	David	sister-in-law				366

Family name(s)	First Name(s)	Maiden Name	Sex	Marital Status	Father's name	Mother's name	Name of spouse	Year of birth	Date and place of death
SOFER			F		Osias				
SOFER	Zigmunt		M	Married		Bracha			
SOFER			F	Married			Zigmunt		
SOFER			M		Zigmunt				
SCHACHTER	Hutka??		F						
FLEISCHER	Chaya		F						
FLEISCHER	Asher		M						
FLEISCHER	Hersch		F						
TAENZER	Sidonie		F						
TAENZER	Emil		M						
TAENZER	Henrik (Dr.)		M						
SONNENBLICK	Rivka		F	Married			Yeshayahu		
SONNENBLICK	Yeshayahu		M	Married			Rivka		
SONNENBLICK	Klara		F		Yeshayahu	Rivka			
KNOLL	Malka		F						
KNOLL	Frida		F			Malka			
KNOLL	Yocheved		F			Malka			
HALPERN	Bluma		F	Married			Pinchas		
HALPERN	Pinchas		M	Married			Bluma		
HALPERN	Yehuda		M		Pinchas	Bluma			
HALPERN	Tziga		M		Pinchas	Bluma			
HALPERN	David		M		Pinchas	Bluma			
HALPERN	Ester		F		Pinchas	Bluma			
HALPERN	Mala		F		Pinchas	Bluma			
DANNENHERSCH	Pepi	SCHWARZ	F	Widow			Yakov	1871	1942
DANNENHERSCH	Avraham		M					1895	1943
DANNENHERSCH	Yosef		M					1901	1943
DANNENHERSCH	Mattis		M					1901	1943
DIG?	Leonie	DANNENHERSCH	F					1896	1943
DANNENHERSCH	Yanina		F					1933	1942
SPRUNG/SPRING	Meier		M	Married			Pesha		1942
SPRUNG/SPRING	Pessya		F	Married			Meier		1942

Addit'l family	Eulogizer 1	Eulogizer 1 first name	Relationship to deceased	Eulogizer 2 last name	Eulogizer 2 first name	Remarks	Page
	SOFER	David	uncle				366
	SOFER	David	brother				366
	SOFER	David	sister-in-law				366
	SOFER	David	uncle				366
	SCHACTER	Binyamin					366
	SCHACTER	Binyamin					366
	SCHACTER	Binyamin					366
	SCHACTER REGER	Binyamin					366
	KORN REGER	Zeeva					366
	KORN REGER	Zeeva					366
	KORN REGER	Zeeva					366
	BARACHU?? SONNENBLICK	Yocheved	daughter	FUSS SONNENBLICK	Sara		367
	BARACHU?? SONNENBLICK	Yocheved	daughter	FUSS SONNENBLICK	Sara		367
	BARACHU?? SONNENBLICK	Yocheved	sister	FUSS SONNENBLICK	Sara		367
	BARACHU?? SONNENBLICK	Yocheved	neice	FUSS SONNENBLICK	Sara		367
	BARACHU?? SONNENBLICK	Yocheved	neice	FUSS SONNENBLICK	Sara		367
	BARACHU?? SONNENBLICK	Yocheved	neice	FUSS SONNENBLICK	Sara		367
	HALPERN	Tzila	daughter	HALPERN	Asher		367
	HALPERN	Tzila	daughter	HALPERN	Asher		367
	HALPERN	Tzila	sister	HALPERN	Asher		367
	HALPERN	Tzila	sister	HALPERN	Asher		367
	HALPERN	Tzila	sister	HALPERN	Asher		367
	HALPERN	Tzila	sister	HALPERN	Asher		367
	HALPERN	Tzila	sister	HALPERN	Asher		367
	DANNENHERSCH	Moshe					368
	DANNENHERSCH	Moshe					368
	DANNENHERSCH	Moshe					368
	DANNENHERSCH	Moshe					368
	DANNENHERSCH	Moshe					368
	DANNENHERSCH	Moshe					368
	STIEGLITZ SPRUNG/SPRING	Bilha	daughter				368
	STIEGLITZ SPRUNG/SPRING	Bilha	daughter				368

Family name(s)	First Name(s)	Maiden Name	Sex	Marital Status	Father's name	Mother's name	Name of spouse	Year of birth	Date and place of death
SPRUNG/SPRING	Mendel		M		Meier	Pesha		1918	1942
SPRUNG/SPRING	Sara		F		Meier	Pesha		1923	1942
SPRUNG/SPRING	Feiga		F		Meier	Pesha		1927	1942
SIEGEL	Fischel		M	Married			Malka		
SIEGEL	Malka		F	Married			Fischel		
SIEGEL	Arnold		M		Fischel	Malka			
SIEGEL	David		M		Fischel	Malka			
SIEGEL	Meier		M		Fischel	Malka			
SIEGEL	Moshe		M		Fischel	Malka			
EISNER	Hinda	SIEGEL	F		Fischel	Malka			
WALD	David		M	Married			Tzipora		
WALD	Tzipora	MARK	F	Married			David		
WALD	Alter		M		David	Tzipora			
STRICKS	Arye		M	Married			Chana		
STRICKS	Chana	METZGER	F	Married			Arye		
STRICKS	Yoel		M		Arye	Chana			
METZGER	Hindel		F						
WASSERKRUG	Eliezer		M						
STELZER	Chaim Leib		M						
FRIEDBERG	Sara Yehudit		F	Married			Yitzchok		
FRIEDBERG	Yitzchok		M	Married			Sara Yehudit		
FRIEDBERG	Yakov		M		Yitzchok	Sara Yehudit			
FRIEDBERG	Sheindel		F		Yitzchok	Sara Yehudit			
FRIEDBERG	Mina		F		Yitzchok	Sara Yehudit			
FRIEDBERG	Zagosh		F		Yitzchok	Sara Yehudit			
KRAMEISEN	Itta	FRIEDBERG	F						
SALZBERG	Tzirel	FRIEDBERG	F						
SOCHABESKI?	Ester		F	Married			Chana		
SOCHABESKI?	Chana		M	Married			Ester		
WINTERGRUEN									
KURZWEIL									

Addit'l family	Eulogizer 1	Eulogizer 1 first name	Relationship to deceased	Eulogizer 2 last name	Eulogizer 2 first name	Remarks	Page
	STIEGLITZ SPRUNG/SPRING	Bilha	sister				368
	STIEGLITZ SPRUNG/SPRING	Bilha	sister				368
	STIEGLITZ SPRUNG/SPRING	Bilha	sister				368
		Chaya	daughter				368
		Chaya	daughter				368
		Chaya	sister				368
		Chaya	sister				368
		Chaya	sister				368
		Chaya	sister				368
		Chaya	sister				368
	WALD	Chaim	son	WALD	Moshe Yari?		369
	WALD	Chaim	son	WALD	Moshe Yari?		369
	WALD	Chaim	brother	WALD	Moshe Yari?		369
	STRICKS	Sela	daughter				369
	STRICKS	Sela	daughter				369
	STRICKS	Sela	sister				369
	STRICKS	Sela	niece				369
	POLANI??	Mondek	son				369
	POLANI??	Mondek	nephew				369
	FRIEDBERG	Mala	daughter				370
	FRIEDBERG	Mala	daughter				370
	FRIEDBERG	Mala	sister				370
	FRIEDBERG	Mala	sister				370
	FRIEDBERG	Mala	sister				370
	FRIEDBERG	Mala	sister				370
	FRIEDBERG	Mala	niece				370
	FRIEDBERG	Mala	niece				370
	FRIEDBERG	Mala	niece				370
	FRIEDBERG	Mala	niece				370
family	WINTERGRUEN	Pinchas				Eulogisers from Rehovot	370
family	WINTERGRUEN	Pinchas				Eulogisers from Rehovot	370

Family name(s)	First Name(s)	Maiden Name	Sex	Marital Status	Father's name	Mother's name	Name of spouse	Year of birth	Date and place of death
KRANZ									
STEINBROCH									
AMSTER									
REISBERG									
NEISS									
BLODINGER	Sara		F	Married			Yitzchok		
BLODINGER	Yitzchok		M	Married			Sara		
BLODINGER	Tzvi		M	Married	Yitzchok	Sara			
BLODINGER			F	Married			Tzvi		
BLODINGER	Naftali		M	Married	Yitzchok	Sara			
BLODINGER			F	Married			Naftali		
BLODINGER	Moshe Fischel		M		Yitzchok				
WEISSMANN	Avraham		M						Russia, 1943
WEISSMANN	Henrik (Dr.)		M	Married	Avraham		Ella		Russia, 1943
WEISSMANN	Ella	LIEFERNER?	F	Married			Henrik		1942/43
WEISSMANN	Falk		M		Henrik	Ella			1942/43
GOLDSTEIN	Franya	WEISSMANN	F	Married	Avraham		Yosef		Lublin
GOLDSTEIN	Yosef		M	Married			Franya		Lublin
ACHSELRAD	Sosha	HABENSTREIT	F						Russia
HABENSTREIT	Fonda??		F						Russia

Addit'l family	Eulogizer 1	Eulogizer 1 first name	Relationship to deceased	Eulogizer 2 last name	Eulogizer 2 first name	Remarks	Page
family	WINTERGRUEN	Pinchas				Eulogisers from Rehovot	370
family	WINTERGRUEN	Pinchas				Eulogisers from Rehovot	370
family	WINTERGRUEN	Pinchas				Eulogisers from Rehovot	370
family	WINTERGRUEN	Pinchas				Eulogisers from Rehovot	370
family	WINTERGRUEN	Pinchas				Eulogisers from Rehovot	370
	BLODINGER	Zelig	son				370
	BLODINGER	Zelig	son				370
	BLODINGER	Zelig	brother				370
	BLODINGER	Zelig	sister-in-law				370
children	BLODINGER	Zelig	brother				370
children	BLODINGER	Zelig	sister-in-law				370
	BLODINGER	Zelig	brother				370
	WEISSMANN	Z. O.	brother			Uncertain if killed	371
	WEISSMANN	Z. O.	brother			Uncertain if killed	371
	WEISSMANN	Z. O.	brother-in-law				371
	WEISSMANN	Z. O.	uncle				371
2 children	WEISSMANN	Z. O.	brother				371
2 children	WEISSMANN	Z. O.	brother-in-law				371
	SCHERE ACHSELRAD	Mina	daughter			Uncertain if killed	371
	SCHERE ACHSELRAD	Mina	niece			Uncertain if killed	371

יִזְכּוֹר

תהיינה דמויותיהם
הקדושות והטהורות
של יקירינו חקוקות
בליבותינו וצרורות
עם הנשמות של כל
קדושי ישראל
שנרצחו בשואה
ושמותיהם יאירו
לנו את הדרך
לגאולה השלמה

ENGLISH

[Page 7]

Preface

The Editorial Board

The Remembrance Yizkor Book of the Jaroslav Jewish community is one of the numerous volumes dedicated to the many communities in Poland destroyed in the Holocaust. It is part of the general project of remembrance books intended to memorialise the extinct Jewry of Poland.

The Jaroslav Remembrance Book is the collective effort of scores of contributors, townspeople who drew on their memory and information about the splendid Jewish community and the city of Jaroslav itself. The pages of this book contain the annals of one of Jewry's oldest settlement points in Poland and much work has gone into penetrating the records of the history of the community as well as of its personalities and leaders of all types and colorations.

The book represents an attempt to summarise the 500 years of the community's existence in Jaroslav. While presenting this community as an ancient and influential community in the overall context of Polish Jewry, we have also depicted the uniqueness and individual image.

The book has been written chapter upon chapter in Hebrew and Yiddish, so as to make its contents known to the older generations as well as to Israel's native born. Inasmuch as we have found it impossible to publish most of the material also in English, we have decided to present a general abbreviated survey of the history of the community, its achievements and public affairs between the two World Wars.

[Page 8]

Introduction

The Committee of the Jaroslav
Townspeople in Israel

This volume, the Book of Remembrance of the Jaroslav Jewish community, is making its appearance much belatedly. By this time, hundreds of such communities in Poland and the lives of their Jews have been memorialised through monuments and books of remembrance. We were greatly disturbed by the thought that unless an adequate effort was made now, at the very last moment, to publish such a volume in memory of our Jaroslav, no trace would remain of one of Poland's outstanding Jewish communities. As is known, our town contained a Jewish population for five hundred years. It was the seat of the "Synod of the Four Lands", and it was known far and wide for its sages and leaders; more than once its Jews were chosen to represent Polish Jewry.

The work involved in the publication of this volume was not easy. The material in its pages was compiled thanks to the perseverance and diligence of several of our townspeople. At first, we turned to all of them with a request for articles, memoirs and diaries. The response, we must admit, was weak. People claimed that their memory had failed them; some promised to furnish material but did not keep their word, for several reasons. Only a few score from among the hundreds responded and sent some material, which we studied carefully, selecting whatever was appropriate for the purpose. We received material in Polish, Yiddish and English, all of which had to be faithfully translated into Hebrew.

It should be said that the memoirs, few as they were, reflected a great love and affection for our town. Many of its Jews, we found, still carried about with them the memo – ries of their childhood days and they wrote with great pride about the excellent and splendour of Jaroslav.

[Page 9]

The Jaroslav Book of Remembrance deals mainly with the history of Jewish life in our town during the last 50–60 years of its existence. It does not engage in Jewish life prior to World War I, and concerns itself only slightly with Jewish life under the Nazi in the period during World War II.

The Jews of Jaroslav were expelled from the town by the Germans in the first weeks of the occupation, to the other side of the San River – to the boundary line separating the Polish territories occupied by the Germans and by the Russians. Thenceforth, the fate of Jaroslav's Jews was not that of an entity but as of individuals, who shared it with Jews from other towns and cities under Soviet rule. In those cities our townspeople found temporary respite as refugees until the outbreak of the Russo–German fighting in 1941. In Jaroslav itself, only a handful of Jews was left. It is for this reason that the volume does not contain memoirs from the Nazi occupation period other than a brief story of the Jews in the town during the short period until the expulsion, as well as accounts of several individuals who found their way to Soviet Russia and the anti–Nazi partisans.

This volume comes to fulfil a sacred duty, to serve as a witness to what was once the Jewry of Jaroslav. It comes to serve as a monument to the town's splendid Jewish community so that future generations may get an inkling of its Jewish life – gracious, warm and fruitful.

It is our pleasure to acknowledge, at this point, the help and assistance tendered by the members of the Editorial Board:

[Page 10]

Moshe 'Mundek' Hebenstreit, Chairman of the Jaroslav Townspeople Association in Israel. Stirred by the proposed publication of this volume, he contributed much to its realisation, sparing neither time nor effort in compiling and sifting the material. He also wrote much of the material and was always available for meetings and consultations.

Moshe Kalcheim. Blessed with a phenomenal memory, he has retained every detail of public events in Jaroslav and of its daily life. He wrote a good deal of the material, spent much time preparing it for the press and left the imprint of his own comments on every page. Without his active assistance, we could not have achieved the exactness of the facts and events related in this volume.

Special appreciation is due to **Dov (Berek) Fruchtman**, for his diligent work in translating some of the material and helping the undertaking to come to fruition. He also did some of the writing.

The Jaroslav townspeople in Israel wish to thank one of their distinguished members, **Rabbi Moshe Steinberg** of Kiryat Yam for his gracious consent to the inclusion, in this volume, of a large portion of his comprehensive essay on the history of Jaroslav Jewry. Thanks are also due to **Yosef Palant** and **Avraham Königsberg** for their diligent work in Haifa on behalf of the volume.

Our gratitude also goes to **Raiska Kostman** and **Asher–Simcha Graf** for their work in carrying the volume through its final processes. We wish to pay tribute to the memory of the late **Yosef Narziesenfeld**, one of the first initiators of the Jaroslav Book of Remembrance. Finally, we wish to express our thanks and gratitude to **Mr. Yitzhak Alperowitz**, the editor of the volume who spared neither time nor talent in seeing it through the production stages, to its attractive and admirable publication.

[Page 11]

We extend our thanks to all who toiled in the task of creating this Book of Remembrance, those in Israel and those abroad.

May this volume be an everlasting memorial.

[Page 12]

From the Editorial Board

It is with great reverence and respect that we present this Book of Remembrance of the Jaroslav Jewish community to its survivors in Israel and abroad.

This volume commemorates one of the oldest and most resplendent Jewish communities in Poland whose existence was terminated by the Nazi foe. Many generations, long gone and recent, meet our eyes from its pages; generations of Jews of all kinds and types: rabbis, scholars, intellectuals, Zionist leaders and community workers – they, who for centuries, illumined Jaroslav and its surroundings.

Jaroslav was a bustling, effervescent town. It raised devoted Jews, were they sages and dignitaries or plain folk, full of love for Israel and deep attachment to Zion.

Jewish Jaroslav! You were our abode and our mother for you gave birth to a unique way of life and conduct, in your desire to become an exemplary cultural centre for all and everyone around you. Your people created your coloration, bringing into it the new culture of the west, of those days. You were a town of commerce and craftsmanship, of Torah and intellect. You raised generations of proud Jews, self–respecting and reliant, permeated with Jewish and human values.

This magnificent edifice has been demolished and destroyed.

Images long forgotten emerge in the pages of this volumes; yesterday has come to life. Particles of the community's way of life rise to the surface. In this volume, we have attempted to tell about the values with which we were reared, the synagogues, educational institutions, youth movements and the political factions. We have tried to restore chapters from the life of the town, material and spiritual, creative and constructive.

[Page 13]

This volume does not presume to reflect all the variegated forms of life, as lived by the Jews of our town – merely a tiny portion of its experiences, nor do we presume to have succeeded in depicting the entire gamut of life, events and accomplishments. The sources have not sufficed nor do the limitations of this volume allow it. Withal, we have striven to have the volume encompass and mirror Jaroslav Jewry in all its ramifications, currents and movements from the inception of the community to its final destruction. We have also see to it that every bit of writing should be as authentic and authoritative as possible.

It should be said, however, that despite all our efforts, we have not been able to obtain appropriate material about several personalities, institutions, organizations and societies which occupied positions of importance in the life of the Jaroslav Jewish community. May the virtues of commission redeem the faults of omission.

Special attention is given in this volume to comprehensive articles about outstanding and unforgettable periods in the history of the Jaroslav community. Also included are brief articles by the survivors of the community who thus expressed their feeling of longing for the homes where they were born and the community in which they were raised, now in ruins.

May this volume be an Eternal Light to the memory of the saintly martyrs.

Tel–Aviv, 1978 (5738)

The Editors

[Page 14]

Jaroslaw: Its History and Jewish Community

Yitzhak Alperowitz

Jaroslav is one of Poland's oldest cities with a history which goes back 800 years and a Jewish community which existed there for five centuries exerting a marked influence on Poland's entire Jewry during those generations.

The exact date of Jaroslav's founding is not known but it is surmised that its name is derived from the Russian Prince Jaroslav who annexed the lands of Przemysl to his principality and gave his name to the place. However, there is no historical vindication of this assumption.

Jaroslav was known as a major commercial centre. This reputation was established already in the 16th century thanks to the big fairs which it held during the summer months. These lasted three to four weeks and attracted merchants not only from Poland itself but also from Turkey, Persia, Spain and the Arab lands. On this occasion, Jaroslav housed 30,000 merchants, among them many Jews from Poland and elsewhere. The outstanding fair was held in the month of Elul when the "Synod of the Four Lands" held its sessions.

In the Jewish world, Jaroslav was known for many centuries as a centre of rabbinic scholarship. Its rabbis and sages served as the spiritual leaders of the Jaroslav Jewish community, but their work and influence extended throughout Poland. We know of their activities from the books and manuscripts which have come down to us, as well as from the community records of their participation in the sessions of the "Synod of the Four Lands" held in Jaroslav.

The image of the community is reflected in internal and external information gleaned from many sources, and its own history of progress and change is a faithful replica of the changes which took place in Polish Jewry. At the same time, its own vicissitudes were outstanding both in their communal/economic development as well as its social/cultural growth. The Jaroslav community took active interest in the affairs of its sister communities in Poland and Russia. Its character showed the impress of both Hasidism and Enlightenment. Most of all, Jaroslav was one of the cities in which Zionism was more than a popular movement; for many individuals, this movement was a personal experience.

Left: Rose Stern Kirschbaum (born Jaroslaw 1828, died 1911); Right Toba Kirschbaum Schwartz (daughter of Rose Kirschbaum, born Jaroslaw 1853, died 1912). Both photos are not in original book.
Courtesy of Dan Rottenberg

Jan Brillant in front of the family pharmacy in Jaroslaw.
Photo is not in original book. Courtesy of Avigdor Brillant

*

[Page 15]

The beginnings of the Jaroslav Jewish community are shrouded in the mist of the Middle Ages. Up to the middle of the 15th century, there is no mention of any Jewish habitation in its confines. The first authoritative information about the settling of Jews in Jaroslav dates back to 1464. Growth, however, was very slow: in 1561 there were only two Jews in the town. For many years the town fathers denied Jews the right of domicile using as a barrier the privilege of "de non tolerandis Judaeis" which the other residents received in 1571 from the town's governor. This measure stipulated that no more than one Jewish house, two at the most, would be allowed in the town. The Jews were forced to submit to this edict and to settle in the suburbs, particularly the Russian suburb of Flakinia.

As of the beginning of the 17th century, however, there was a continuing stream of Jews into the town. It may be assumed that in the 1630's there already existed in Jaroslav a Jewish community worthy of the name. As the number of Jews increased, King Wladislaw IV issued a privilege in 1638 which made the Jaroslav Jewish community an independent branch of the Przemysl central community.

[Page 16]

The Chmielnicki riots in 1648–49 caused an upheaval in Polish Jewry. Jaroslav's Jews were among the victims of the Cossack savagery. No less harsh were the incursions of the Swedish forces in 1656 and the Rakoczy gangs, which pillaged and destroyed the property of the town's residents. Beginning with 1772 and for 150 years thereafter, the city was ruled by the Austrians. This transfer of authority was accompanied by many essential changes: the city was detached from Poland, with which it had strong economic ties, and this led to a decline in trade and commerce.

In the second half of the 18th century, the Jewish community of Jaroslav blossomed forth, numbering 1,884 souls, according to statistics dating to 1765. Originally forbidden to live in the centre of the city (on such streets as Spitka, Opolska, Lubelska, Sobieski and especially Rynek), the Jews slowly began to penetrate into the area. The Jewish population increased during the next 100 years; 1872 figures showed more than 4,500 Jews in the city. The Jewish community became organized and elections were held, for the first time (October 5, 1876) to a Community Council of 16. Dr. Frenkel was elected Chairman of the Council and Dr. Emil Gottlieb was the vice–chairman. Also around this time, Jaroslav was given the standing of a free city, and it also became the county seat. It received further impetus in 1860 when the Krakow–Przemysl railway line was extended to include it in the railway network. But while the Jewish population also benefited from this development, its growth caused tension between the Christians and the Jews. As a result, the Jewish community lived in the shadow of constant fear and instability. But even as they had to maintain vigilance in this never–ending struggle, the Jews were able to do well materially and gain control of the commerce branch.

[Page 17]

Part of the market square

The 15 years (1889–1905) that Heinrich Strizower was Chairman of the Council were a period of creative construction. During his tenure of office, a new Bet–Hamidrash replaced the old one. A two–grade school financed by Baron de Hirsch was built on the grounds of the Talmud Torah; an old folks home was erected; the road to the cemetery was paved; the Main Synagogue was refurbished and a resolution was adopted to build a poultry abattoir, put up a new public bathhouse and the like.

World War I years (1914–1918) caused a havoc in the city which was on the front line of the Austro–Russian fighting, near the San River. The urban population suffered from a shortage of food and vital items. The Community Council decided to establish a special fund to help low–income families (regardless of religion) whose fathers and sons were serving in the army.

[Page 18]

In October 1918 when the war ended, Jaroslav again became an integral part of Poland. During the first years after the war, the city enjoyed a swift population growth. From the 1920's to the mid 1930's, despite the atheistic trend of the Polish Government and the anti–Semitic forms which it took, by way of the infamous "Ozon" provisions, the Jews managed to have a deciding vote in the city's economic affairs and left their mark on commerce, industry and other economic pursuits. Most of the industrial enterprises (about 80%), were owned by Jews. Trade, banking and light industry grew swiftly. The city was joined to the electrical grid and a commercial centre, Halla Targowa, was erected. Among the major factories owned by Jews were the Salik–Reif ribbons plant, Gurgul's biscuit factory, the Glassberg and Korn flour mills, a meat processing plant, a brick yard and others.

The end of the fighting also caused an upswing in Jaroslav's national and religious life; Aliya to Eretz–Israel was inaugurated and it was not to halt until the Holocaust. Once life settled down to normalcy and the economic situation became stabilized, elections were held for Chief Rabbi. A joint session of all the community members elected Rabbi Yitzhak Halevy Steinberg to this important post. The election was held on May 25, 1921 and Rabbi Steinberg served as Chief Rabbi of Jaroslav until the outbreak of World War II and the destruction of the community.

As provided by the by–laws of the community, elections to the Community Executive and the Council were held in 1934. Advocate Dr. Shmuel Schor became Chairman; Eliezer Berish Goldman (the representative of "Agudas Yisroel") was elected Vice–Chairman. The Zionists elected Max Salik to head their Council and Shimon Spiegel (representative of the Mizrachi) as Vice Chairman; when the latter went to Eretz–Israel, he was replaced by Adolf Ragger, representing the "Yad Harutzim" faction.

The complete roster of the Executive and Council, until the outbreak of World War II, consisted of: Dr. Shmuel Schor, Chairman of the Executive; Eliezer Berish Goldman, Vice–Chairman. Members: Moshe Hass, Leib Metzger, Max Folkman, Elimelech Reich, Dr. Wilhelm Schwarzer, Mendl Schloefrig and Rabbi Yitzhak Steinberg (Virilist). The Council: Max Salik, Chairman; Adolf Ragger, Vice–Chairman: Members: Yona Evert, Mordechai Orenbach; Abraham Glatt, Shimon Licht, Yeshaya Lang, Dr. Moritz Meister, Eliyohu Sandig, Hayim–Aharon Zilbiger, Adolf Pechter and Aaron Rosenfeld. This was Jaroslav's last community body before the war.

[Page 19]

Central square and the City Hall (Ratusz)

[Page 20]

In the 1930's, the Polish Government placed a heavy burden on the mercantile class, the shopkeepers and the artisans – the principal areas of Jewish economic endeavour. The general policy of the Polish Government was to push the Jews out of the economic spheres and to support fully their competitors – the Polish bourgeois class, which was rapidly growing. On the death of Marshal Josef Pilsudski, Poland moved closer to Nazi Germany and became further infected with the Nazi policy regarding the Jewish people. The Jews of Jaroslav felt the anti–Semitic atmosphere closing in on them.

When war broke out between Germany and Poland in September 1939, the German forces advanced quickly. On September 10, after a brief battle with the remnants of the Polish army, the Nazi captured the city. On Sukkot, 1939, the Jews were driven out to the Russian territory beyond the San River and they scattered throughout the Jewish communities of eastern Galicia. When the Jewish deportations were initiated by the NKVD, some of Jaroslav's Jews were exiled to northern Russia and spent the war–years there in privation and misery. At the end of the war, most of the few surviving Jews of Jaroslav returned to their city; the others met their death in 1941–42.

[Page 21]

Jewish Social Life between the World Wars

Poland's post–war years, constituting a period of political–social upswing in Polish Jewry, left their impress on Jaroslav, as well. An intense and dynamic Jewish life pulsated throughout the community as its members vigorously took part in all facets of its activity.

Jewish social activity centred around three main areas:

1. The religious institutions of the community;
2. The political parties and youth organizations, of all colourations;
3. Jewish/national education.

[Page 22]

The Community and its Economic Pursuits

The formal community was the axis on which all Jewish life in the city moved and functioned. It had the say on all economic and social matters and consequently, there was always intense interest in its activities expressed also in the constant contention among the various segments of the Jewish population, each of which wanted to exert its specific influence on the communal agencies. The struggle was not merely one of economic policies; rather, the Community Council dealt with all–encompassing matters of Jaroslav Jewry: – the rabbinate, ritual slaughtering, vital statistics registry, charity and welfare, the public bathhouse, the cemetery and the like.

But economics did play a major role in the community structure in that Jaroslav Jewry maintained the old traditional practice of the Jews to take care of their own. At the core of such communal activity were "Yad Harutzim", the Free Loan Fund, the People's Bank and such charitable organizations as "Matan Beseter" ("Anonymous Contributions"), "Tomkhei Aniyim" ("Supporters of the Poor"), "Kimha d'Fischa" ("Passover Aid"), and the like.

The Jews of Jaroslav obtained their livelihood from several sources, the foremost of which were commerce, crafts and shop keeping, which served the city's population as well as the peasants in the vicinity.

The business district centred around the so–called "Hala Targowa". Here was the core of the Jewish economic endeavour. Here also was the centre of the Jewish cultural institutions and agencies, and the effervescence of its Jewish–national affinities permeated the entire area.

[Page 23]

Education

The community maintained a variegated schooling network of general and religious education: "Yavneh", "Tarbut", "Beth Jacob", an assortment of Heders as well as technical and business schools. Some young people also attended the Polish high schools – the comprehensive high school, the classical "Red and Blue"), a high–grade technical high school, one for girls, as well as yeshivot and a Talmud Torah.

Among the most popular heders was Rabbi Hersh Mer's, from Alef–bet to Chumosh and Rashi. More advanced studies were offered by the Talmud Torah, which had an enrolment of some 200 pupils.

The "Yavneh" School, Lag Baomer, 1933

[Page 24]

In the early 1930's, a yeshiva was added to the Talmud Torah.

In addition to the larger heders, smaller private ones were scattered throughout the city, each with 10–12 pupils. Such, for example, was the heder of Yosef Yitzhak Shlattiner at 2, Wonska Street; another on Sobieski Street in the "Hakhnosas Orchim" synagogue. Der hoicher Shmuel maintained a heder in his shtibl. Another heder was conducted by Rabbi Yosele Weisstuch (der lomer Yosele).

Many Jewish children attended the Polish governmental schools and a few had the advantage of private tutoring.

Religious Life

The Great Synagogue

The Jewish worshippers in Jaroslav had available to them various synagogues and places of worship all over the city, but their pride was the Great Synagogue, a majestic and inspiring edifice of beautiful exterior and interior. The Great Synagogue was the centre of the community's religious life. Here prayed the Chief Rabbi of Jaroslav, Rabbi Yitzhak Halevi Steinberg. The services were conducted by Cantor Meshulam Lam, assisted by a children's choir. All special events and ceremonies, state observances as well as Jewish, were held here.

When the Germans captured the city, they converted the Great Synagogue into a grain storehouse.

[Page 25]

The Bet–Hamidrash

To the right of the Great Synagogue, and practically annexed to it, stood the Bet–Hamidrash, the entrance to which was through a beautifully wrought iron gate. This gate, it was said, was set into the wall surrounding the Jewish ghetto, in the Middle Ages.

Prayers in the Bet–Hamidrash were according to the Sephardic rite and most of the worshippers came from the "courts" of several Hassidic rebbes. The atmosphere was Zionist, and during the reading of the Torah, some of the worshippers gathered in anteroom for a stormy session of debates on Zionist issues.

The Khos Kloiz

One of Jaroslav's most famous synagogues was the Khos Kloiz, located at the "small Rynek" (market place) not far from the Municipal Building.

The Khos Kloiz enjoyed this reputation because of its chief cantor, Rabbi David, who literally charmed his listeners with his beautiful voice. He kept to the traditional liturgy of the prayers and the congregation was well familiar with his melodies.

The Kloiz was not distinguished in its exterior but inside it was simple and intimate. On the High Holidays, the Kloiz was packed with worshippers who came from all over the city to listen to Rabbi David. On Simchas–Torah the synagogue rocked with the fervent prayer and dancing of the worshippers, in sheer ecstasy.

The Talmud Torah Synagogue

A synagogue for the daily prayer existed in the Talmud Torah building. It was well–filled on the Sabbath and the High Holidays also thanks to its excellent cantors, the melamed Reb Hershele who was highly respected and appreciated and Reb Moshe Hass. The worshippers were truly inspired by them.

[Page 26]

The Tchortkover Kloiz

The Tchortkover Kloiz on Lubelska Street not far from Grunwaldzka, was frequented by the Hassidim of the Tchortkover Rebbe. Many among the 70 or 80 worshippers belonged to the "Mizrachi".

In the early 1930's, work was completed on the new and modern Main Synagogue, Hessed Ve'Emet, on Wengerska Street.

Minyanim

In addition to the synagogues, there were several minyanim scattered all over the city. The best–known among them were the minyan of Reb Shiele, the youngest son of the Belzer Rebbe, Steinbok's minyan in his home, and those in the homes of Moritz Halberthal and Reb Pinhas Hemerling (the religious magistrate) at 2, Wonska Street. All of the minyanim accounted for many worshippers, particularly on the Sabbaths and holidays.

Reb Lozer Diller's Synagogue

The minyan was located in the Christian neighbourhood, on the main street opposite the offices of the County Commissioner and the post office. On the Sabbaths and holidays, this synagogue was thronged with Jews of all categories: Hassidim in shtreimlach and kapotes, misnagdim, and the more affluent merchants, property owners, members of the free professions and students.

[Page 27]

Zionist Activity

Jaroslav was a decidedly Zionist city. Thanks to their various parties and youth organizations, the Zionists set the tone for the community's social life. The Zionist clubs were filled with young and old, and the programme extended beyond pure Zionist activity to all facets of cultural endeavour – talks, lectures, and discussion evenings on a variety of subjects. Naturally, the main efforts were to further the up–building of Eretz–Israel.

Among the Zionist youth organizations which exerted the greatest influence on Jewish academic and vocational youth groups were: "Akiva", Bnei Akiva", "Hashomer Hatzair", "Hanoar Hatziyoni", "Hechalutz", "Hechalutz Hatzair", "Freiheit", "Hechalutz Haklai Hatziyoni". The Zionist parties were the General Zionists, "Poale Zion", "Mizrachi", the "Revisionists" and the "Grossmanists". The socialist Zionist parties established a roof–organization – the "League for Labor Eretz–Israel". The most vigorous Zionist activity was carried on by the Jewish National Fund in its continuous collection of funds for up–building the land. "Yad Harutzim" annually sponsored JNF bazaars, always a highlight on the Jewish community calendar.

Among the other political parties which conducted lively campaigns in the community were: "Agudas Yisroel", "Poalei Agudas Yisroel", "Tze'irei Agudas Yisroel", the "Bund", assimilatory circles and various illegal leftist groups.

The "Bnei Zion" (General Zionists) Club was an important social centre for hundreds of the city's Jewish young people.

[Page 28]

Sports

Jaroslav's Jewish young people were highly charged with a love of sports. They belonged to many sports clubs, the most popular being "Dror", "Maccabi" and "Hapoel". All the clubs had several sections: soccer, basketball, ping–pong, cycling, athletics, tennis and the like.

In the 1920's the drills and competitions were held at the Wandoles and on the vacant parcel of land behind the Great Synagogue, or on the Targowica near the city park. In the 1930's these events were held in the municipal stadium near the railway station.

Jewish young people not attached to any of these clubs used to enjoy sports under the aegis of the Zionist movement – "Akiva", "Betar", "Hashomer Hatzair" and others. "Dror", the largest of the clubs in all sections, extended membership to all Jewish sportsmen regardless of their political orientation or party affiliation.

יִזְכּוֹר

תְּהָיֶינָה דְמוּיוֹתֵיהֶם
הַקְּדוֹשׁוֹת וְהַטְּהוֹרוֹת
שֶׁל יַקִּירֵינוּ הַקְּדוֹקוֹת
בְּלִבּוֹתֵינוּ וְצַרְוֹרוֹת
עִם הַנְּשָׁמוֹת שֶׁל כָּל
קְדוֹשֵׁי יִשְׂרָאֵל
שֶׁנִּרְצְחוּ בַּשּׁוֹאָה
וְשִׁמְוֹתֵיהֶם יָאִירוּ
לָנוּ אֶת הַדֶּרֶךְ
לַגְּאוּלָה הַשְּׁלֵמָה

NAME INDEX

*Please Note: Names on the lists on pages 208 – 229 are **not** included in this index*